TAKE IT ALL ON BOARD

8 STEPS TO MASTERING THE SLOPE & LIFE WITH CONFIDENCE

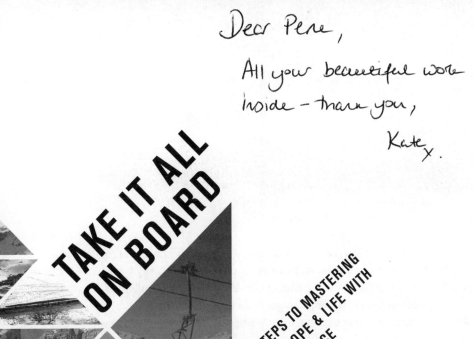

TAKE IT ALL ON BOARD

8 STEPS TO MASTERING THE SLOPE & LIFE WITH CONFIDENCE

KATE MACKAY

MuMac
Dedicated to Improvement

Published by MuMac, 2017

enquiries@mumac.co.uk

www.mumac.co.uk

ISBN: 978-1-9998618-0-3

1 3 5 7 9 10 8 6 4 2

Cover design © 2017 by AM SMYTH Branding and Design
Interior design © 2017 Pene Parker
Interior photographs © 2017 Kate Mackay, unless otherwise stated
Printed and bound in Great Britain by York Publishing Services

TAKE IT ALL ON BOARD
8 Steps to Mastering the Slope & Life with Confidence
www.takeitallonboard.com

For Freya,
may you always follow your heart and be happy,
and
For Gordon,
who encourages and challenges me
in equal measure.

TABLE OF CONTENTS

At the end of each chapter is a series of exercises. Much of my coaching work involves clients who want something more than abstract notions of understanding themselves – goal-oriented people find it easier to move forward with a measurable program of achievement indicating their progress.

The exercise sections are intended, firstly, to help you increase awareness of yourself, of your life, and to stimulate different thought patterns. Just as we get into physical habits, e.g. those relating to exercise and eating, so we also adopt particular thinking habits. We're not always aware of them, however, and just as some patterns of thought serve us, so others can hold us back.

Secondly, these exercises are graded according to difficulty – just like a piste – indicating where more effort maybe required to provide an answer. The easiest exercises are those with no black diamonds present, a single diamond denotes an exercise that is marginally harder to complete and a double diamond represents the hardest category of exercise, one where you will need to think more deeply and honestly.

Thirdly, if the exercises are completed consistently throughout the book, you will be able to see from your work on the page what changes to thought and behaviour may be needed. Collectively, they provide the scaffold for an action plan to take you safely towards your goals.

Similarly, the scoring system will help you assess your progress in a measurable way. The initial score tally will be a baseline metric against which you can compare the subsequent progress you make after practising the work. Your scores should increase and you will gain a meaningful understanding of your performance and achievements over time. The scoring does not aim for perfection, a perfect grade, but rather it establishes a quantifiable means of understanding your progress towards goals that you define for yourself. The difference will be the measure.

Please note, within the book, some names have been changed at peoples' request, and some have been changed to protect their identity.

A note on local place names; throughout the book where there are multiple names for a single place, I have used the local name. The exceptions are where the local name would be unrecognisable to most readers, and I have opted for a commonly used, or recognised, name.

Ten percent of the profits from the sale of *Take It All On Board* go to Snow-Camp – the UK's only registered charity offering participation in snowsports to provide life skills training and vocational opportunities for inner-city young people. Since 2003, the charity has been empowering at-risk youth, increasing motivation and encouraging aspiration in its participants who have the opportunity to gain accredited qualifications and employment in the snowsports industry and beyond. Snow-Camp programmes run right across the UK and there are many ways in which you can get involved with their work; please visit www.snow-camp.org.uk to find out more.

As with all endeavours, process is mostly a team effort and the production of this book is no exception.

To Rebecca Strong, my editor, your dedication, knowledge and experience are beyond compare, and your patience, kindness and integrity have meant working with you has been one of the most fulfilling professional relationships of my life. You may have been more than 3,000 miles away but you walked beside me, and held my hand, every day. From my heart, thank you.

My good friend and coach, Sabrina Brown – without your belief and encouragement this book may never have got off the ground. I enjoy every minute of our very long telephone conversations and constantly wish that we lived nearer each other. Thank you to Ann-Marie Smyth for your beautiful book cover design, and to Pene Parker for your fabulous interior design. You both excelled.

Thanks go to the following people who helped with early drafts of the manuscript: Tina Diddee; Rahul Nayar; Victoria Wyndham-Lewis; Frank Gillespie; Bonnie Green and Nikki Holdsworth. Others have helped in many ways offering practical support, guidance, and general encouragement: Tiana Wilson-Buys; Joanne Dolezal; Deb Sharratt; Natalie Eminae; Ann English; Emma Lambourne; Emma Jameson; Tom Moore and from Snow-Camp, both Dan Keeley and Dan Charlish.

A huge thank you goes to my snowboarding instructors without whom I'd still be flailing around on the nursery slope. You have inspired and supported me in so many ways. Without you, there would be no book. Total respect to Tammy, Ash, Keith, Neil, Donnie and Ben. My girl crew – Claire Adams, Kirsten Dent, Ann-Marie Smyth, Tina Diddee, Gabrielle Stokes – you are fabulous and I love you all. And of course, thank you to all who have appeared in the book and to everyone with whom I have ridden over the years. There are too many of you to mention.

My parents, Anne and Charles Mudge, you have always encouraged and supported me in all of my endeavours. Thank you for always being there for me, no matter what.

And finally, my husband, Gordon, without whom I would never have strapped on a snowboard, you opened up a chapter in my life which I never knew would be so much fun. You truly are my Prince of Pleasure! And Freya, thank you for giving up your mum and for being patient when I was so often at my keyboard. You have such a big heart. I love you.

My heart skipped a beat with the sudden realization of what I was being asked to do. Our instructor had said, 'I want you all to go over that jump, and then we're all going to slide down that box rail.' And I'd panicked. My immediate thought was, 'I can't do it. I'm neither ready nor skilled enough to do this.' Friday evening music pumped out of the sound system at the indoor snow slope, and surrounded by other snowboarders shredding their way towards the weekend, I eyed the obstacles before us. The jump looked steep and the box rail narrow. I was worried I'd hurt myself, and thought I'd probably look an arse, too. However, since my early days on a board I'd always thought that I'd love to be able to ride a box rail and prove to myself and to my husband (who snowboards well) that I had it in me – that I could do this. I had to make my mind up quickly: do I wimp out, or tough it out? It's in such critical moments of decision that our futures can be shaped, and at that instant I thought, 'What've I got to lose? I'm here and I may as well give it a go.' I rode the jump and performed it quickly so that the little devil on my shoulder didn't have time to say, 'Who d'you think you are? What makes you think you can do this? You'll never be any good at it.' But do you know what? I did make it over that jump; I didn't get any air, but at least I didn't fall and what's more, I was grinning ear-to-ear as I high-fived one of my fellow female snowboarders.

And then, without waiting for my luck to change, I manoeuvred into line for the box rail and, although I had no style whatsoever, I slid down it without falling off. I felt immensely pleased and just a bit proud.

I'm not exactly a typical snowboarder. That first kicker and box rail were both achieved by a 39-year-old mother. I'm married to Gordon, mum to Freya, and have a portfolio career running several businesses. Confidence has proved to be a fickle companion over the years. At times it has walked beside me, strong and buoyant, helping me to achieve what I need and want to do, but at other times it has proved elusive, vague and slippery

– I've doubted myself and also doubted my abilities. I've spoken in front of hundreds of people at national conferences feeling empowered and confident, but I've also felt nervous picking up the phone and having a difficult conversation. I can feel sure of myself in work situations and hold my own in meetings, however, there have been several times I've trembled going on a first date. Many of us can feel confident in various aspects of our lives, but that certainty can be threatened by a negative experience that turns everything on its head.

Snowboarding is classed as an extreme sport and it's more usually associated with teenage boys wearing their pants half way down their backside, shouting, 'Yeah man, this is sick!' as they throw themselves off cliffs. Think of a snowboarder and the image most people conjure up would not be me. I'm not a dude, I didn't start snowboarding until I was past the age of thirty, I don't launch myself off cliffs (and have no intention of doing so) and at my age I certainly don't wear my pants half way down my backside! I'm not particularly fit, I'm definitely not brave and I hate the cold. And yet despite all the above, I'm a snowboarder. I love riding my board. It has taken years of bruises, sweat and tears, as well as all the fun, learning and enjoyment, to legitimately say that, but, yes, I can now put my hand on my heart and proudly state…'I am a Snowboarder.'

However, it took a while to earn my stripes, and I spent many years on the nursery slopes trying to learn. In the early days my biggest goal was to master the simple button tow that would take me to the top of the baby slope. And essentially the process, in line with the construction, is a simple one – the lift carries an individual rider up the side of a piste and consists of a vertical pole with a circular disc at the bottom, its top attached to a moving cable. The rider places the pole between her legs and allows the pull of the circular disk behind her to drag her up the slope. What distinguishes the button tow from a standard chairlift is that the gentle gradient of the slope means feet and board can remain on the ground, thereby affording greater stability. However, it was invented in the days of skiing, and for the rider strapped onto a single board (rather than bound into two skis) the particular logistics of embarkation and balance become an interesting challenge.

Meanwhile, off the button tow, the best I felt I could ever hope for was to become sufficiently skilled to snowboard down a blue (graded as 'easy') run without falling over too much. My confidence level alternated between non-existent and a state of enthusiastic optimism, but although I had few role models, I remained positive and found people who could support me. If someone had said to me back then that I would go on to snowboard with world-class British snowboarders, to write articles promoting women's snowboarding, to jump kickers, perform on rails and snowboard off-piste, I would have laughed. It was so far beyond my capability and vision that I may as well have considered flying to the moon. But...that is exactly what has happened. And if I can achieve this from a starting point of zero, then I know that you can achieve it, too. We all have mountains to climb; we just need to know how to get there.

01

TIGNES

JUMPING ON BOARD

how to get up the mountain

You may not be surprised to know that I started snowboarding because of a man. Not just any man, but the man who later became my husband. Gordon. We met at a party in Leeds, in February 2000. I could say the rest is history, but then I'd deprive you of getting to know him, which would be a shame, because he's a rich character, one of life's lovable rogues, and someone who has been hugely influential in my life. Gordon is charismatic, warm, romantic and funny; he's also rude, undiplomatic and loud. How he has never been punched I do not know, and although I can use many adjectives to describe my life with him, dull is certainly not one of them. Gordon is a Geordie, raised in Newcastle, but at the time we met he had lived in Leeds for almost 20 years after graduating from college, there. He runs two companies and although he is a driven and astute businessman, he is a bit of a hippy at heart. His first love – and the one to which he is probably most loyal – is surfing. He has hung ten in many beautiful parts of the world and even when living in land-locked Leeds he regularly managed to get a few surfing trips in each year. When he's not looking for the perfect wave, his mind turns to snowboarding.

After I graduated from Huddersfield Polytechnic, I moved to Sheffield and started working for the National Health Service (NHS) in a job I loved. Professionally, life was good. One of my colleagues, Julie, also a friend, is a Glaswegian who is a dead-ringer for the Australian singer Natalie Imbruglia. Her husband, Daniel, is a northern lad who'd rebelled against the medical traditions of his family to work in the music industry, and had been the drummer in a band Gordon used to manage in his youth. Daniel had known Gordon for fifteen years. Julie was, and still is, a great matchmaker, so it was my friend who introduced me to Gordon at the party in question. I was supposed to be going back to Suffolk to see my folks that particular weekend, but the prospect of a get-together with single men in attendance was too much to forego, so I duly blew off Mum and Dad, and headed to Leeds with hope in my heart and some lippy in my pocket. There were nine of us staying overnight, we met more people in the restaurant, and more in the nightclub, afterwards. Even before the end of the meal, Gordon had caught my attention and, unbeknown to me, the feeling was mutual. He spent the next three hours in the club telling me all about surfing and snowboarding, and the more drunk he became, the more I struggled to understand him; the combination of a Geordie accent and a slight speech impediment tangled my understanding of the words. But the party continued back at his house, and it was suitably depraved and debauched, as any party worth its salt should be. However, so that I don't implicate myself and others in print. I'll gloss over the next few hours.

Daniel and Gordon's other male friends described him to me as a cross between Peter Stringfellow and Shaun Ryder from the band, The Happy Mondays. In my mind, then, potential husband material Gordon was not. But despite these warnings I continued to see him, and it was obvious from the early days of our relationship that this was not a casual fling. During our first year together, he organized a trip to Tignes in the French Alps, and there was never any question about my attendance as part of the group. However, my understanding and knowledge of snowboarding was poor to non-existent, limited to the awareness that, unlike skiing, one plank of wood might be used, rather than two.

After Christmas that year, we headed off to Tignes, via Geneva, on an obscenely early flight from Manchester. Tignes is one of the highest resorts in France and is rather more functional than charming in nature. It is, however, known to be snowboard friendly. As one of the highest resorts in the Alps, it also has a longer season than many other places, a fact that makes it appealing to those travelling pre-Christmas and post-Easter. In the Rhône-Alpes region of South East France, it is made up of five villages: Tignes Val Claret; Tignes Le Lac; Tignes Le Lavachet; Tignes Les Boisses and Tignes Les Brévières. The first three are situated close together at a high altitude of 2,100 metres, whereas Tignes Les Boisses and Tignes Les Brévières lie further down the valley at 1,800 metres and 1,550 metres, respectively. They are separated from one another by a vast hydroelectric dam, the largest in Europe at the time of its completion in 1952, after decades of circulating rumours and huge resistance by the residents of old Tignes village whose homes had been flooded as part of the scheme. The Chevril dam was intended to deliver 10 per cent of France's post-war energy but, ironically, became redundant after a few years with a national policy shift in favour of nuclear power. Forty years later, as part of the preparations for the 1992 Olympics which were held in nearby Albertville, street artist Jean-Marie Pierret painted a huge fresco of Hercules on the front of the dam in order to symbolize its lasting expression of force. And every ten years, as the lake held back by the giant concrete barrage is drained, the old village of Tignes re-emerges. The acclaimed 2013 French zombie series, *Les Revenants* (known in the UK as *The Returned*) was filmed in and around this region of France, and the dam plays an important role within the plot, maintaining a haunting background presence in each episode.

Off-screen, the compensation paid to the local community when their village had originally been submerged, funded the creation of the new village, including the areas of Tignes Val Claret, Tignes Le Lac, Tignes Le Lavachet and Tignes Les Boisses which were all developed in the 1960s, above the level of the dam. The architecture of that era is still dominant today, and in contrast with the surrounding alpine scenery, the postmodern buildings of these first three villages can make for a stark, slightly sterile environment. However, above Tignes lies the Grande Motte glacier extending from 3,030 metres up to 3,545 metres and that altitude makes Tignes a year-round, snow-sure resort; it's a safe choice for international events, including, from 2010 to 2013, the European Winter X Games, where skiers and snowboarders launched themselves off huge kickers and down a halfpipe, performing tricks and spins in pursuit of air and glory.

TECH TIP

BASIC GEAR

When starting out, beg, borrow (but don't steal) snowboard outerwear from friends. If you cannot borrow, then buy your:

1. jacket, and
2. pants

in TK Maxx, Trespass, or any other value store you can find.

Our group of fifteen people was staying in a chalet-hotel in Tignes Le Lavachet. I knew some of our party well, including Julie and Daniel, others were acquaintances, and some people I hadn't known previously at all. We were a typical mixed bag of snow enthusiasts, then, including both skiers and snowboarders, but no one knew everyone. I'd borrowed and hired most of my equipment and snowboarding clothes, and that was totally fine by me. One of the first things to establish for a newbie, is her snowboarding type – is she a 'regular' or a 'goofy' snowboarder? The terms regular and goofy indicate whether you lead naturally with your left or right foot. Most people don't know so a good determining test is to have a friend stand behind you, and when you have your eyes closed, have him or her push you gently but firmly forwards. Whichever leg you put out in front of you to stop yourself from falling is your leading foot. Another good indicator is to observe your leading leg while practising other sports (such as hurdling), or to note which leg you raise first when stepping into a pair of trousers. Whichever leg it is, that's your dominant leg and it should be your leading foot on a snowboard, the one you strap in first at the front of the board. After several solid pushes (just for good measure) from various friends, my initiation was complete and at the start of the holiday I now knew my first, personal snowboarding fact – I am a regular rider. And another fact – as with most sports, when it comes to wardrobe aesthetics, the rule of thumb is this: 'Do not stand out.' That is, unless you can snowboard well, and are able to pull off the look of high-vis threads with some similarly high-vis moves, the risk of appearing 'All the gear but no idea' runs high. It was only after my dark, understated jacket and pants received the thumbs up from His Snowboarding Greatness that I ventured out into the snow, and towards the nursery slope for my first lesson.

My early lessons usually started with mastering the chairlift that carried us to the top of the short nursery slope. Riding onto a regular lift is essentially pretty easy whether you're a snowboarder or skier: shuffle quickly forward when you see the people ahead of you

swept up and away; stand facing forward on the line provided; wait for the next chair to swing around behind you on the mechanized cable; plonk your backside on the seat when you feel the cushion against your calves; and remember to keep the front rail of your board or ski tips up, up, up! Riding off a lift, however, presents additional challenges for the rider. For those of you who ski, I'll allow a snigger because I know that skiing off a chairlift is comparatively easy. On a snowboard the logistics are very different, or should I say difficult. Balance is no longer an 'equal and opposite' Newtonian experience as it is for a skier. The parallel forces of energy created as a skier pushes her legs sideways away from each other (first one, then the other), and that work in tidy unison to keep her upright and moving forwards, simply do not exist on the board. I can no longer count the number of times I've fallen over when riding off a chairlift, the massively unbalanced weight and width of the board supported by

TECH TIP

READ THE LABEL

Snowsport gear varies in its waterproof ratings
from 5,000 millimetres up to 20,000-plus millimetres
where the units are a measure of pressure. A fabric with a
rating of 5,000 millimetres signifies that a standard, square,
one-inch tube can be filled up to a height of 5,000 millimetres
(5 metres or 16.4 feet) before water would leak through.
The higher the number the more waterproof the fabric,
but also the more expensive:

1. Ensure snowboard outerwear has a minimum of 5,000 millimetre rating
which means it will withstand light rain and dry snow, but no pressure

2. Equipment with a 20,000 rating or greater will tolerate
heavy rain, wet snow and high pressure

3. The choice made when purchasing winter sports gear
will be a balance between the types of conditions
you are likely to be exposed to and affordability

In short, check the label. As a newbie,
you'll spend a lot of time sitting
on the snow!

my leading foot at odds with the weightlessness of the other foot, free of its bindings, but grappling for purchase on the ice that usually forms around the much-flattened lift area. I've lost control and hit people (and yes that does include small children, too), I've pulled others over by hanging onto them in an attempt to stay upright, and I've been pulled over by others falling onto me. Chairlifts are centres of drama on the best of days: clothing or equipment can get caught and panic ensues as a passenger realizes she's trapped and about to be transported back down the mountain; some riders simply fall off; others who ride off too slowly may be caught unawares and hit by the lift chair as it whips back round. I once came across a snowboarder who had been knocked unconscious when the chair hit the back of her head. And there's the infamous tale told by Gordon's mates, which describes my husband dangling from a chairlift by his hood, his feet scrabbling in the air. The Liftie had not noticed that he had become hooked to the seat rails in time to stop the chair before it had swung around to turn back down the mountain. And in the realm of personal mishap, I've had a glove caught in the rail along the seat-back, which does not sound too bad by itself, but during a January blizzard and half-way up the Grands Montets in Chamonix, there was a real risk of frostbite; the ride down the mountain would have taken me at least 30 minutes. I've also caught the bindings on my board in the footrest, unable to raise the security bar. My cry of panic, 'Stop! Arrête!' brought swift action from the Liftie and an abrupt, swinging halt to the ride. Already past the exit point, I had no choice but to jump three feet down into the snow. Only my front foot remained strapped into its binding, an imbalance that could have resulted in any number of twists

and tears to knees and ankles, and my saving grace was the depth of soft snow on landing. But the worst incident I've heard about was told by my instructor in Chamonix who witnessed two children fall off a chairlift in Flégère. Fortunately, neither was too badly injured, but fall over while riding off a chairlift, and I have mastered the art of standing up on my front leg and gently pushing off the chair seat, able to manoeuvre between those foolish enough to stand in direct line of its exit. However, on the board as in life, travelling up the mountain doesn't always go smoothly and occasionally, despite years of experience and practise, I still end up on the deck.

During that first trip to Tignes, a routine established itself — we all went our separate ways first thing, but various friends appeared from their morning activities to join the beginners for lunch. They listened to our progress and, in turn, we heard about their adventures beyond the confines of the nursery slope. After lunch we would head back out onto the snow to put into practise what we'd been taught in the morning. Sometimes Gordon would grace us with his presence for a short while in order to offer encouragement; it was the kind of yelling and guidance that a Sergeant Major might hurl at his squad. My husband has a number of virtues, but patience is not one of them. One afternoon, after I'd fallen over for the seven hundredth time — my core muscles gripped by lactic burn — I told Gordon, 'I just can't do it!' To which he replied, 'There's no such word as "can't" Angela, now get up.' Stunned silence spread through the surrounding crowd. I took a deep breath, inflating my aching ribs, and told him, 'There is such a word as "can't", and don't ever bloody call me Angela again!' At which point I stomped off as best I could on a snowboard that I could not master and in a fit of equally untamed rage, inflamed by the easy reference my boyfriend had made to his first wife. I was seriously pissed off with life in general. But with snowboarding and with Gordon, in particular.

By midweek I was bored, frustrated and fed up. Learning to snowboard seemed ridiculously hard. I decided to spend some time by myself so that I could see what I might be able to achieve on my own. I spent the afternoon walking a small way up the nursery slope, strapping in and putting the board in the fall line, pointing it downhill, and letting myself go. And this was where everything fell into place, it was the first time I could understand what all the fuss was about — for a few, short seconds I could feel a sense of speed, the exhilaration that comes with freedom and from play. The light was dull and flat, and with very little contrast in the surrounding environment I felt cocooned in my own world. It felt good to be alone without any other distractions; no Gordon barking orders; no friends volubly chattering; just me, absorbed in the feel and flow of the board. I completely lost myself in the moment and the experience was a form of active meditation; from that point on, snowboarding had me in its grip.

Towards the end of the week, Gordon made the decision to take me away from the nursery slope full of beginners, and up the mountain to a slope where experienced skiers and snowboarders roamed. The previous day, he'd seen me make one turn from my toe edge to my heel edge, and believed I was proficient enough to graduate. In his eyes, I would be able to repeat the move again and again.

We woke to a dull overcast sky, and I was quite nervous to be going somewhere new and unfamiliar. Julie and Daniel accompanied us. Like me, Julie was still a novice, and I think Daniel felt guilty that he'd not spent much time with her on the slopes. After breakfast, we boarded the free shuttle to Val Claret and as the bus took us along the road beside the frozen lake I could see the vast, white, treeless landscape high above. In order to venture beyond the nursery slope a ski pass would be required, and I'd 'borrowed' one from a friend in our party. In the era before electronic lift management was introduced, all passes had a photo attached, and fortunately my friend and I looked sufficiently similar to get away with the ruse. I was through and onto the chairlift.

Panic can set in at such a moment. I turned my head down behind me towards the village of Val Claret well below the lift, and any optimism plummeted with my gaze. I wondered how I would ever get down. 'I can only turn in one direction and I can't do that very well,' I thought. And in that jumbled climate of fear, when the moment came to ride off the lift, I fell. By the time I was upright again, Julie and Daniel had ridden off, leaving Gordon as sole provider of instruction, guidance and general encouragement. Hmmm.

> CONFIDENCE TRICK
>
> ## *OVERCOMING INADEQUACY*
>
> Feelings of inadequacy are natural during the 'conscious incompetence' stage of learning. Do not berate yourself – instead, be kind.

My confidence was low, a mental state which did not provide a solid context for the physical and mental demands of riding unfamiliar terrain. I did not feel I would be able to turn, even though I had managed one successful attempt the previous day, and my general approach was to sideslip using the back edge of my board, to hell with the calf-burn. Down I went, then, digging the heel edge of the board into the snow and sliding haltingly across the piste. Although the method gave me hope that I'd be able to descend any slope too steep for my pay-grade, the downside is that riding this way for too long or too far, floods the leg muscles with lactic acid; it is a constant test of the quads and calves. At that time in my life I used to ride horses twice a week, and my calf muscles were like rock, yet I still struggled to slide for the length of time needed to get even part-way down the piste. I knew I had to get down, but couldn't see apath towards that outcome. Gordon, switching tactics, tried gentle encouragement for about two nanoseconds before resorting to type. 'You could do it yesterday, why can't you do it today?' he demanded. I had no conscious idea how I'd managed to make that turn, nor any established muscle memory of it, and under the weight of pressure and accusation I couldn't replicate it. We were both getting frustrated and I was starting to get frightened. I really didn't feel safe. 'Take your board off, because you obviously can't do it,' he told me. And then just as quickly admonished me to 'put it back on. It's dangerous to be up here without a board on.' Gordon threatened to ride off and leave me. 'Leave me then, go away,' I suggested, tears steaming my goggles. My vision blurred and I realized I needed to stop crying because I couldn't see where I was going. Physically and mentally exhausted, I still had no idea how I was going to get down to the base of the mountain. Julie and Daniel lapped us several times, on each occasion giving us a wide berth, no doubt eager to avoid the meltdown.

Time and time again I fell. The numerous attempts to get up were sapping my energy. I could have used the toe edge, rather than the heel edge of my board, and it would have been possible to sideslip directly down the mountain by facing into the slope, digging into the snow that way. Unfortunately, I couldn't find my toe edge for the simple reason that I couldn't turn, and as with my heel edge, I was evidently not strong enough to sideslip over the distance needed to get down the piste. And so I continued the slide on my heel edge, testing all the muscles in my stomach, arms and shoulders. They were hurting badly. Eventually, Gordon decided the only way I would be able to get back to the village was to follow him off-piste. For those of you who can ski, or who have some experience of snowboarding, this idea probably sounds like madness, and even today I would not suggest that a beginner venture away from the piste. At the time, I felt a great deal of pressure, and I also didn't know any better. Fortunately, plenty of snow had fallen and the depth of the powder supported my board. I found I could follow my boyfriend, floating down behind him in the path that his board had cut before me. It was actually quite easy to do, but reaching the bottom a small stream ran across our path, and there was no bridge. I had almost made it, I was so close to safety, but this final obstacle seemed a challenge too far. I would've screamed if I'd had the energy, but instead the tears flowed. Was there no end to this infernal, knackering, soul-destroying task? In a final burst of rage-fuelled energy, I threw my snowboard as hard as I could across the stream and hurled myself after it, collapsing on the opposite bank. I felt completely drained both physically and mentally. It was the worst day of the entire holiday; I hated Gordon, I hated snowboarding, but more than that, I hated myself for not being able to do it.

> CONFIDENCE TRICK
> ## MAKING A PLAN
>
> *If you feel inadequate,*
> *start putting a plan in place*
> *to move forward towards*
> *'conscious competence'.*
> *Working your way through*
> *the book will*
> *help you to do this.*

It was a bad way to end the trip, but after a few weeks at home, and some time to reflect, I decided I did, in fact, want to master snowboarding. That solitary afternoon spent practising on the nursery slope had given me a glimpse of the joy and liberation that this sport could bring; I wanted to feel that way again. But there was also an element of sheer bloody-mindedness, which is an inherent part of my character. I was not going to be beaten and I wanted to show Gordon that I could do it. I usually learned new skills (such as driving a car, or operating computer software) pretty quickly and this was a sobering, new experience. At the beginning of the holiday I had been unaware of how unskilled I was while snowboarding; I was unconscious of my incompetence, it was the 'ignorance is bliss' stage of learning. From my work, I knew about the learning model referenced in 2011 by Linda Adams, the Conscious Competence Ladder. Developed by Noel Burch of Gordon Training International, it identifies this as the first of four distinct psychological stages experienced within a person's learning curve, and Burch calls it 'unconscious incompetence'. But by the end of the holiday, I had moved into the second stage he identifies, one of 'conscious incompetence.' It's an uncomfortable place to be for any length of time, and I recognized the deficit in my snowboarding skills. The second stage is a period of vulnerability, of psychological distress and unless I was prepared to put some steps in place to work towards the third stage, 'conscious competence', I knew I would be stuck here for months or years. So, instead of burying my feelings of inadequacy, I decided to embrace them. I knew I needed some professional input, rather than limiting myself to the particular gifts and charm of my boyfriend who was a talented amateur. I just needed to be humble enough to seek it out, and ask for help. Truth be told, I wasn't sure I'd be able to make it as a snowboarder, but my heart was telling me that I had found something right and true, and I felt I had to pursue my new goal. Experiencing the freedom these mountains offered had brought me fully alive. The pressure of everyday life had been stripped away,

---

CONFIDENCE TRICK

BEING CLEAR IN YOUR PURPOSE

Having purpose helps drive confidence development. Do you know what your purpose in life is?

1. *Start by thinking about your values and which of these you hold dear. This is about you, not what you think others expect from, or of, you. They could include family, connecting to others, faith, adventure, pursuing excellence, or something else*

2. *Live by those values, follow your passion, and strive to make a difference in life*

3. *Set your priorities according to your values and passions, you will wake each day with a sense of purpose*

4. *Write your values down on a piece of paper (or draw a picture, or use a photo or a song). Look at them often to connect yourself to your higher purpose.*

and in its place the beauty, peace and harmony of the natural world could reach through to my spirit and touch my soul.

Living life on purpose and doing what I felt to be right was an important part of developing confidence. Inner drive was a motivating factor on my path to success. Several years later I returned to Tignes with Gordon, and on this trip we brought our daughter, Freya, with us. My experiences this time around were completely different. Tignes is linked with the resort of Val d'Isère, popular with British winter sports enthusiasts, and together they form the Espace Killy ski area, which covers 300 kilometres of pistes. On this occasion, I was able to make the most of the terrain, riding powder, nipping into the snowpark to jump kickers, enjoying off- piste adventures and pounding the slopes with my husband. Before leaving the UK, I'd hooked up with Alliance Snowboarding and had signed up for four 3-hour group lessons over the course of the week with instructor, Ben Kinnear. Ben was the GB Junior Team Coach, and in 2013 he was appointed the UK's first, specialist Freestyle Development Coach. He is also a British Association of Snowsports Instructors (BASI) Snowboard Trainer. With a busy family life, I'd had no time to preconceive any ideas about my instructor, and when I met him at the beginning of my first lesson by the Palafour chairlift, I was rather taken aback. As a happily married woman I didn't fall into the classic cliché of young student drooling over an authority figure, but Ben was without doubt the epitome of a tall, dark, handsome stranger. More to the point, during that first morning it also transpired that he knew Tammy Esten, the Director of MINT Snowboarding, which is based in Morzine. By the time of this second trip to Tignes, Tammy (whom you will hear more about later) had taught me numerous times and had become a friend; if Ben knew Tammy, then he had to be pretty sound.

Ben taught us the technical aspects of riding, starting with stance and position on our snowboards, before he graduated to foot steering, or foot pedalling, a technique for riding smooth, sophisticated turns. For some in our group this was a consolidation of previous learning, but for others it was new. Riding 'fakie' or 'switch' (both of these are snowboard-speak for riding backwards) is a skill that has to be mastered for freestyle purposes. It allows the rider to turn 180 degrees in the air and travel safely away; essentially it is riding with your least-favoured foot in the leading position. For me it meant riding goofy rather than regular. When first practising the technique, it feels alien and counter-intuitive; the body screams to revert to old muscle memory. And so as we fought against our subliminal selves, skidding and crashing down the slope, Ben gently encouraged us to stay positive and determined.

He also took us into off-piste territory, which for some in our group was a completely novel experience. Travelling off-piste, whether as a skier or snowboarder, carries its own dangers. No longer are you riding on terrain that's been groomed by skilled workers, and patrolled by people whose job it is to look out for the safety of all slope users. Away from the pistes you are on your own. The unadulterated snow lies just as it has fallen from the sky. The risk of avalanche is higher and topography has to be read successfully to keep everyone safe. No one should venture away from the piste unless she is experienced in, and knowledgeable about, those conditions. Ben is a highly qualified instructor and his presence allowed us to escape the crowded pistes and to explore a little further out onto the natural slopes, where the mountain was pristine, unspoiled by human interference. Riding in off-piste conditions is a very different experience, and technique needs to be adjusted for deeper snowpacks.

During one foray away from the groomed runs, we came upon an open, untouched field of powder. The warm spring sunshine beamed down from a cloudless sky and turned the snow into millions of sparkling diamonds. The vista was pure, snowboarding heaven and we had a chance to make our path over a perfect alpine blanket. As Ben called us one at a time to make our way through the diamond field, I thought, naively, that he was allowing us each to carve our own path uncluttered by one another. Wrapped up in my own thoughts, marvelling at the quiet, majestic beauty, I had failed to take on board that Ben's actions were keeping us safe; he was mitigating the risk of avalanche by ensuring the slope only received the weight of one individual at any one time. The combined weight of the six members of our group could have caused the snowpack to fracture and slide en-masse down the mountain, taking (and potentially burying) us with it.

In addition to taking us through on and off-piste terrain, Ben also led us through the boardercross course. The term originates from motocross, reflecting similar features and tests that require the rider to stay in control along a course of banked turns taken at high speed. Competitors usually race together with four or six people per heat, navigating drops, steep sections, flats, rollers and each other, with various opportunities for jumping, riding, and catching air along the way. Boardercross, also known as Snowboard Cross, is an official Winter Olympic sport, and given the risks that terrain and speed throw up, it is thrilling to watch both the men and the women race for a position on the podium. Needless to say the performance standards of our group were not quite at that level. And none of us was racing another, but we got through the course albeit a bit battered and bruised. I'm not really brave enough to embrace boardercross, and although it can be an enjoyable TV pastime the reality is just too adrenaline-fuelled for me. It is a discipline that has to be attacked fearlessly, and I am far too tentative.

One day I asked Ben about his other work training the GB Junior Team, and whether there was anyone to lookout for in the future. The first name he mentioned was Katie Ormerod, whom I had not heard of, but who in 2014 was the first woman to land a backside double cork. She was sixteen. As of autumn 2016, no other woman had landed this trick. She has a real prospect of competing as a slopestyle event medal contender for Team GB in the 2018 Winter Olympics in PyeongChang, South Korea. Ben was not teaching future Olympians whilst leading our group, but he was generous with his knowledge and his experience shone through.

Hidden Valley lies somewhere between the peaks of Tovière and La Daille at Val d'Isère; I'm not sure exactly where it is, and, like Brigadoon, I would probably struggle to find it again. Towards the end of the week, I woke to a day of low cloud and poor visibility. My heart sank — snowboarding in these conditions is more challenging than fun. Navigation and avoidance of obstacles, including other slope users, necessitates higher levels of concentration and spatial awareness. This particular day Ben suggested to the group that we might like to explore an off-piste route. treeline there is almost no definition to the landscape, there are few landmarks by which to gauge progress or with which to aid orientation. Our intended route down, however, was through a gully in the form of a natural halfpipe where boulders and the odd tree lined either side, and so at least we could descend using a clearly delineated path. But once we committed there could be no turning back. Once we were through the channel – that was it, and the only way was ahead. It sounded intriguing, and I was all for getting out of the low cloud. It was impossible to see into the gulch from the gentle terrain above its entrance, but we were warned that the entry was steep. Ben called us in one at a time, and I made full use of my heel edge, gripping the snow as I began to sideslip down — falling would have been a painful experience. Once through the stomach-churning, buttock-clenching entrance, the terrain became easier to read and there really was only one way to go. The path wound around high, rock cliffs creating an s-shaped descent. In places it was narrower than the length of my snowboard which meant that sideslipping on my heel edge was no longer an option. Careful control of my board was needed, and many times I clung with gloved hands onto the abrasive rock in order to ease my passage around the boulders. Twice we had to remove our boards, once to clamber down a steep section surrounded by high, narrow cliffs, and on another occasion, towards the lower section

---

CONFIDENCE TRICK

REMAINING POSITIVE

Developing a gratitude attitude for what you have and experience helps build positive attitude. At the end of each day, think about the positive things that happened (even those small things such as hearing a bird sing or a passing stranger who smiles at you) and feel thankful.

of the route, we had to crawl on our stomachs, commando-style, through a tiny tunnel at the base of a cliff. At 4 metres in length, it was a sustained effort to crawl through in full snowboard gear, propelling our snowboards in front of us as we inched along. But the passageway was our only access point to the other side of the cliff, and once through we could continue our descent. We cheered each other on the whole way down, offering encouragement to everyone to try their best, and as we blasted out of the trees and onto the piste at the end of our journey, huge grins expanded across our faces. It had been extremely fun and we had shared a real sense of camaraderie. The time I had with Alliance noticeably improved my snowboarding, giving me greater confidence to ride powder and go off-piste; it built upon what I had already learned, consolidating my turning technique and ability to ride switch. It remains among one of several favourite snowboarding adventures.

The difference between my two trips to Tignes was the difference between night and day. And the contrast had been achieved by mastering snowboarding technique, by becoming more familiar with the mountain (learning its terrain and weather patterns) and by feeling greater comfort within the snowboard culture. Importantly, in the intervening time, I had also found an instructor, Tammy, at MINT Snowboarding, who understood me and knew how to get the best from me. I had learned to manage my fear, develop positive coping rituals, and to meet and learn from many other individuals. I had continued to push myself so that I could ride more of the mountain. And as time had progressed, my self-belief and confidence had gradually increased. My learning curve had started at zero, and had sunk to an even lower point before climbing back up. The trajectory is not uncommon, and it highlights a universal truth that no matter how little self-belief you possess in a given moment, an opportunity to improve always exists. And from that decision to trust in opportunity, confidence will result. You just need to make that decision to be the best you can be. And to take that first step.

1. Choose one or two areas of your life in which you would you like to be more confident. Write them down in the appropriate column headings in the table, below.

Area of Life 1	Area of Life 2
1.	1.
2.	2.
3.	3.

♦ 2. What is holding you back from being confident in those areas? These could include skills, people, self-belief, finances, health or body-image. List your reasons in the rows under each heading, above.

♦ ♦ 3. It is important to think about living with purpose and with passion. Imagine your ideal life and ask yourself:

Who would be in it?
Where would you live?

Write your answers in the rows of the following table.

Who	Where
1.	1.
2.	2.
3.	3.

As you consider your answers to 'Where', think about:

a. chosen geographical location, including which part of the world and whereabouts in your chosen country.

b. the nature of your perfect home. Is it: a chic mountain hideaway; an urban contemporary loft; a cosy country cottage; or something else?

   Describe the style it would be decorated in, how many bedrooms it would have, what the garden would be like, and as many others aspects as possible that you see in your mind. Be as detailed as you can.

4. What would you be doing for pleasure? Think about how you like to spend your spare time. In the table rows on the following page, write down which hobbies you do now, or those you'd like to take up in the future.

5. Think about what you would be doing for work. Think about the type of job and which inherent characteristics it would need for you to be happy. List the characteristics in the tables rows on the following page.

Hobbies	Job characteristics for work happiness
1.	1.
2.	2.
3.	3.

You need to feel totally stoked and get feelings of pure pleasure when you look at your answers. Jump on board right now. Drop in, and write your answers down.

Scoring

Exercise 1. Give yourself one point for each area of life you mention.

Exercise 2. Deduct a point for each item holding you back.

Exercise 3. Give yourself one point for each detail described.

Exercise 4. Give yourself one point for each hobby you do now, and reward yourself with one point for each hobby you want to take up, when you achieve this.

Exercise 5. Give yourself a point for each inherent work characteristic you achieve.

Total chapter points................

02

INDOOR SNOW SLOPE

STRAPPING IN

learning where and how to stand

Contemplating the gentle gradient of the slope in front of me, my world felt different — there was no sunshine, no wind and no trees. But the colourless landscape was irrelevant because I felt a familiar excitement pump through my veins as I prepared to descend. Moments later, however, I was far less self-aware and definitely in the thick of it. Desperately trying to force my body to make the unfamiliar movements, using my feet to steer while keeping my body balanced, I fell a number of times, usually onto my backside. The disconnect between my head and body was frustrating, although I knew I was making progress because I was, in fact, falling less often. Upon reaching the bottom, encouraged by the instructor, I cheerfully grabbed the tow taking me back to the top of the slope to complete the exercise all over again.

After my first snowboarding experience in Tignes, I had made a considered decision to help myself by ensuring I moved on from the second stage of 'conscious incompetence', away from all its associated feelings of inadequacy and failure, towards 'conscious competence.' I knew a good place to start would be to gain skills from a qualified snowboarding instructor, from someone who knew how to teach, from someone who was not Gordon, basically. I just needed to find that someone. Not such an easy task in the UK.

In its short history, snowboarding has not been readily accessible in Britain. With the exception of parts of Scotland in the winter, such as the Cairngorms and Glencoe, the only other outdoor venues in which to participate included a handful of ski and snowboard clubs in the North of England and a smattering of dry slopes across the rest of the country. However, during the past fifteen years, a number of indoor snow slopes have opened their doors to the public. These include the Snow Centre at Hemel Hempstead, Snozone at Milton Keynes, Tamworth SnowDome in Staffordshire, Chill Factore at Manchester, Snozone at Castleford and Snow Factor in Glasgow. An indoor snow slope is not scenic, there is no natural light and they have no windows. Amongst regular users a snow slope is affectionately known as the Fridge — cold inside and illuminated by electricity. It may not sound attractive to spend time in such places, but the facilities allow UK residents to take occasional or frequent lessons. They give people the chance to try snowboarding, or skiing, before investing in an expensive winter holiday, and for those like me who were stuck in a state of conscious incompetence, they offer a valuable experience on snow before heading abroad again. And at the upper level of competence, our indoor snow slopes have enabled many of the younger GB Park and Pipe Team to practise and develop their skills on a regular basis. In other words, if you visit an indoor slope, you are likely using the same facilities as the nation's best, and that puts you at the heart of the snowboarding world and its culture.

When I first started snowboarding back in 2001, the only UK indoor snow slopes were the SnowDome in Tamworth, which opened in 1994 as the country's first recreational indoor snow slope, and Snozone in Milton Keynes which opened six years later. Most indoor snow slopes are about 170 metres long with a width between 30 metres and 100 metres. Beginner areas and the main slopes are serviced by any combination of button tows, travellators, and in some places, even a rope tow. The incline of the slope is gentle, its steepest gradient equating to a European blue-graded slope. The snow is 'real' and generated by forcing water and compressed air through a series of snow guns situated around the slope. This usually happens at night and the snow is maintained by keeping a cold environment below 0 degrees Celsius. The condition of the snow can vary depending upon how often the centre grooms and maintains it — sometimes it is soft and fluffy while at other times it can be hard and quite icy. As part of larger commercial complexes with other facilities under the same roof, Britain's indoor snow slopes are located next to shops, ice rinks, cinemas, restaurants and even climbing walls. Through the first decade of the twenty-first century, after Milton Keynes threw open its doors, various other snow slopes sprung up. My local is the Snozone in Castleford (otherwise known as Cas).

I had considered an outdoor dry slope — these are numerous across the UK — where many professional snowboarders were introduced to the sport. Their surface material varies but commonly used webbing consists of plastic bristles bordering empty hexagons, the acre or so of these polygons creating a vast mat that blankets an outdoor hill. It's not uncommon, when taking a tumble, for fingers and thumbs to get caught inside the webbing, which can result in broken digits. And trying to avoid injury, I ruled out the dry slope experience.

At Cas, lessons were graded from one to four and each lesson took two hours to complete. Usually, after two hours, a student could progress to the next level, but occasionally, a level would need to be repeated. Level one was intended for beginners and covered the set-up of bindings and an introduction to basic movements, including balance and stance on the snowboard. In this area, my experience in Tignes gave me a distinct advantage over my fellow students. Moving up to level two consolidated learning from level one, additionally introducing heel edge control and a sideslipping manouevre called 'falling leaf', when the alternating release of heel pressure propels the rider downwards. During level three, I learned how to turn my snowboard, shifting my centre of gravity from heel edge to toe edge, and from toe edge back to heel edge. At this stage I was not able to link my turns, and there were lots of falls as a result, most of which hurt nothing but my pride. Typically, most learners shift their weight towards the rear as they start to turn the board from one edge to the other, and when it comes into the fall line (this is the direction of gravitational pull down a slope) which is essential for the turn, its speed increases. Most

TECH TIP

STANCE #1

THE WIDTH OF YOUR BINDINGS WILL NEED TO BE SET UP

1. Your feet should be sufficiently far apart to enable you to direct pressure towards the front and the back of your snowboard, equally

2. If your feet are too close you will make unnecessary body movements when trying to steer your board; and if your feet are too wide apart, your body will be restricted and you will feel uncomfortable

3. Play about with the width of your stance until the distance feels right to you

TECH TIP

STANCE #2

THE ANGLES OF YOUR BINDINGS WILL NEED TO BE SET UP

1. Point the toes of your front foot slightly outwards from the hip to a positive angle of +15 to + 20 degrees from the midline of your board

2. Again point the toes of your back foot slightly outwards from the hip towards the back of your board. The back foot will have a lesser negative angle of -3 to -15 degrees

3. Play about with the angles of your stance until the position feels right to you. If in doubt start at +15 and -15

people instinctively want to slow down, and the natural inclination is to lean back even further. Physics can be a hard-knock lesson in the world of snowboarding, and it's one that is learned early. What happens, in fact, is that with the increase of pressure to the back of the board, it subsequently slides out from under the rider's feet, depositing her squarely on her backside. Because acceleration unnerved me, mastering the skill of the turn took a long time. However, eventually I was able to progress to level four, at which point I started to link my turns together.

A word on lifts, again. At indoor snow slopes lifts can vary in nature. And in Cas, the beginners' area is serviced by a rope tow, which requires the rider to grab and hold onto a moving rope that forms a rotating pulley at the side of the piste. The initial jerk can swoop people off their feet, so preparation is key, but the real irritation is the damage to gloves or mittens – the friction of the rope running through grasping palms causes fraying. Other mechanisms for transporting people to the top of a slope are installed elsewhere, and a travellator (similar to those seen in airports and probably the easiest 'lift' to use) adjoins some runs. But travellators are not evident on many parts of the mountains with the exception of the nursery slopes at a few resorts, and as a snowboarder, it was therefore good practise using the button tow at Cas, which was introduced at level four. It not only gave us access to the larger recreational slope away from the beginners' area, but I could take the essential, but time-sucking competency into the first day of my next snowboarding holiday on the mountain.

TECH TIP

GET UP THE NURSERY SLOPE

1. Prepare for the initial jerk of a rope tow or button lift by tensing your core muscles as you grab ahold so that you are not pulled over.

2. The friction of a rope tow damages gloves. Use cheap gloves or mittens to avoid the expense of replacement from wear and tear.

The indoor snow slope instructors obliged my thirst for knowledge with buckets of encouragement and unbridled enthusiasm. The four levels of lessons provided a clear path of progression with each level building upon the foundation of its predecessor. I was taking small, incremental steps, pushing gently beyond the limits of my comfort zone via a strategic plan. It was a radical difference in approach to that fateful day in Tignes when Gordon had pushed me too hard and too fast, shifting me into my panic zone, and damaging my confidence. Whenever anyone is pushed this way, if they're 'thrown in the deep end', no meaningful learning can take place. The student switches into survival mode. It may be tempting to rush learning to get to the final destination of mastery but taking this route has the potential to knock confidence rather than build it.

> CONFIDENCE TRICK
> ## TAKING BABY STEPS
>
> When putting your plan in place to become 'consciously competent', think of the smallest steps you can possibly take to get there. Build them into your daily or weekly routine. Giant steps can damage confidence.

I transferred my learning from Cas to the Alps whenever I got the opportunity. And for a week at a time, I practised and practised and practised. In fact I spent many an hour on the nursery slopes trying to embed these early skills into muscle memory. But as a UK resident, I resigned myself to spending the majority of my time in rainy, blustery Old Blighty where snow-clad mountains are somewhat scarce. However, the indoor snow slopes provided a laudable substitute and enabled me to learn and to build upon what I'd learned. Eventually, there came a time when I was sufficiently competent to attempt freestyle. Performing tricks, however, came rather more by accident than design.

Sarah, the Marketing Manager for Snozone throughout the country at the time, had invited me to join her one Friday evening, and to spend some time on the recreational slope as part of Castleford's

Girls' Academy. I had been introduced to Sarah by a mutual friend and warmed to her quickly. She had a wicked laugh, wild hair and was the adventurous middle child of a conventional family. We were of a similar snowboarding standard and often spent time together on the slope. This particular evening I bucked my usual trend of diligence and turned up expecting to have a bit of an easy ride, chatting and laughing with my friend on the slope, then slipping onto a bar stool for a swift drink before heading home. I had no idea what the Girls' Academy entailed and was in for a rude awakening.

As I strode through the doors, feeling the familiar cold blast of air, I noticed a few freestyle features out on the slope — kickers and rails. Kickers are the shaped mounds of snow that snowboarders or skiers use to propel upwards into the air, whilst rails, usually made of metal, are designed to challenge a rider's balance. There are a number of different types of rails: a box rail has a large flat surface area, making it much easier to balance a board that essentially slides flat across its upper surface; a narrow rail is just that, and requires greater skill and balance. Even though I'd spotted the features off to the side of the slope, I still hadn't figured out the reason for their presence, and when, after a couple of warm up runs down the slope, Ketia, our instructor, announced that we were all to go over the small kicker near the base, I turned in panic to Sarah. The horror on my face contrasted nicely with her broad grin. She knew exactly what we were there to do. Sarah and I had spoken previously about wanting to be sufficiently skilled to ride a box rail because we thought it was something that neither of our respective partners had done. We thought they would be impressed by our achievement and, at the time, it seemed like the pinnacle of snowboarding success to us. Secretly, it was something we both thought we would love to achieve, and now was our chance. I hesitated, aware of the adrenaline surge through my system, but, with heart in mouth, I set off, rode up the kicker and made it over the top. I did not get any air but nor did I fall over, and I got a real thrill from doing it. I wanted to do it again: I loved it. Next up, I rode a small (very small) box rail where I fell on landing, but the second time around

I stayed upright. Result! I was so thrilled with what I had achieved and had enjoyed it so much, that I went back to the Girls' Academy, later that year.

On this occasion, the kickers and rails were far higher and therefore more daunting. I had to step up a gear. While riding a larger box rail, about 50 centimetres high, I kept falling on landing, but with practise, by the end of the session, I had nailed the trick without taking a tumble. I avoided the kickers that appeared to be much larger and didn't want to damage hard-won confidence by scaring myself stupid; the attempt would have pushed me well beyond my comfort levels and into my panic zone. It would have been a leap too far. But rather than berating myself for not even attempting them, I used my time constructively and concentrated on developing some flatland tricks that are performed without the need for kickers or rails. An Ollie is one of these, a technique to lift a snowboard from the ground without the need for a kicker. A rider shifts her weight to the tail of her board whilst lifting its front and then springs off the tail, her board level in the air before she lands again. And of course it should be performed as one smooth sequence of actions, a takeoff into the air from the ground. A basic freestyle skill that has to be mastered, an Ollie enables progression to a variety of freestyle moves including a 180 from a kicker (a half-spin rotation in the air landing the opposite way from takeoff). As I huffed and puffed, trying to force my muscles into the correct sequence of actions, I was ungainly and could not produce the dynamic energy required to lift the board beneath me. The session was videoed, and all the errors and falls were replayed in glorious Technicolor afterwards. Squirming, I could see all my faults clearly, but also, from them, where a path to improvement might lie. I needed to lower my centre of gravity, to bend my knees more and to accelerate (an enduring theme over the years). Despite the unexpected nature of my introduction to freestyle, an indoor slope had proved a far less intimidating context for learning than a mountain resort — it's smaller than most outdoor snow parks, and there are generally fewer spectators watching the action. Without the distraction of others, then, I'd been bitten by the freestyle bug and wanted more.

The company, Definition, is the brainchild of Gav Learmonth. Gav is the former coach to the British World Cup Halfpipe Team, the man who took them to the Winter Olympics in 2006. Importantly for me, he believes anyone should have the opportunity to learn freestyle. I'd read about his company in 2011, and suspected that spending some focused time over a couple of days would advance my learning. Firstly, I wanted to overcome my anxiety around box rails (I had fallen backwards off a small rail a few months previously) and secondly, I'd set myself the goal of getting enough air to enable a simple grab of my board.

The weekend course was held indoors, at Snow Factor in Glasgow. Julie and Daniel lived on the outskirts of the city and were generous hosts during my trip. Rising early on Saturday, I was keen to get started but also feeling somewhat nervous. The risks involved in freestyle snowboarding are similar to the risks encountered while jumping horses; whether on a snowboard or on horseback, once I start leaving the ground, the stakes rise for me, and in turn that tension makes injury more likely. We were nine students, four women and five men. Ranging in age from teenagers to forty-somethings, our experience varied from dry slope learners to accomplished mountain riders with a love of freestyle. After warm-up runs and a refresh of general riding technique, we concentrated on fakie or switch techniques, riding the opposite way to our favoured stance. Riding switch is an important skill to master, or at least to embrace, and adding on the lift of an Ollie means that aerial 180 half-spins are then only one further step. After riding switch for a while, we were ready to progress to the features, a couple of small box rails — a straight rail and an A-frame. The A-frame has a ramp up to a flat section that then descends into a second ramp descending off the rail, and I had never ridden one before. Waiting in turn with the other students, as my time drew nearer to ride, I felt the butterflies return and my palms turn sweaty. I was moving outside my comfort zone again, but not too far beyond it. I knew technically what I had to do because the process had been clearly explained to me. Fully in the moment, I focused, dropped in, and rode smoothly over the rail, landing evenly, then riding cleanly away from the feature. My nerves had been unfounded and to my own surprise, I had thoroughly enjoyed the ride. As my anxiety decreased, I realized I had achieved my first goal.

With my confidence riding high, I was momentarily tempted to try the even more challenging rainbow box rail that arced before us to a 1.5-metre apex. Any fall from that height would have consequences more serious than a bruised backside. I could easily have been swept along by earlier euphoria, but in my heart I knew the rail was beyond my capabilities. I watched as students lined up to drop in, wrestling with myself. And then Caroline, one of the four women in our group hit the deck, falling hard. Although I was very concerned for my peer, my own self-awareness had not let me down, and I felt a degree of relief. Caroline had broken three ribs.

CONFIDENCE TRICK

EMULATING THE TORTOISE, NOT THE HARE

Do not be tempted to rush learning. Solid foundations of knowledge and experience constructed over time build confidence and future competence in ways that are structurally sound.

Sunday dawned, and with it the prospect of nailing my second goal, the grab trick. Fortunately, day two introduced us to kickers. With aching limbs, we started practising over a roller, a mound of snow from which we could pop and get air. At the time I booked the course, this particular indoor snow slope had a kicker built and shaped from a raised part of the slope, not from an addition of snow. Its structure meant that it could not be varied in height, and its size intimidated me. I agonised about making the attempt, but in the end passed up the opportunity. Although disappointed, I enjoyed riding faster over the roller, getting air and starting to try for a grab. By the end of the day I still hadn't succeeded, but I was content with my progress. Developing confidence by practising competence, and moving away from my comfort zone in small steps, ensured I was building solid foundations on which to consolidate future gain.

Being outdoors and snowboarding in the mountains is the perfect way to experience the sport, but for those in the UK, trips to the Alps can be curtailed by reasons on the ground (parenting, work, both) that are further compounded by geography and time. The indoor snow slopes are never going to replace the pull and power of the mountains, but they can have distinct advantages when learning. An indoor slope surface is relatively even, and a snowboarder or skier can concentrate on her skill rather than keeping an eye out for surprise changes to terrain up ahead. When riding in the mountains the topography on the same run can vary with changing weather and the time of day; conditions can transform a fun and enjoyable piste into difficult slog, something that's hard work. Snow can become icy, particularly first thing in the morning during springtime, or it can become pockmarked with moguls at the end of the day as everyone skis and rides back to base, mashing the snow on their way. At an indoor slope on the other hand, such worries do not exist and conditions in the Fridge more or less stay the same. The other distinct advantage is that whenever you find yourself missing the sport, especially in summer, you can get a quick snow fix, and as winter beckons, it feels good to get your snowboarding legs back before heading out to the mountains. And as the presence of the younger GB Park and Pipe Team members attest, even once you've passed the immediate learning phase, certain elements of snowboarding can always be tweaked and refined.

Between forays abroad, I decided that I wanted to be able to continue tweaking and refining, and looked into the dedicated teaching delivered at the indoor slopes. I came across a company called Snowboard Coach that seemed committed to raising standards of riding for anyone wanting to improve. It was started in 2002 by former professional snowboarder, Ash Newnes, who had previously been a rider for K2, one of the snowboard manufacturers to sponsor its own team. More recently, Ash has been the resident snowboard coach on Channel 4's *The Jump*, in addition, he trains instructors for each of Great Britain's snowboard governing bodies, and he holds full, worldwide accreditation from the International Ski Instructors Association (ISIA). Snowboard Coach has a number of instructors and while Ash taught me in preparation for the BASI Level 1 instructors exam at Cas, Snowboard Coach's local instructor, Mike Vaiksaar, was an important influence for me when it came to technique and outlook.

Mike is a Yorkshireman with the ubiquitous male snowboarder's beard, and although he's softly spoken, he carries an air of quiet authority. Congregating by the equipment hire section at Cas, Mike talked to every group member individually, asking about their riding experience and their aims for the session. We started on the slope, going over the basics of snowboard stance, ensuring everyone began from the same knowledge level. Once we'd all grasped the concept and had practised it, we then moved on to our individual goals.

It was during one of my many sessions with Mike that a thought popped into my head. I was uncertain whether to slap it down immediately, or to give it room to breathe. In the end, I plucked up the courage to ask his opinion. 'I was just wondering, do you think it possible that I might be good enough, maybe with lots of practise, sometime in the future, to gain my BASI Level 1 Snowboard Instructors qualification?' Was I good enough to become a snowboarding instructor? That voice in my head, you know the one which always nags and tells you off, said, 'Who do you think you are to be so bold as to ask that question? You spent years on the nursery slopes, you still get nervous at times and you are too slow to be a proper snowboarder. Do you really think BASI are going to give you a qualification?' But Mike didn't laugh, he didn't have an incredulous look on his face, and nor did he roll his eyes. He just said, 'Yes, you can do that. Just practise next summer, register for the instructors' preparation course and take the qualifying exam in twelve months' time.' Just like that. You could have bowled me over with a feather.

So that's what I did. Ash is the instructor for that preparation course, and in May 2013, at Milton Keynes' Snozone, I took further steps with him towards the BASI Level 1 Instructor's qualification. As the founder of Snowboard Coach, Ash dictates the culture and ethos of his company, so it was no surprise that he started the day just as Mike started his sessions, with an off-snow briefing followed by a refresher of the basics concerning stance and board steering. Ash is slim, sports a beard, and the uniform headwear of the snowboarding culture, the Beanie, is ever-present when he's off the slope. Before lunch we covered the topic of foot pedalling, experimenting with the differing degrees of pressure required to articulate varying scopes of arcs and turns. Smaller, sharper turns, also known as 'pivots' require greater dynamic foot pressure, whereas broader, turns require the same manoeuvre, but with much less pressure. And post-lunch we were joined by sponsored rider, Skyla Baily, who is now an Elite Junior with Great Britain's Snowboard Cross Team. Just as we were working towards ours goals, Skyla was working towards her own.

At the top of the recreational slope, I contemplated the task Ash had set. We'd been asked to try snowboarding with straight legs and, as

I dropped into the fall line, I felt unstable. Despite slowing my speed, turning was almost impossible. On the next descent, and in contrast, we snowboarded with excessively bent legs, and I understood Ash's intent was to allow us each to discover the feeling of optimal leg position, and why too much, and too little, knee bend is detrimental to a rider's ability to control her board. Rather than telling us what to do, he let us experience the physical sensation ourselves. We also covered carving turns, gripping the snow, and worked on individual skills regarding body alignment. The weekend finished with video analysis, and although I learned that I needed to be more progressive (riding faster and being more assertive) Ash pointed out that speed can mask skill. Anyone with enough bravado and nerve can go fast on a snowboard, but it doesn't make them skilled.

CONFIDENCE TRICK

KNOWING YOUR OWN LEARNING STYLE

Seek out learning activities which suit your learning profile and preferences – it will help build confidence more readily.

On the snow as in life, every rider has her own particular hurdle to conquer. Over the years, mine has been to master different techniques so I can snowboard more smoothly and efficiently. Both Mike and Ash raised my game gradually. In their hands, I have never felt pushed beyond comfortable limits, but have been encouraged instead to master smaller steps that then navigate towards a greater passage of confidence and capability.

Whatever topic or subject we learn, on and off the slopes, we all need to be aware of our own preferred learning style if we're to save money and time. When Gordon tried to teach me in Tignes on that very first trip, he assumed I learned similarly to him. If I had recognized our differences sooner, I might have saved myself some heartache. Using the model set out by psychologists, Peter Honey and Alan Mumford in their 2000 book, *The Learning Styles Helper's Guide*, Gordon is considered an Activist and I am more of a Theorist. In simple terms, Gordon learns by doing, whereas I learn by thinking things through in logical steps. Where I am more cerebral in my learning, Gordon is action-focused. There are a

number of different learning style models which have been presented over
the years, of which Honey and Mumford's model is just one. However, I've
found it useful to draw on their research when considering why I react
a particular way myself when I'm learning, or when I'm observing in my
work how I can best help others who learn differently.

Honey and Mumford have identified four distinct learning styles within
their model — the Activist and the Theorist I've mentioned, and they're
joined by the Reflector and the Pragmatist. These high-level personality
traits and preferred learning methods can be understood as follows:

1. Activists are gregarious, seeking challenge and immediate
    experience; they learn by doing, by breaking things apart, and
    by getting their hands dirty. In a learning context, Activists can
    thrive on role play, group discussions and competitions.

2. Reflectors are thoughtful people who avoid leaping in to
    situations, preferring to watch from the sidelines and to view
    things from a number of different perspectives before drawing
    any conclusions. They think things through before acting,
    gathering data and analysing before reaching conclusions.
    Appropriate learning activities for Reflectors include the possibility
    for observation, feedback and paired discussions.

3. Theorists aim to understand the reasons behind actions,
    absorbing information through the use of stories, illustrative
    metaphor and quotes. They benefit from models and facts in
    order to engage successfully with the learning process.

    And finally, but by no means least,

4. Pragmatists. Pragmatists tend to be down-to-earth, practical
    people who seek and try out new ideas. They put learning
    into practise in order to see how tasks relate to real life and they
    learn best through case studies, via the application of method to
    a relevant real-world context.

But no single individual will manifest just one type of learning style, and most people tend to favour one or two. It's also important to consider that a person's learning style can also vary over time.

Coming across the Honey and Mumford model while working as a junior manager in the NHS, and completing the questionnaire, I was very evidently a Theorist and Reflector. I had some of the traits of the Pragmatist, but scored very low in the dimension of the Activist. If someone scores evenly across different styles it means she can benefit from whichever activity is being used to facilitate learning. I knew that I hated role play, similarly anything that meant I had to act without having the chance to think things through, first. However, I decided to work on my Activist learning style and sought out activities that meant I did not have time to think and just had to do. Interestingly, as my roles at work changed I was exposed to a greater array of experience. During training, and when presenting to groups of people, there were times when I had to engage with material as an authority, but without time for preparation (either someone was off sick, or had not been not performing well and I needed to step in). On other occasions I had to step in and facilitate meetings with no prior warning. While I generally work at quite a fast pace, and make decisions quickly, this took me out of my comfort zone and I felt awkward and anxious. But the big learning point was that the experience itself was never, in fact, as bad as I thought. And the more I did it, the easier it became. Now, I can stand in for others when required, and I have gone on to train and teach more than a thousand people.

It was not until I started training to be a life coach that I completed the Learning Styles questionnaire again. On the revisit, a more equal balance between the four styles was evident. I also had the chance to reconnect with my Reflector self – that trait had been buried and suppressed during the last ten years as a result of the roles and jobs I had performed. I am still a Theorist and Reflector with some Pragmatist thrown in, but I can assume Activist traits if required. Self-awareness helps me understand why I do things the way I do, so I tend to ask lots of questions about why things are done a certain way and I need to understand a set of parameters if I'm to piece together an outcome in my mind. But I also know that I can get caught up seeking too much clarification and can think things through too much — sometimes I just have to get on and try things out for myself.

When Gordon learned to snowboard he did it by watching others and giving it a go, and so perhaps it's unsurprising that this was the approach he took with me. But research has shown that men learn differently from women, too. Women's brains are wired differently to men according to Dr Ragini Verma, Associate Professor at the University of Pennsylvania's Section for Biomedical Image Analysis. The 2013 study of the connectomes of the human brain, which she completed with colleagues, is one of the largest of its kind. There have been numerous books about the differences between men and women, but when it comes to the specifics of distinct learning systems, a much-cited article by Gabe Keri (2002) found that there is a clear difference between the genders in this respect, and that women prefer abstract learning, favouring organized learning materials, many reading assignments and an instructors' knowledge. Gordon had struggled to understand why I could not watch him and then translate form into action, magically performing the way he did. Not only did we have dissimilar learning styles, but we also had gender differences that both played out perfectly. For Gordon to teach me successfully, he would have had to adapt his method. My learning style and gender dictated the necessity for lessons where an expert could explain why things were done a certain way and how everything fitted together. It's commonly understood that when the sport of snowboarding first took off, it was almost exclusively practised by men. More interestingly, perhaps, it also took a number of years before official teaching systems were introduced. This raises the question that if more women had been involved in the sport during its early days, would formal, organized instruction have been introduced earlier? And by which circular argument would more women have been involved earlier, too?

Learning and practising new skills of course helps us move further away from the uncomfortable second stage of 'conscious incompetence' towards the more desirable stage of 'conscious competence'. And the quicker we can find ways to facilitate this the better, but when it came to my own learning, I always bore in mind that the smaller, incremental gains of competence would build the type of lasting confidence I desired. I knew that one means of accelerating the process would be to demystify the subject area. When I first started snowboarding, I knew almost nothing about the sport and its associated culture. It was time to start studying. As noted above, for women, reading assignments are a favoured way of learning, and so I subscribed to magazines such as the *Daily Mail Ski and Snowboard* magazine (now the *Telegraph Ski and Snowboard* magazine). I read nonfiction accounts from professional snowboarders including Tina Basich's autobiography, *Pretty Good for a Girl*, and I devoured instructional manuals like *Go Snowboard*, by Neil McNab. I took to watching snowboarding DVDs including *Proper and Bad Ass Big Airs* produced by Lockdown Projects for The Snowboard Asylum (TSA). As tongue-in-cheek recordings of various British snowboarders doing their thing set to some classic and cheesy 1980s and early 1990s tracks, it proved that learning was fun. And now it goes without saying, the internet is there for anyone at all curious to know more about their chosen topic.

Back in the 1980s when snowboarding was first gaining in popularity, it was seen as a radical new sport that conflicted with the well-established sport of skiing in almost every way. During that period, resorts did not have snowboard instructors and therefore most riders were self-taught. Invariably young, and dressed in baggy clothing that was at odds with the style of the skiers around them, the new kids on the mountain were perceived to have a bad attitude, they were deemed a safety risk and for the most part excluded from the slope-side Establishment. In fact, the solid majority of resorts even banned snowboarders in the USA, and there is a small number that still run with the prejudice today.

In the 1960s, Sherman Poppen bound two kids' skis into one and saw how quickly his young daughters took to the slopes on his surfboard for the snow. Refining the idea, he cut and planed a single plank of wood that was shorter and broader than a pair of skis, attached anti-skid padding for both feet (which were to be placed sideways-on) and added a rope at the front for steering. From that act of fatherhood, snowboarding history began. The first boards were called, perhaps unsurprisingly, 'snurfers'. The early prototype was further developed in the 1970s by Dimitrije Milovich who manufactured the Winterstick, and it has been further enhanced by the more recent and better-known innovators, Tom Sims and Jake Burton, whose influence and creativity shapes the snowboards ridden today. As technology advances, the impact of both these brands on the sport and on its adherents continues.

A fierce rivalry developed between Tom Sims and Jake Burton who was to become the dominant force and manufacturer of snowboards. Sims was based on the West Coast of the USA, and Burton on the East. Sims was a skateboarder, surfer and snowboarder who wanted to have fun, whereas Burton was a businessman with a passion for snowboarding. Today Burton is a leading designer, innovator and manufacturer within the industry, and he's been instrumental in persuading resorts to accept snowboarders. The company sponsored the creation of organic rather than man-made parks, and the Stash, as these parks have become known, offers riders a more natural aesthetic in which to play. In place of steel and glare, logs and tree stumps provide challenges to balance, agility and stamina. By the time Tom Sims died in 2012 at the age of sixty-one, the worldwide rights to his brand, Sims Snowboards, were owned exclusively by Collective Licensing International, LLC. But he is credited with a number of snowboarding firsts including the first snowboard with metal edges,

> CONFIDENCE TRICK
> ## IMPLEMENT YOUR PLAN
>
> Start putting your plan in place to move forward towards 'conscious competence' in aspects of life that have caused you to doubt yourself. Think about:
>
> 1. the specific areas where you want to attain competency, and
>
> 2. how you will become familiar with your chosen sphere of confidence – which books, magazines, and online material will you read?

the first professional model and, significantly, the first women's-specific snowboard, designed for a lower centre of gravity. Sims is an integral part of snowboarding heritage without whom the sport may have taken a very different direction.

Skiing is a traditional winter sport with a long, stand-alone history of its own and it is governed by firmly-established rules and etiquette. Snowboarding is a modern, relatively new sport influenced by surfing and skateboarding. It has no set rules and remains free from strong historical connections. Skiing was perceived as an upper-class activity pursued by yuppies and rich kids whilst snowboarding was seen as a youth subculture, populated by disrespectful, rude teenage boys whose behaviour endangered others on the slope. Mainstream media (and also snowsports' own news outlets) fuelled the division between slope users, and ridicule between both groups became the norm. In resorts, frequently heard gripes became, 'Bloody skiers think they own the slope, waving their poles around and standing in front of the chairlift exits,' while skiers might have been heard to complain, 'Stupid 'boarders always sitting around on the slope blocking the piste, scraping the best snow off.' And off the slope but online, the prevalence of numerous YouTube videos, including *Shit Skiers Say* and *Shit Snowboarders Say*, provide a window into a lingering rivalry. 'I hate the flats,' and, 'I haven't waxed my board in soooo long' or, 'Hold up I haven't strapped in' might be the skier's slam to taunt the snowboarder, whose retort in turn might echo back, 'I think I've got like fifty days already,' 'Cool poles,' or, 'I hate stairs in ski boots.'

A number of people believed snowboarding would be nothing more than a passing fad, fizzling out, allowing the slopes to return exclusively to skiers. However, some resorts were more forward-thinking and developed areas where snowboarders could perform jumps and ride on rails. By encouraging snowboarders, who turned up with plenty of cash to splash, other ski areas soon realised the opportunity cost and started to follow suit. Over several years, skiers began to enter the snow parks and freestyle skiing became popular.

In further cross-pollination, snowboarding started to influence skiing equipment – carver skis have broader tips and tails than earlier designs, and the shape, which is developed directly from snowboard technology, permits skiers to turn more efficiently. The boundaries separating the two cultures and that line in the snow between their associated stereotypes continue to blur. Today, you are just as likely to see skiers jumping kickers and riding rails like snowboarders, and wearing the same baggy clothing. Skiing has become cool again, and there are as many rich kids who snowboard as there are bad ass dudes who ski.

However, there will always be technical differences between the two on the mountain. Skiers will always attain faster speeds on the piste, while snowboarders will continue to dominate in powder, off-piste. I have friends who ski, and we often holiday together. There is good-natured banter between the two groups, often playing out according to stereotype, but we generally get on well and help each other out. I have frequently been pulled along by a kind skier who has watched me struggle along a flat section of the mountain, and have been thankful. But I have been known to shout at those less courteous if they ski over my precious snowboard, and to grumble in frustration when a skier, who is able to manoeuvre more quickly on the flat, pushes in front of me in crowded chairlift queues. However, today's snow enthusiasts share a far less grudging respect for one another.

Snowboarding has come a long way in the past thirty years. Views gradually changed over the decades, particularly with the expansion of the sport in the 1990s, and official sanctioning came with its inclusion in the 1998 Nagano Winter Olympics. However, controversy arose even then. Terje Haakonsen, then one of the world's leading snowboarders, and someone still revered today, boycotted the Games. He believed collaboration with the IOC (which he viewed as a global enterprise distinctly for profit) would have a damaging effect on snowboarding's culture of free spirit, and on the sport's ability to govern itself on its own terms. The Canadian, Ross Rebagliati, won the first snowboarding Olympic gold medal, but it was subsequently rescinded after he tested positive for marijuana. To make matters more confusing, the medal was later re-instated because at the time, 'weed' was not a banned substance. Technically, it didn't enhance performance. And to further exemplify the sport's amusing growing pains, it later came to light that Team USA's Olympic snowboard coaches did not actually snowboard. Despite the conflicts and questions, snowboarding is no longer seen as a subversive craze, and is now considered a mainstream winter sport.

By immersing myself in all-things snowboarding, then, whether it was taking formal lessons, watching DVDs, or reading, I became more familiar with my new world. It seemed less exotic, more accessible to me, more of my own reality. Gradually, I began to yearn for the snow and the chance to jump on my board. In the early days, moving out of my comfort zone, from the safe place in front of the TV or from behind a magazine, I felt something akin to dread, it all felt so very strange. But, over time, I knew the anxiety would diminish until this recent passion of mine felt fully normal and an integral part of my life.

1. On which occasion were you pushed out of your comfort zone?

   Write the name of the occasion here:...

   ....

   a. How far were you pushed?

   Place an 'x' on the scale below to indicate how far you were pushed.

A little	Somewhat	A long way

   b. How did it feel?

   Place an 'x' on the scale below to indicate how you felt.

Very comfortable	Somewhat comfortable	Very uncomfortable

♦ ♦ c. Write down what you think you learned in the table below.

Were you stomping it or face-planting?

What I learned	Stomping it or Face-Planting
1.	1.
2.	2.
3.	3.

2. What three things can you do to become more familiar with your chosen area(s) of confidence building identified in Chapter One?

Area of Life 1	Area of Life 2
1.	1.
2.	2.
3.	3.

◆ 3. List three things you can do to gain greater practical competence in your chosen area(s) of confidence building.

Area of Life 1	Area of Life 2
1.	1.
2.	2.
3.	3.

4. Name three small goals that you can set for each area. This could be registering for a local race, signing up for a weekend course, or simply talking to a friend about your plans and making yourself accountable for them. But there should be a time-frame, or an end date, attached to each goal.

Area of Life 1	Area of Life 2
1.	1.
2.	2.
3.	3.

◆ ◆ 5. Consider which of the four learning style/s covered in this chapter that you think you may manifest. You may have one or up to four. Identify three specific areas for each where you think it helps and hinders you.

Identify your learning style/s below, and then complete the table for each:

a. Learning Style 1:..

Helps	Hinders
1.	1.
2.	2.
3.	3.

b. Learning Style 2:..

Helps	Hinders
1.	1.
2.	2.
3.	3.

c. Learning Style 3:..

Helps	Hinders
1.	1.
2.	2.
3.	3.

d. Learning Style 4:...

Helps	Hinders
1.	1.
2.	2.
3.	3.

You need to strap in to your learning to understand where and how you stand in relation to your confidence goals. Prepare for life's snow park! Write your answers down.

Scoring

Exercise 1. If you have marked your 'x' between 'A little' and 'Somewhat' give yourself one point. If you have marked your 'x' between 'Somewhat' and 'A long way' deduct a point. If you have marked your 'x' between 'Very comfortable' and 'Somewhat comfortable' give yourself one point. If you have marked your 'x' between 'Somewhat comfortable' and 'Very uncomfortable' deduct a point. For each item of learning give yourself one point.'

Exercise 2. Award a point for each of the things you can do to become familiar with your chosen area(s) of confidence building.

Exercise 3. Award a point for each thing you list you can do to become more competent in your chosen area(s) of confidence building.

Exercise 4. Award a point for each goal you set within each area of confidence building.

Exercise 5. Award a point for each listed area of help or hindrance.

Total chapter points.................

03

SCOOTING ALONG

how to balance

The hotel was relatively small, clean and functional. Dumping my snowboard bag beside the bed, I felt the wall of mountains tower over the length of the valley beyond my window. I had arrived. The sky was leaden grey, threatening snow and moving towards the glass I looked upwards thinking about all the snowboarders, skiers and adventurers who would now be making their way off the slopes as dusk approached. Turning back into the room, I began unpacking my gear. For a moment, I sat on the bed contemplating the week ahead, wondering what it would bring. Not wanting to dwell too much on the uncertainties, I made my way downstairs to the hotel restaurant where, after a long day without much to eat, the aromas from the kitchen beckoned enticingly.

I hadn't seen anyone whom I thought resembled my fellow snowboarding students, so I chose a small table close to the restaurant entrance, to eat alone. Halfway through dinner, my mobile phone rang. Neil McNab was ringing to find his last remaining student who had not shown up in the bar for her course debrief. I had assumed we would all get together after the evening meal, and I hadn't called the McNab office on arrival to check in. Neil told me to turn around, and with the phone still to my ear I looked over my right shoulder; ten men, including Neil, looked back my way.

This was my first snowboarding course in the mountains, as opposed to an indoor slope in the UK, and in 2008 I was excited to be visiting this corner of the French Alps. Chamonix sits within a fist of mountains, clasped by the furl of Switzerland to the north, with the Italian border at its wrist, to the South. Globally renowned as a destination for hard-core adrenaline junkies, the flat valley floor is surrounded and dominated by lofty peaks including the highest summit in Western Europe, Mont Blanc, which rises to 4,810 metres. A year-round resort, attracting climbers in the summer, and snowsport enthusiasts in the winter, it is on many adventurers' bucket list. Chamonix is also home to L'Aiguille du Midi, a cable car boasting the world's highest vertical ascent of 2,807 metres. L'Aiguille takes visitors up to 1,000 metres below the summit of Mont Blanc, providing access to the classic 20-kilometre off-piste route, the Vallée Blanche. The route is littered with crevasses and the threat of avalanche ever present; for most people, travelling off-piste here requires the presence of a mountain guide. The frozen expanse of Europe's largest glacier, La Mer de Glace, snakes for seven kilometres at the run's end, and for less advanced riders, the brilliance of its icy sweep can also be reached via the funicular railway from the valley floor. Below the glacier's surface, a sparkling grotto lined with ice sculptures is cut into the shifting mass, each year.

Climbers and mountaineers are also drawn to the region; Les Drus (3,754m), Les Grandes Jorasses (4,208m), L'Aiguille Verte (4,122m), and Les Droites (4,000m), are all peaks that draw extreme adventurers to an area known for the challenges of its ascents and descents. Those challenges have also turned it into a similar mecca for mountain bikers, trekkers and trail runners. In fact, Chamonix hosts a number of extreme events, including the Ultra-Trail du Mont-Blanc, an iconic ultramarathon of 166 kilometres that boasts an elevation gain of more than 9,500 metres.

The Chamonix-Mont Blanc Valley stretches for 17 kilometres and cradles multiple towns, which are parenthesized by Le Fayet to the West and Le Tour to the East. In between, communities live and die with

TECH TIP

IN YOUR POCKET

CHECKLIST FOR ITEMS TO CARRY
EVERYDAY ON THE MOUNTAIN

1. Tissues

2. Lift pass

3. Sun screen

4. Lip balm

5. Small bottle of water
(to combat altitude sickness and dehydration)

6. Cereal bar

7. Money & credit card

8. Medical insurance details, as well as

9. Gloves, goggles, piste map, and helmet.

the snow — every year, the resort of Les Houches hosts the Kandahar World Cup, a ski race in which competitors can reach thrillingly high speed thresholds of 160 kilometres per hour, while in 1999, areas of Montroc were buried under the force of a terrifying avalanche in which 300,000 cubic metres of snow accelerated to almost 100 kilometres per hour and caused the deaths of twelve people who were killed inside the assumed safety of their homes.

In the world of backcountry snowboard guiding, Neil McNab is a leader. He has more than twenty-five years of experience as a professional free-rider, teacher, and high mountain guide. Even before turning to freeride, Neil had won no fewer than eleven individual British Snowboard Championship titles. He has been instrumental in setting up the BASI teaching qualification for snowboard instruction; for his part in the 2004 rescue of an injured Korean climber he was given the Denali Mountaineer of the Year Award; and in 2008, he received the US Department of the Interior's Citizens Medal of Valor. McNab Snowboarding has been in business since 1995, and its base in Chamonix allows Neil to combine his passions of snowboarding, climbing and mountaineering. At the time of my first trip, I wasn't aware of all the accolades that my instructor had received, a brochure in Gordon's office had simply advertised Neil's technical snowboarding courses. I knew he'd developed the McNab 'Pressure Control System,' that in 2006 he'd published a book, *Go Snowboard*, and I felt confident that this system would suit my theoretical learning style. I knew I wanted to spend some time dedicating myself to learning and practising my skills beyond the indoor snow slopes, and so I booked myself in.

I'd been to Chamonix several summer's previously, but had never seen it in winter conditions. And although I'd been aware of its reputation for extreme adventure, I hadn't really appreciated the scale of its extremes. With hindsight I could have chosen a more mellow resort, but I had faith in Neil and his team, and I put my trust in them to keep me safe.

Prior to his call in the hotel restaurant, I hadn't met or spoken to Neil, but before my week was out, I was to get to know him much better. Feeling self-conscious with ten pairs of eyes looking at me, I sidled over to the boys' table. An additional chair was found and I squeezed into the space made for me. Everyone started talking, pulling me into their conversations, asking various questions. But I also had a question, 'Where is the other woman who is supposed to be on the course?' I was told she backed out at the last minute. 'Oh,' I said, the disappointment perhaps evident. The nerves crept in. I wasn't quite sure how this was going to work out — I had left Gordon at home, looking after our 22-month-old baby girl, and despite the chance to escape sleepless nights, I began to question whether I had made the right choice to come away. But I was here now and would have to get on with it.

Tiredness overtook me, and I did not hang around much after the meal. I needed to calm my nerves and absorb the fact that I was the only woman. Ringing Gordon when I got to my room, the panic flooded out. 'What if I can't do it? What if I can't keep up? What if I'm really crap and hold everyone up?' I had never learned in a wholly male environment before. My husband tried to reassure me, but the seeds of doubt had been planted, and on this occasion the ground for their successful germination had been prepared by others. During the first of my trips to Tignes, Eileen had been the sole woman who rode with the boys. She was a long-time friend of one of the group, and I viewed her as a snowboarding goddess who could rip with the men, an athlete who could hold her own. But I'd also heard the men talk about her, and it hadn't always been complimentary. For her skills and for the intrusion into a male enclave, they sometimes referred to her as Guyleen. What were this lot going to say about me?

When my alarm went off at 7.00 am it was dark. The sun had not yet risen over the mountains and I felt cosy under my duvet. I was tempted to roll over and go back to sleep, but the butterflies in my stomach chased me out of bed. I dressed hastily before heading downstairs to a substantial breakfast. My usual staple is porridge, which allows for a slow release of energy and this, along with a mid-morning energy bar, can sustain me until lunchtime. With breakfast complete I returned to my room to gather the last bits and pieces ready to tackle the day. But it was as I entered the hotel's Boot Room, where all boots and boards are kept overnight, that I realized there was no going back. I was all fingers and thumbs as I bent down to put on my boots, the nervous anticipation of the day playing out in clumsiness visible to everyone around. But I also noted that many of the boys carried harnesses, transceivers and shovels with them – they would be going with Neil to do a separate, off-piste course. And suddenly, for the first time since arriving, I started to feel a bit more relaxed – that left only myself and three other men on the beginners' course, and Keith McIntosh, who worked with Neil, as our coach. An experienced and well-qualified instructor, Keith was in his mid-thirties and taught the talented British youth team. He hailed from Scotland and lived in

Chamonix with his family. As I stepped outside and inhaled the crisp air, looking up at the mountains as the sun started to bathe the valley, I felt alive, keen to get started. By 8.30 am we had thrown our boards in the back of the transit van and were heading up the Chamonix Valley towards Le Tour. I sat in the front of the freezing van, with Keith at the wheel, and he started to tell me, in his strong Scottish accent, about Mel, and about his 1-year-old son, Arren. My sleep had taken a serious battering prior to the trip, but I found a fellow sympathiser in Keith who understood the demands a baby can make, and with whom to exchange tales of exhausted fallout. For the rest of the ride, we chatted amiably about parenting young children.

First days at anything new can be daunting, and this was no exception. Before I even strapped into my snowboard, Keith examined its set-up, passing his experienced eye over the width and angle of my bindings. Stance is one of the foundations of snowboarding, and a weak stance will translate into poor riding. It's impossible to ride well with incorrectly-set binding angles and width. After some adjustments to my snowboard — widening the bindings and tinkering with the angle for my back foot — came the acid test, and Keith asked that we all take a couple of warm-up runs on the lower slopes. Nervously, as I descended the gentle, green run and some slightly steeper, blue slopes, I was fully aware that my instructor's keen eye was scrutinising every move. I turned my board from toe to heel edge in quick succession. By flinging a shoulder and arm across my body, I was able to throw my weight from one side to the other, and force my board to 'turn'. With rough shimmies, I scraped down the slope instead of using the toe and heel edges to slide across the snow. I had no idea about carving, certainly no knowledge of snowboard design and was roundly ignorant of that science translating to efficiency and style. The way I rode the board meant I had to expend a lot of effort. It felt aggressive, not graceful.

The bright, cloudless sky made for great visibility, and as we ascended the mountain after lunch, there were clear views from the cable car and Arve chairlift. We could see the length of the Chamonix Valley, and looking up, the height of the snow-clad mountains above. With Keith's patience and engineering background shining through, he explained the science of snowboard construction, and how we could all benefit from using our understanding of design to improve our personal snowboarding technique. Above the treeline, the upper pistes were wide, open expanses with very few skiers or snowboarders in evidence; we could practise all afternoon in peace. Usually this terrain would be littered with beginners, but January is one of the quietest months in the Alps, and Chamonix is not renowned as a beginner's paradise. At the end of the day, we had a choice — to descend in the cable car, or snowboard a red run back to the bottom of the slopes. A red piste is steeper than a blue, and I dithered. In the end, worried it would prove too difficult for my capabilities, that I would fall and hurt myself, I elected for the cable car. Did it make me appear weak or was it expected because of my gender that I'd choose the easier option? These thoughts crossed my mind. But the first day had been good; I had kept up with the boys and, more importantly, I'd remained injury-free. To risk an accident so early in the week would have been a risk too far for me. I knew it was better to end on a positive note.

Once off the slope, with the sun disappearing fast, the air turning colder by the minute, we clambered into the van and returned down the valley to a warm drink and some cake before heading to the hotel's sauna and swimming pool. At the end of the day, after six hours strapped into my board, I was stiff, but the intense heat of the dry sauna began to relax my muscles. The first day, just like at school or a new job, had not been as bad as I had feared. No one had laughed at me, and I had not been scared stupid. Nor had I burst into tears.

Back in the van on day two, we headed across the valley to Flégère. The area is only accessible via a cable car from the village of Les Praz, and it's impossible to ski or snowboard all the way back to the valley floor. As we rose above the treeline, the vehicles and buildings in Chamonix below began to look smaller and smaller. I turned away from them to gaze up, and the wall of sheer, plummeting cliffs stopped my heart, briefly. The steep ascent took about five or ten minutes, and stepping outside into fresh air, the sudden expanse of reflected white light forced me to reach for my goggles.

All ski slopes are colour-graded according to degrees of incline, and within the European classification system, a green slope presents the gentlest run, through blue, red and finally, black, which presents the steepest challenge. A different system operates in North America, but wherever you are in the world, it is always advisable to ski or ride within your limits. However, and it is a big however, there is large variability within each colour grading. The resort management decides how its own pistes will be marked, and a blue run in one resort is not always comparable to a similarly-graded run in another; some resorts adopt a more mellow approach than others, and this is reflected in their piste classification. Variation can also exist between countries, so that a blue run in France will be steeper than an Italian blue. Nor is it unknown for a resort to mark a run blue if that particular piste acts as a link to another resort, even if the run might be considered red in the context of it's own classification system. Owners know that fewer skiers and snowboarders will attempt a steeper slope, and so they downgrade it.

At Flégère, Keith took us to a green run. It was, and still is, the steepest green slope I have ever seen. Most green pistes are almost flat and, as a snowboarder, I hate them, avoiding them at all costs. Gaining momentum is a challenge, and green is not synonymous with easy, it usually means taking my board off and walking. However, this run was perfect for what our instructor wanted to teach, and it made the point of his lesson very well. We stood at the top of the piste, looking down to the chairlift below while we contemplated his question. 'What can you

TECH TIP
READ THE LAY OF THE LAND

Struggling to get going on a piste? Or completely stuck?

1. Look at the slope, and

2. Ask yourself, 'Where is the fall line?'

see?' Keith asked, as we wondered if there might be some kind of trick to the enquiry. 'Tell me about this piste,' he encouraged. 'Explain the topography and tell me where the fall line is.' I was stumped. In the past, I'd often run into trouble on a piste because I hadn't understood where the fall line lay. A ball that is dropped anywhere on a slope will roll down in the direction that gravity pulls it, but the direction of that fall line doesn't always correspond with the direction of the piste. It was my inability to grasp the distinction between the two that had resulted in previous frustration. I found the easiest way to think of it was to imagine the steep camber on a road – the road may travel east to west, but towards its edges, the contour of the fall line is north to south. On a piste a rider can inadvertently travel off course as the gravitational pull along the immediate fall line sends her sideways, away from the general direction of the piste itself. In the past, I'd ended up in deep powder at the side of a slope, unable to understand why I'd run out of available snow. Keith took me through it one more time. 'Look at the direction of the fall line in comparison to the direction of the piste. You need to stay high to one side in order to take account of its sideways gravitational pull.' A light-bulb snapped on in my head. By reading the slope correctly, I could avoid strapping into my snowboard in the wrong place, trapped on the wrong side of the gradient. Many slopes will present interesting pairings of fall line and piste direction, but these are often isolated to shorter sections within the run. This particular slope was an extreme example, the visibly steep slope illustrating Keith's point well. By examining piste topography, I could now use it to best effect.

Prior to lunch, we kicked it up a notch and headed up a small chairlift to a short, blue run. The wooden-slatted seats looked old and they made for an uncomfortable perch as we moved slowly upwards. Over the next rise, the small wooden hut at the exit came into view and with it, that familiar anxiety surrounding the dismount. Today my anxiety was heightened further, I could see several people spread-eagled on the ground ahead of me. Lifting the bar, I froze, worried about finding a path through the mass of arms, legs and snowboards, and in the moment I was too slow. The wooden seat whipped around behind me, and before I could think, I joined everyone on the ground. Conscious that the next two riders were about to be deposited, I scrambled away as quickly as I could. Fortunately, these old-fashioned and aging chairlifts are being replaced, but occasionally they can still be seen, and whenever I ride one I make a point of alighting swiftly before the chair catches me out.

Once we had untangled ourselves, Keith instructed us to slide down the slope on our heel edge for a distance, and then to switch to our toe edge. We were to experiment with pulling our knees in towards the centre of the board and then pushing them out across the ends of our boards. He wanted to know which stance gave us a better feel of the slope, a truer grip of the board beneath us. I set off, alternately pulling my knees in and then pushing them out. The difference was stark. With my knees extended, engaging the side of my quads to my hips, I could more surely control the entire length of the board's edge. With my knees pulled in, however, I only had control and feel for the edge between the bindings, which made it harder to grip the snow and to control the snowboard fully. This is one of the best exercises I know for beginners, demonstrating as it does the fundamental importance of stance.

In the afternoon, Keith pulled out his video camera, capturing on film what we'd learned. And once we'd finished for the day, back at the bar where it was quiet, we could review the footage, critique our own performances and contribute observations on the stance and style of each rider in the group. Dreading this part of the process, I had no choice but to watch my mistakes. However, on-screen, any errors were not as glaring as I'd perceived them to be in the moment. I've been videoed falling and face-planting many times now, and the alternate reality screening inside my head is a recurring theme. But the cold light of an objective lens adjusts the inner distortion, scaling it down and the discrepancy is something I try to remember when away from the mountains and back at work. Recently, after a week's holiday, feeling off my game during a meeting, and kicking myself afterwards for not giving a good account of myself, nor of the work I'd done, I recalled the video playback. Most people would have been oblivious to my below-par performance, and I really didn't need to be so hard on myself. We all do it. We can all learn to be kinder to ourselves.

On day three, our luck with the weather ran out. It was snowing hard as I pulled back the curtains, and the cloud was low. In the Boot Room at 8.30 am sharp, Keith announced that we would adapt to the conditions and would still find opportunities to learn. 'Today we'll be going to Les Houches,' he said, "cause we can use the tree-lined runs to help with visibility.' The drive was short and at this early hour, with less than favourable weather, the resort was quiet; only a few people were around to interrupt the eeriness that had descended on the mountain. I jumped on the chairlift settling next to Keith, and we passed over trees whose snow-laden branches hung heavily. In silence we ascended higher, moving through the low cloud that thickened around us. I was transfixed by the swirl of snowflakes, hypnotized by their slow, rhythmic dance. The rattle of the chairlift as it passed over each pylon was the only interruption to the magic.

Exiting at 1,900 metres, the snow continued to fall thick and fast around us. Our run was blanketed with 6 centimetres of light, fresh powder, and this was a perfect piste. Earlier, I had panicked when I saw we were to take a chairlift servicing a red piste, and I'd tentatively asked Keith, 'What colour run are we going to do?' He turned to look at me with a twinkle in his eye, and delivered his answer in a deadpan Scottish accent. 'White,' he said. I almost fell for it, and could now see his point. The impact of the weather and environment effects the slope, an easy blue run can turn gnarly, chopped up with moguls by the end of the day, and conversely, under deep powder, a challenging slope can offer a mellower ride. We lapped our run several times as the snow continued to fall around us, and it must have been a struggle for Keith to see our moves, but we all managed to get feedback from him, and we'd made progress on our technique. Significantly, the morning had been my first experience of these conditions. I'd also snowboarded a red run for the first time, and my confidence had grown as a result.

Towards the end of the day, I started to tire, however. Heading back up the chairlift, our task was to descend the entire mountain from our starting point near its top, down to the car park at the bottom where we had left the van first thing that morning. The vertical descent was approximately 600 metres and it would be the longest run I had ever attempted. Snowboarding the first 300 metres of descent along tree-lined runs, the tranquil grace of the scenery lifted my spirits, but then the landscape changed. Our broad piste narrowed to the width of a road, bordered by a sheer mountain wall to my right and a steep drop-off to my left. The incline became much gentler as it rounded the curve of the wall. A number of mountain roads that are otherwise passable in the summer are incorporated into the ski map during the winter months, and they become pistes under snowfall. Trying to maintain my speed across the narrow stretch, I panicked whenever I judged myself to be going too fast, and struggled to find an even pace. I didn't have the width to control my speed with the broad turns of a beginner, and invariably I'd dig into my heel edge, applying the brakes. Frustratingly, I came to a dead halt. Removing my snowboard, I carried it until I reached a point of sufficient incline to regain some speed. Strapping in again, setting off down the run, I accelerated, only to panic, dig in, and come to another, abrupt halt. I repeated the exercise. Although my group had gone on ahead, I was aware that somewhere in front of me, they would all be waiting. Around every corner I expected to see some relief, a chance to sit and rest with the others before carrying on. But none came, just more of the same. How much further could it be?

I was tired, my muscles ached, I was hot and sweaty, but mostly I felt disheartened. Feeling the pressure to catch up, I ploughed on alone, pushing the weariness I felt to the back of my mind. Approaching the next curve in the run, I hoped to see the car park, and at the next, but it never seemed to come into view. More walking. More strapping in. More speed, more panic, more stopping. Always more. At last I rounded a bend, the piste widened, and I saw Keith and the others sitting in the snow at the side of the run, chatting amiably to each other. Relief flooded through me as I reached the group, and I

TECH TIP

SCOOT ALONG

Sometimes you need to unstrap for short distances.
In which case:

1. Keep your front foot strapped in, placing your
back foot on the snow, behind the front binding of your
heel edge, and push off in the direction of travel

2. Continue this manoeuvre several times to get
to where you need to be

3. Over longer distances, after pushing off,
place your back foot on the snowboard,
tight against the back binding (not in it)
and glide until you stop,
then repeat the process
until you can strap in.

flopped down on my back in the snow, absolutely spent. Keith turned towards me with his good-natured smile. 'You're lying in goat poo,' he said. 'Shit,' I muttered, sitting up and moving sharply to one side. 'Exactly,' he replied. Where I'd collapsed was a neat circle of small, round droppings, like buckshot. I noticed how each pellet had sunk into the snow. 'Are we nearly there, yet?' I asked aloud, sulking. When times are at their hardest, the end is most frequently in sight. I just needed to find that extra bit of strength and determination to see it through. Riding under the tunnel, the van came into sight. I'd done it. Exhaustion, relief, pride, all of them tumbled into the van with me. During the drive back to the hotel, and ready for a well-deserved sauna, there was no hiding my glazed smile, that flushed state of grace shared by every snow enthusiast who has pushed herself to achieve.

The degree of mental energy needed to absorb facts and turn them into physical reality is high when learning any sport, but this is particularly true at altitude. Beginners can become easily tired and a recuperation period is often needed. By midweek, I knew I needed a timeout and decided that unless I woke up the next day feeling rested and relaxed, I was going to take the day off. It is strange, in hindsight, how mind and body can seem to work in subconscious tandem – feeling unwell the following morning, I remained in bed, sleeping and reading. And it was the reboot I needed.

CONFIDENCE TRICK

EMERGING FROM A MENTAL CLOUD

If you are having a bad day and things are not going well, consider taking a break. Use the time out to engage with an activity you enjoy. It will boost morale.

Heading to the sauna and swimming pool had become something of a routine before the evening meal, and that rest day was no different. The sauna was small, allowing a maximum occupancy of four people, and when the off-piste group of men returned, three joined me in the dry heat. Despite my fears earlier in the week, I had never been made to feel like the odd one out, and I was treated with respect and courtesy. Relaxing in to the easier intimacy of the heat and pine, talking our way through the day, I was suddenly asked a more probing question, 'Why did you come here all on your own?' 'It was either that or not at all,' I replied, and my answer was laced with acid; I was irritated by the intrusion, which seemed to bear judgement, and I felt I had been caught on the defensive. I realized it must have looked rather strange, a married mother away in the mountains for a week, unaccompanied. I had chosen to leave my husband and baby daughter at home, and had come away without friends. However, the reason was exactly as I'd said. If my goal was to become a more accomplished and proficient snowboarder, the practical reality meant I was going to have to sacrifice time with my family to learn my skill. At the time, I didn't know anyone who wanted to do the same, and so it was either do it on my own, or not at all. Procrastination, the excuse of motherhood, these were not valid reasons. I'd made a plan, I'd prepared, and I'd organized. I had the strong desire to make this happen, and the patience to wait for the right moment. I was also fortunate to have a supportive husband, encouraging parents and a flexible childminder. Not all women have this network. But if the opportunity presents itself, then I believe you reach for it, because seizing the day marks the difference between living and existing.

'Seize the day' — its promise is never uncomplicated. During the evening meal, Gordon called me on my mobile. In the middle of dinner and reluctant to take his call, I nonetheless felt guilty he was at home without me, and I made my excuses, the phone to my ear as I scurried out of the restaurant. He cut straight to the chase, sounding frazzled. 'I've had no sleep,' he began. 'Freya's not going to bed until late, and I cannot get my tea before nine o'clock. She wakes up in the night and I'm battered.' I wasn't sure what he expected me to do about it from the Alps, but I made sympathetic noises, appreciating that he probably needed to let off some steam. Going to bed that night, I felt unsettled. Was it a sense of foreboding? At any rate, I buried my face in the pillows.

The next day came with an executive shake-up, our instructors swapped groups and this time Neil led us out to the slopes. I had heard that he was a perfectionist, that nothing but the best would do and I felt anxious as I climbed into the cable car. Neil is tall at over six feet and his snowboard was large, as a result. We squeezed into one of the first lifts of the day, and as the ground fell away beneath us he took a thermos out of his backpack for a quick slurp of something warm. I could feel my phone vibrating inside my jacket pocket and the display, upon retrieving it from within the many layers of my clothing, showed Gordon's number. 'Hiya,' I said, but after our discussion the previous night, it was a forced greeting. 'I've had a terrible night,' he said, opening the conversation. 'I'm exhausted, and now I've got to get to work.' Inside the cable car, I was aware that everyone could hear, but after several exchanges, I asked him the killer question, 'Do you want me to come home?' There was a pause down the line, and holding my breath I waited for his response. Eventually he spoke. 'No, you stay there. Work hard, become a better boarder and come home when it finishes. I'm alright, really.' And I exhaled. Feeling thankful and relieved, I could now turn my full attention to the week. A small part of me was concerned about what I might have to deal with on my return, but for now, all that could wait.

Putting my phone away I looked up, and noticed for the first time that the day was a glorious 'bluebird' – brilliant sunshine beamed across bright cobalt, cloudless skies and through the cable car window. Compared to the previous day at Les Houches, when it had been snowing hard, this was a different landscape entirely. The cathedral of mountain spires and distant summits made me feel glad to be alive. I could taste the day's promise.

It was early, and we had the privilege of being the first on the slopes. Overnight, the piste bashers had performed their magic, crenellating the snow into its pristine early-morning corduroy. Standing at the top of a perfect, unscarred red run, Neil's words rang in my ears, 'If you want to go as fast as possible use skis, but if you want to experience the mountains and appreciate their feel and flow, then strap on a board.' I achieved my first gripped turn, shifting the pressure of my weight from my heel to my toe. A huge grin swept across my face and I announced excitedly, 'I want to do it again.' Turning had always presented a challenge for me (and for many new riders) that prior moment of hesitation, a common downfall. I had to commit to the fall line to make the turn, and starting the process with my leading leg, roll my foot pressure from heel to toe. For once, I'd completed the transitions smoothly. With that initial deposit into cellular memory, I knew I needed to replicate it again and again. Neil led us over to the first red run I'd completed under Keith's supervision two days previously, when the snow had been falling heavily, and today we were in for a treat.

The Kandahar Alpine Ski World Cup is held each year on La Verte piste, accessible from Les Houches. The race is part of the Alpine Ski World Cup circuit, and competitors endeavour to perform consistently over four disciplines: Downhill; Slalom; Giant Slalom and Super-G.

Giant Slalom and Slalom are considered technical races, whereas Downhill and Super-G are speed events. Competitors in the technical races ski two runs, both of which are held on different courses on the same piste. Those racing in the speed events only ski one run. A fifth event, the Super Combined, demonstrates skiers' ability to shine technically and at speed; it allows competitors one run of Slalom and one of Downhill or Super-G, and these are both raced on the same day. The World Cup began in 1966, but the first Kandahar race predates it significantly. That event was held in 1928 and hosted by the Ski Club Arlberg in St Anton, Austria, the race moving in the early thirties to Mürren, Switzerland, where it was held on alternate years. Its name comes from the British military commander Frederick Roberts, Earl of Kandahar, who was the major benefactor of the British Kandahar Ski Club. And as time passed, other locations were added to the event including Les Houches in 1948, Sestriere, Italy in 1951 and Garmisch-Partenkirchen, Germany, in 1954. These races were considered to be among the most important alpine skiing events besides the Olympics and the World Championships. In 1966 they were incorporated into the World Cup circuit, but the Kandahar retained a particular mythology. La Verte is a black run (not green as its French name suggests), and its vertical drop plummets 870 metres along its 3,343-metre length. Competitors hurtle to the base in times between two to three minutes, their speeds often exceeding 100 kilometres per hour.

From our chairlift passing over the upper part of the Kandahar, we could see and hear the organisers and skiers preparing for the race below us. The voices and the noise of competitors practising over the frozen snow reverberated around us as the sound-waves echoed off the terrain. The course was doused with water, which turned to ice on contact with the cold slope, and the new surface enabled competitors to reach their top speeds. The piste had been outlined with bright blue spray, a visual cue for the racers, and it was easy to see the skiers fly the length of a football field as they hit a bump. I had watched downhill racing on television (the BBC's *Ski Sunday* had been a perennial attraction for me) but viewing the action live was very different. My admiration for their skill and sheer guts reached new levels. In equal measure the spectacle was inspiring and nerve-wracking to watch.

Throughout the morning, the sights and sounds of the Kandahar drew our attention from the chairlift as we returned after each run to ascend the mountain and practise on the slope adjacent to the race. But once off the lift, our focus returned to the immediate lesson, and to our own progress. The contrast was undeniable, but slowing down, taking things step-by-step is a process that itself needs mastering. Neil was very precise about what we were aiming towards. 'I want you to carve your board, using your edge to make as thin a line as possible in the snow between each turn.' In his demonstration, Neil made the theory appear easy, but the practise for us proved harder. Despite attempts to force my body to create a pencil-thin line, my old muscle memory took over, and my path in the snow was much wider than the one Neil had made. No matter how much I tried, my thoughts would not translate to the correct body movements. It was frustrating, but for someone like me who sideslipped her board everywhere, I was making progress, and with that hope came confidence. Over lunch, and from our mountainside restaurant, we could see the details on the surrounding peaks at Les Houches, which traced their jagged outlines high into the cloudless sky. Two days previously, whilst here with Keith, they had been shrouded in low cloud. Neil spoke more about his life in the area, showing us the routes he had taken during his climbs on the neighbouring mountains. Here and there, he pointed to the overnight refuges used by climbers, hikers and ski tourers, huts that are only accessible on foot, but where they could find food and shelter. 'How many times have you climbed Mont Blanc?' I asked. 'I don't know,' he responded, 'I've lost count.' And I was in awe.

Waking up on my final day, I wanted to pull the duvet over my head, to roll over and disappear into sleep again. My muscles ached, I had bruises where I didn't know it was possible, and to make matters worse, my period had arrived. With a cramping stomach, quelled briefly by painkillers, I climbed gingerly into the van and hunkered down in the front passenger seat as we set off for Italy. Chamonix sits at the mouth of the Mont Blanc Tunnel and at its Italian end lies the town of Courmayeur in the Aosta Valley. The tunnel, which was completed in 1965, is more than 11.5 kilometres in length and serves as a major transit route for regular and commercial traffic between the two countries. In 1999, a lorry carrying margarine and flour caught fire and burned for fifty-three hours reaching temperatures of 1,000 degrees Celsius. Thirty-nine people died in that incident and the tunnel closed for three years while major repairs and renovations took place. International media coverage of the disaster meant I was well aware of recent history, and whilst travelling through, it was sobering and unsettling to think of the people who lost their lives in such a tragic and horrific manner.

The bright sunlight was dazzling as we left the darkness behind. On the southern side of Mont Blanc, Courmayeur sits at the far end of the large open valley, and the town is often bathed in sunshine when Chamonix lies in shadow. Popular in summer and winter alike, the cobbled, pedestrianized village centre offers charm and Italian chic. Inside the large cable car, waiting for it to ascend, several Italian women entered, variously sporting full-length fur coats and Gucci sunglasses, or designer ski-wear. The clientele was noticeably different to that on the French side. Keith had returned as our instructor, and he charged all four of us with putting into practise on the wide open slope what we'd learned through the week. My efforts were very half-hearted. Lunchtime could not come soon enough. With aching muscles we trudged through the doors of a traditional Alpine restaurant where a waiter led us through to the rear and out onto a narrow wooden terrace, high above the valley floor. Perched on the side of the cliff, it felt like I could see 100 miles away, to the flat Turin plains in the hazy distance. Feeling the sun's gentle, warm restorative powers, even in late January, I sat back, taking in the view, all the while making my pizza last as long as possible. Spring was around the corner, and I wanted to have an afternoon nap in the beckoning deckchairs out at the front of the restaurant rather than pick up my snowboard and head for the lift. I had reached my limit. Mentally and physically tired, I realized my capacity to absorb new information was severely diminished and in the afternoon I went through the motions, following Keith's instruction, but I couldn't focus. I was ready for home.

My experiences with McNab Snowboarding had increased my exposure to the mountains and I'd had the opportunity to learn from highly qualified instructors. I'd been able to practise, obtain feedback, practise again and build upon each acquired skill. I was beginning to develop competence, but I still understood that the foundations of my learning were not solid. More work was required. The following year I returned to Chamonix, this time as part of a group of five women, but again with McNab Snowboarding. After riding for a week with an exclusively male group, I wanted to experience learning with other women. Expecting an easier ride, I was in for a shock.

Sitting in the transfer bus from Geneva towards the Chamonix Valley, I felt elated to be back, and getting ever closer to the mountains, my excitement grew. The flatlands soon gave way to higher altitudes and as the bus climbed, so did my anticipation for the week ahead. Not knowing who my fellow students would be, I was assured, at least, that they would be women. At the restaurant over our first dinner, I met Heidi and Sarah-Jayne, and learned that they were both travelling with their partners, who were attending a parallel McNab course. They spent much of the evening talking together.

Eager to get going on the first morning, and in contrast to the year before, there were very few butterflies chasing around my stomach. Lacing up my snowboard boots in the basement I got my first glimpse of Jacky and Lucy, two other riders who had finally arrived that morning on a flight that had been delayed. Jacky was small, curvy and wore her long blonde hair tied back under her helmet, whilst Lucy was tall and dark, and cracked jokes from the start. Per my previous trip, Keith was our instructor and we headed up to Le Tour in the van with which I was now quite familiar. The cloudless sky made for good visibility but a vicious wind delayed the cable car and chairlifts which operate only when conditions are safe. With disappointment on our faces, we made our way into a café and drank the first hot chocolate of the day.

It wasn't too long before the lifts were opened and we ascended up to the top of the Arve piste, a blue run named after the river that runs the length of the Chamonix Valley. Within any official snowboarding group, a nervous pecking order establishes itself among riders while everyone sizes each other up — who are the most proficient riders, and who are the least? We were no different, and by the end of the day our individual rankings was clearly set. Most companies group riders together by ability and will often go to extensive lengths to get this right, but inevitably there will be variation within any group. In the morning, Keith covered familiar ground of snowboard set-up and stance, and, just like 12 months previously, we lapped our first run swiftly, practising the basics under review.

After lunch on the sunny restaurant terrace, we returned to the familiar piste we had been snowboarding that morning. Only on this descent, Keith wanted us to try the off-piste to the side of the groomed slope. Watching Keith, followed by Sarah-Jayne, Heidi, Jacky and Lucy, I warily tailed them into the powder. Apart from my foray into the off-piste on that disastrous day in Tignes with Gordon, I had steered away from ungroomed slopes, and was steadfast in my adherence to marked pistes only. As the others rapidly whooped and hollered their way down the mountain, I lost sight of them. I attempted to turn my snowboard and promptly fell. The powder felt very different to the snow on the piste. I seemed to float over the surface, and when I caught an edge it was like falling into soft cotton wool. Momentarily I lay there, laughing. Snow had entered my goggles, scurried up my back and trickled into my gloves. How exhilarating and funny it seemed. My laughter died down and I tried to get up on my heel edge. Putting my hands behind me, I sunk down to my armpits in deep snow, with no solid ground or hard purchase to push against. Floundering, and trying to scrabble for leverage in the aerated blanket of snow, I began to sink deeper. Everyone would be waiting for me at the bottom of the slope and I could feel the pressure mounting. Shouting down to Keith, 'I'm stuck, I can't get up. Don't wait. I'll meet you at the bottom,' and not knowing if anyone, in fact, could hear me, I tried a different tactic. The weight of the built-up snow made the process of lifting my snowboard much harder; I couldn't roll onto my stomach, and after several aborted attempts, lay back to recuperate, exhausted. I was boiling hot, and as sweat began to trickle from my arm-pits, I gave way to rising panic. It was impossible, I thought. I can't get up. There was no way I could make it down the rest of this slope in the off-piste powder. What if I fell again? I looked to the piste about 6 metres away, and decided to focus my efforts on returning to familiar terrain. Sitting up again, I cleared the snow from the top of my board, and taking a couple of deep breaths, I twisted onto my stomach, grunting with the effort. Face down in the snow, I reached beneath me, arms outstretched. Focusing on the problem, quite literally before me, and eliminating a worry I could not control (namely, what would the others think?) I discovered that compacting the snow underneath my hands, starting to build it into a small platform, gave me the solid base I needed to push myself up. At last I was making progress. Eventually ready to make my move, I looked over my right shoulder at the piste. It looked tantalisingly close. Pushing upwards, desperate not to fall, balancing on my toe edge and pointing my board towards the fall line I started to move. Gathering just enough speed, looking towards the piste it came nearer until at last my board made contact with its hallowed, groomed surface. Totally spent, I lay down, closed my eyes, and, after a few minutes, felt my breathing gradually return to normal. It had taken me twenty minutes to get out of the powder. Opening my eyes, seeing the azure sky above, I reminded myself where I was, and how lucky I was to be here. After all, I could be at home, in front of my computer, working under a dull, grey English sky. Sitting up, I could see Keith waiting for me a bit further down the slope — he had remained behind whilst the others had gone on. I rode down to him to apologize for my lack of ability and for keeping everyone waiting. At

CONFIDENCE TRICK

LOOKING FOR THE SUNSHINE

Seek out and spend time with positive people – positivity rubs off.

1. Ask a trusted, positive person to help you look at the facts.

2. Consider what's real – is the situation really that bad?

the time, recognizing I was the least able snowboarder in the group, I felt my place on the course was unjustified. I worried others would think badly of me. But Keith just smiled and gave me a big hug. 'Not to worry,' he said. He also pointed out that I had now outgrown my short, 145-centimetre Fanatic snowboard. It was too small to cope in the powder, and it would hinder my progression.

Driving back to the hotel we stopped en route to buy new snowboards for Jacky, Lucy and myself. Not having a lot of money to splash around, I chose an ex-rental Burton Feather snowboard. It was a little larger than I wanted at 154 centimetres, so a bit of a step up from my current board, but I really didn't have much choice — at eighty euros it was one-fifth of the price of Lucy's new Ride board. Arriving back at the hotel, Lucy, Jacky and I retired to the sauna. Jacky wore the tiniest bikini I had ever seen, it barely covered her nipples, and that in many ways suited her full-frontal, out-there attitude. As we reviewed the day, it became clear that Jacky was annoyed that Heidi always seemed to hang close on the slope and in her path. We could feel the group fracturing in two, Heidi and Sarah-Jayne joining forces. They were both on holiday with their partners, they both snowboarded at a similar level, and it seemed inevitable they would become pals. Back in my room, reflecting upon my own performance, I still fretted about holding everyone back.

By midweek, the weather had turned. A low cloud hung over the valley and I woke to snow flurries beyond the window. Expecting to return to Les Houches, as we had done twelve months previously when the weather closed in, I was surprised when Keith announced we would be heading to the Grands Montets, accessible from Chamonix's neighbouring village of Argentière, further east. This was new territory for me. Its north-facing, steep slopes are the stuff of legend, and the area is an off-piste mecca, attracting ambitious intermediate, advanced and expert snowboarders and skiers. With a vertical descent of 2 kilometres, it presents the most challenging terrain in the valley. Exiting the chairlift, we scooted further along a short, flat section before heading further again up the mountain. I tried to rush, feeling that constant pressure to keep up. We spent most of the day on the red piste of Pierre à Ric, snowboarding from the mid-station down to Argentière village. The steeper slopes meant practising initiation of our turns from a higher point within their arc, and changing onto our new edges sooner, before we got into the fall line. With this early turn, speed can be controlled and a consistent momentum maintained.

TECH TIP

ON THE FLAT

When riding along flat sections of terrain it's hard to sustain momentum.
Keep:

1. Your weight centred over your snowboard

2. Even pressure over both feet, and

3. Your knees bent, loose so you can absorb any lumps and bumps in the snow.

Sitting half-way down the run, towards one side, Keith was explaining the technique in more detail, the physics of our acceleration, when a posse of young men came hurtling down, careering past us and shouting our way. Keith paused momentarily, watching the spectacle, and then he turned to us and said, 'Every one of you girls is better than that lot. All it takes is balls to strap on a board and point it downhill. It'll only take you so far.'

Approaching the base of the run, the slope levelled out as it curved towards the chairlift. I had always found it difficult to gather sufficient speed to cover the flatter sections, struggling to run on the broad base of my board alone, unable to grip and maintain control with its edges. It takes practise to keep an even pressure between toes and heels, an even balance between front and back foot, and without it the ride can be squirrelly. Catching either edge of a snowboard results in a quick, unceremonious meeting with the ground, often occurring so fast the rider has no chance to put her arms out to break her fall. I didn't relish the prospect of face-planting. It's possible anywhere on the mountain, but on these sections around the lift base, where the rider has picked up speed to compensate for the flat terrain, the falls seem to happen at lightning speed and the pain on impact with the compacted snow feels worse. But Keith understood this area of the mountain was my Achilles heel, and approaching the base of the run, he took both my hands in his, and facing me, rode goofy to my regular stance. As I tensed my muscles, getting ready to speed check with my heel edge, Keith started to shake my hands loosely, 'Relax, it's fun,' he said. 'Let's go faster. Come on, Kate.' With painful memories not so distant, I hesitated. But with Keith holding my hands, I was pulled along. I bent my knees, placed even pressure through my feet and repeated the internal mantra, 'Relax, go with it. Relax, go with it.' Suddenly I found myself smiling and the chairlift was in sight. Freeing myself from the details, I'd been able to 'let go'. I had made it without falling over.

Later in the afternoon, as we took the Bochard lift higher up the mountain, I knew this would be the last run of the day. It was the steepest I had ever ridden, and approaching the crest, I hesitated even more than usual. Too tired to think clearly, I travelled most of the piste sideslipping on my heel edge in fear of turning. At the mid-station I rested in the warm café whilst the others repeated the run, and with a mug of hot chocolate between my hands, I pondered the day. Much of it had been spent outside my comfort zone, on the edge of my abilities. Constantly challenged, I now felt drained (it was not until much later that I appreciated I had ridden more than 2 kilometres of vertical descent, effectively tripling my achievement from the previous year at Les Houches). And I had missed my daughter and husband more than expected. I felt it was unrealistic to expect the girls to understand my situation as a wife and mother, which in turn led to increasing feelings of isolation. On this second trip to Chamonix, even surrounded by women, I still felt like I was the odd one out.

The final day was a repeat of the year before, heading through the Mont Blanc Tunnel to Italy and Courmayeur. Again, I was tired and feeling fragile. Neil was our instructor, and his aim was to build upon our early lessons with Keith. The bad weather was yesterday's business, and that morning the sun shone out of a cloudless sky.

Snowboarding across to the main slope where we were to practise, I could see everyone in front of me. It was a familiar view. I seemed to have spent the past week looking at everyone's back as they stretched their lead away from me. And again, on the shallow slope, I found it hard to get moving and ended up at the side of the piste with no room to manoeuvre further. In my haste to catch up with the others I'd forgotten Keith's topography lesson on the direction of piste versus the fall line. Removing my board and walking back up the slope for 10 metres, I strapped in again, feeling the weight of the day stretch before me. Sighing deeply, I resigned myself to feeling inferior, incapable of keeping up with the others. Snowboarding towards our small group, Heidi and Sarah-Jayne hopped in the small cable car with Neil, leaving Jacky, Lucy and me to ascend in the following télécabine. Whilst they chattered about the day, I could feel tears starting to well. Why couldn't I do what they could all manage? Surely, I should be further along my learning curve by now. If I'd taken time to think about the progress I'd made, instead of comparing myself to my peers (and each of them had their own demons to conquer) I might have been able to feel pride in my achievements. My expectations were unrealistic. But on this final day on the slopes, and with tears spilling, I confessed my thoughts and feelings to the two girls who leant me their shoulders to cry on, and I appreciated their kind words and encouragement. Hastily I wiped my face as we approached the cable car exit.

CONFIDENCE TRICK

REFOCUSING: CONTEXT IS EVERYTHING

If things have gone badly, put them in context and focus on:

1. Solutions

2. Ask yourself what you would do differently next time

3. Visualize an approach to the problem that you can call on in the future.

Neil wanted us to develop feel, and we attempted to translate his instructions into action. Snowboarding is as much about art as science, and developing a natural feel for the board and the mountain beneath it enables a rider to attune herself to her immediate environment and adapt her riding accordingly. By developing her awareness, a rider starts to intuit when something feels slightly off, and to understand when it's quite wrong. Away from her instructor, she can start to recognize her errors and know how to remedy them. After a morning of practise we all had to be videoed for teaching analysis purposes. Waiting for my turn to drop in (I wanted to be the last to descend) I set off as Neil called me down. With a camera pointing my way, I tensed and caught an edge. Bang, down I fell. With a bruised backside and ego, I hauled myself up and snowboarded towards the group. Sitting next to Neil in the snow at the side of the piste, I gave in to my anger and frustration. 'I just can't do it,' I barked, slamming my fist into the snow. By this stage I really didn't care what he or anyone else thought. Completely unfazed by my outburst, he calmly clarified what I needed to do. We both stood upright, and as we snowboarded towards the chairlift Neil made his point more emphatically, 'Remember Kate, ride there, don't slide there.' I needed to be more assertive, to command my board's pace and direction. I tried to adopt Neil's instruction, but wasn't in the right frame of mind, and I struggled.

At lunch I sat quietly, feeling despondent and withdrawing from the others. I tried to remain positive, but was now finding it increasingly hard. Rather than spend the last afternoon slipping further behind the others, I wanted to go home. Back on the mountain, I tried as best I could to persevere. In turn, Neil concentrated on encouraging me to move greater pressure up to the front of my board in order to initiate my turn, but mentally and physically, I had no reserves to call upon. As the day progressed I felt increasingly inadequate. Each time I set my board towards the fall line, attempting to turn, its acceleration unnerved me. My peers were faster and technically better, and as each hour ticked away, so did my confidence. Isolation and weariness fed my negativity.

Climbing into the van, at the end of the day, the sun disappearing and the air turning colder, I sat in silence beside Keith as he drove through the Mont Blanc Tunnel. For the whole journey I hardly spoke.

I was brooding over my week and found it hard not to compare myself against the others in my group, all of whom had made serious progress. I felt as if I'd gone backwards. After two focused weeks of top-quality instruction, I wasn't where I expected to be. I anticipated coming home knowing I could ride with confidence. Caught in my own internal struggle, desperately wanting to snowboard but also feeling like I would never be able to make it, I sat there considering whether I should sell my newly acquired board together with the rest of my snowboarding kit. I considered giving up and stopping altogether. Sad and disappointed, I didn't want to admit defeat and failure to others, but mostly I didn't want to admit it to myself. Lost in the inferno, I did not give much thought to Keith at my side. When I dragged my sorry arse out of the van it was to be the last time I would see him. I didn't say goodbye and nor did I thank him for the help, guidance and patience that he had given me. Expecting him to come in for a drink, I just hauled myself out of my seat, thankful to be getting on a plane home the next day. He put the van in gear, and drove home to Arren and Mel to celebrate her birthday with his family. It is with deep regret that I didn't make the most of this last journey with him.

CONFIDENCE TRICK

CHOOSING TO LISTEN TO THE VOICE ON YOUR SHOULDER

We have a metaphorical devil and angel on each!

1. Remind yourself what you can do well. One mistake or bad day does not necessarily represent the entirety of your progress

2. Promote the voice of Reason over the voice of your inner Critic.

I felt like a failure. By focusing on my inadequacies, measuring myself against my peers, I'd put myself in such a negative mindset that I was blinded to the one fact that mattered – in reality I had progressed hugely since my previous trip. Negativity had played a significant role in holding me back, and I'd descended into that downward cycle of pessimism, where it becomes hard to view anything as constructive. The practise of positive thinking, as described by psychology researcher, Barbara Fredrickson, in her 2008 paper, 'Open Hearts Build Lives', allows people to see more opportunities and choices than they might otherwise consider. And with that practise comes the enhanced cognitive ability to develop new skills. At the time, I was ignorant of my own cognitive potential, and instead of harnessing it to work for me, I let it work against me. I could have chosen to remain positive by focusing on what I could do. I could have been more grateful for having the opportunity to come away and learn in a mountain environment, and I could have looked for the positive people around me to reinforce my practise. I could have been far more kind and patient with myself. Learning is not a linear process, and it's usual to have good days and bad. I didn't recognize this, and punished myself. It wasn't necessarily my fault for not knowing, but I missed out on the wonder and celebration of learning new skills.

EXERCISES

1. Revisit Exercise 3 from the previous Chapter: 'List three things you can do to gain greater practical competence in your chosen area of confidence building.' Rewrite the actions in the tables below and add next to them, where and how often you will practise. Be as specific as you can.

Area of Life 1	Where & how often
1.	1.
2.	2.
3.	3.

Area of Life 2	Where & how often
1.	1.
2.	2.
3.	3.

◆ 2. Think of three setbacks of any type you have experienced in the past. Write them down in the column headings of the table, below.

Setback 1	Setback 2	Setback 3
1.	1.	1.
2.	2.	2.
3.	3.	3.

◆ ◆ 3. What did you learn from each of those three setbacks? Write your answers in the rows under each setback identified in the column headings.

4. How will you remain positive when learning your competence? What is going to keep you stoked?
In the table on the following page, rewrite your chosen areas of competence in the column headings, and in the rows underneath each, list at least three reasonably achievable suggestions for keeping yourself upbeat, ideas that will carry you through the process in your life. Think about spending time enjoying your hobbies or pastimes.

Area of competence 1	Area of competence 2	Area of competence 3
1.	1.	1.
2.	2.	2.
3.	3.	3.

Scooting along to competency means building greater balance into your life, using life's topography to your advantage. Visualise your own fall line! Write your answers down.

Scoring

Exercise 1. Give yourself one point for each item you will practise to gain competence, and one point for each separate example you list regarding where and how often you will practise.

Exercise 2. For every setback listed, reward yourself with one point.

Exercise 3. For every different item of learning identified, give yourself one point.

Exercise 4. Award yourself with point for each item listed that will help you remain positive.

Total chapter points................

04

DAVOS

MAKING YOUR MARK
AS YOU CARVE YOUR PATH
changing direction by looking ahead

Sitting on the edge of my Swiss hotel bed, it didn't matter that I couldn't understand the television commentators. It was 9 February 2014 and the Olympic Slopestyle Women's final was underway. Jenny Jones, the British finalist stood at the top of the course about to drop in. I had snowboarded with Jenny two years previously, and had followed her career for a while. During a holiday in Morzine, in the French Alps, I'd shared a chalet with a group of girls who were on a snowboarding camp, and Jenny had joined them for a brief period. My snowboarding girlfriend had left early and I had no one to go shredding with, so I was invited to join the camp, and Jenny, for an afternoon.

Despite the fact that she was one of the UK's most consistent snowboarders, the snowboarding media had never given her enough credit for her achievements. The men's sport is seen as more exciting – the jumps are bigger, the spins are faster – and therefore receives the majority of the media's attention. On the whole, the mainstream media ignores snowboarding altogether unless it is an Olympic year. Watching her as she made her run, willing her to do well, I shouted at the TV, jumping up and down in my room. It didn't matter that no one could hear me. After her second run, Jenny was in gold medal position and my knuckles were white as I gripped the duvet, but there were a number of other riders still to compete. As the next two competitors made their runs, I watched as Jenny slipped one, then another position down the medal table. If my eyes left the screen it was to text snowboarding friends, the viewing action anxiously conveyed through my fingers. Holding my breath, I could barely stand the tension. Now, in bronze medal position, could she hang on? After a nail-biting last run from Austrian, Anna Gasser, she had done it and Olympic bronze was hers. My joy was explosive and I felt thrilled for her. At the age of thirty-four, Jenny was the oldest finalist by six years, and that tier of victory alone was a fitting tribute to all that had gone before — her dedication and continued effort despite injury and lack of recognition. A woman had become the first British athlete ever to win an Olympic medal on snow.

I had arrived in Zurich airport the previous evening, after a two-leg journey from Newcastle via Heathrow, and was looking forward to my onward travel by train to Davos. Waiting at the baggage carousel, my mobile phone bleeped as I turned it back on. The text from British Airways was concise, 'Unfortunately your luggage hasn't travelled with you today.' I had a four-day course looming and wondered what an earth I would do. 'No snowboard, no equipment and no clothing,' I worried to myself. But, I had a day's grace, because instruction wouldn't start until the day after next. I made a decision to call the airline.

The train left promptly, displaying legendary Swiss efficiency, taking me east along the southern shores of Lakes Zurichsee and Walensee, their surface black in the darkness. We trailed gently through the mountain valley to its end before climbing abruptly through Alpine passes that glowed blue in the moonlight, and finally, three hours later, I was delivered to Davos, 1,560 metres above sea level, and Europe's highest town. It was 11.30 pm and Lauren came marching along the snowy pavement calling my name and a loud, 'Hello!' in greeting before segueing without pause into the details of her day. As soon as she started talking I recalled her love of colourful language – she swore like a trooper.

I'd met Lauren in France, two years previously, when we had shared a group chalet in Morzine. At the time, she had come to the Alps with a girlfriend for a women's snowboarding camp, and I had been holidaying separately with a friend of my own. Lauren was average height with sleek, dark bobbed hair but in all other respects, she was anything but average. Everything about her was expressive. She was also the best recreational female snowboarder I had ever seen and appeared to have no fear, tackling anything that was asked of her. Concerned about coming away with a snowboarder of that level, I wondered how far I'd be left in her wake, and if that would be a problem. But my usual holiday partner had deserted me this season, and Lauren had had no one to go away with either, so we'd teamed up. It was late when we arrived at the hotel where we were sharing a room, and we both got ready for the night. Lauren apologized as she stripped naked and walked around the room getting her things together before jumping into bed. Rather startled by the lack of inhibition, or perhaps it was exhibition, I looked the other way and undressed myself discreetly.

Progress had been made since leaving Chamonix, and several years had passed. Looking back, I had learned some lessons from the snow, including the need to practise, which I'd drawn into my larger life perspective. I'd become better at harnessing optimism, focusing on solutions, and creating a positive atmosphere in which I could remain confident. I could seek out activities to complement my favoured learning style, and that meant working with technical instructors who could explain theory and support its translation into practise. On my board, I was competent in many ways, and likely to be considered unconsciously competent on a blue piste. My confidence had become second nature, and very little conscious effort was needed to perform the task. I had developed 'feel' by now, per Neil's instruction, knowing when turns were awkward, particularly on steeper terrain where I still reverted to prior mistakes, usually as a result of old fears of falling… and failing. Importantly, I recognised that I could move in and out of unconscious competence, even regressing a stage, to conscious incompetence when conditions or terrain changed dramatically, and when that happened it had an adverse effect on my state of mind. And so my identified goal for this trip was to become more solid in my confidence riding blue runs, and to embed that unconscious competence more thoroughly. I also knew I needed more exposure to the off-piste on steeper slopes in order to gain the kind of conscious competence that comes with practise. Some parts of my riding were more developed than others, then, and by broadening my exposure to different types of terrain and conditions I wanted to develop greater competence and ultimately confidence.

In the morning, we met the other members of our group at breakfast. To a man they were all keen to get on the mountain and work their snowboarding legs, prior to instruction the next day. I, on the other hand, would be kicking my heels courtesy of British Airways. However, the forced rest day meant I could now watch the Olympic Slopestyle Women's final and take some time to explore Davos. After watching Jenny's triumph, I grabbed my hat and coat and headed out the door for some discovery. Davos is probably best known for hosting the World Economic Forum. Every year, 2,500 global leaders, including politicians, economists, business leaders and a smattering of influential celebrities, descend upon the town in January in order to discuss the world's urgent matters of the day and to shape agenda. It's a working town, situated in Switzerland's eastern Alpine region, fewer than 30 kilometres from Austria's southern border, and as the crow flies, it lies roughly half-way between Munich and Milan. The year-round population of approximately 11,000 swells in the winter as snow enthusiasts looking to participate in their chosen sport overtake the local residents in number. As well as downhill skiing and snowboarding, cross-country skiing is popular, and the area offers more than 70 kilometres of prepared trails. The town is also famous for its ice hockey team, Hockey Club Davos, established almost 100 years ago, and the sport's international invitational, the Spengler Cup, is held at the local ice hockey stadium. Davos is also home to several world-class scientific research institutes. The World Radiation Centre sits towards Lake Davos at high elevation and under deep blue mountain skies. Since its founder Carl Dorno observed more than a century ago that TB patients were healing more quickly at altitude than at sea level, it has been advancing our understanding of the biological influences of UV light, and its primary research today, into radiation measurements and instrumentation, is a successor to that original mission and is a field of global relevance. The area is also home to the WSL Institute for Snow and Avalanche Research SLF, which provides key research into mountain ecosystems, and develops advanced risk management tools (in the form of apps and data) for use throughout the Alps.

Separated into two distinct areas, Davos Dorf and Davos Platz, the main town is spread out along the Landwasser River valley. Unlike its smaller northern neighbour, Klosters, famous for its British Royal visitors and as a classic Swiss chocolate-box resort, Davos has fewer architectural delights than many may expect of a Swiss ski town. If Klosters were a Vogue supermodel assured of her beauty and enduring popularity, then Davos would be a highly organized, middle-class, Boden-clad mother juggling work and childcare with alarming efficiency. One of the world's most scenic railways, the Glacier Express, can be ridden year-round from Davos. The route tracks south through the mountains to Filisur, connecting there with the main line from St Moritz. It then pivots north and west through twisting tunnels and over precipitous viaducts to Zermatt, the town synonymous with the iconic Matterhorn. The 257-kilometre route takes patience, a head for heights and 7.5 hours to complete.

Davos is one of the largest ski resorts in Switzerland and, like Chamonix, it is split into several skiing areas. For both Chamonix and Davos, travel between mountains is made possible by bus rather than connecting through the pistes and chairlift system. To the north, Parsenn is accessible from both Davos and Klosters and is probably the most popular; to the south-east, Jackobshorn's slopes are where freestylers congregate for the snow park and superpipe; Rinerhorn is further south, still, along the valley, while Madrisa rises north beyond Klosters. And finally, Pischa nestles east off the main valley road, and is known for its freeride opportunities and as a place to go for snowshoeing or winter hiking.

The group had opted for Jackobshorn. Still high from watching Jenny clinch her medal, I walked to meet Donnie Macleod for lunch. Donnie is the owner of Synergy Snowsports and was to be our instructor for the week. As I sat in the restaurant, choosing the cheapest lunchtime option on the menu (Switzerland is one of the most expensive countries in the world) in he walked. Lauren had made the holiday booking on my behalf, so I'd had limited contact with Donnie and didn't know what to expect. Dark-haired, with a strong Scottish accent, he explained he wanted to listen and to learn a little bit more about my snowboarding experience, to hear what my goals and expectations were for the week. At this stage in my snowboarding 'career', most people would regard me as competent. I had been asked on more than one occasion why I continued to have lessons, but I didn't see it that way. The top tennis players in the world all have coaches, and I am sure they would not be so arrogant as to believe coaches are not needed. I knew I could benefit from continued instruction, and Donnie had worked with riders at the highest level. His background in slalom racing meant he had worked with three-time British Olympian, Zoe Gillings, who placed ninth in Snowboard Cross (also a racing discipline) at Sochi that year. I was ready with my goals for Donnie, and explained the lack of confidence I felt riding steeper slopes, particularly those off-piste. 'I know that with greater skill comes increased confidence and subsequently tonnes more fun,' I said. My pursuit had to include a sense of play and fun – it was a given for me. And while most people have a level of riding in mind, a limit that they are happy to attain, without aspiring further, I remained unsatisfied and felt the drive to achieve more. I had made a mark, in other words, but didn't feel I had made my fullest mark. 'I'd like to become a more competent snowboarder overall,' I summed up, 'and

CONFIDENCE TRICK

ESTABLISHING GOALS

Plan ahead and establish incremental goals:
1. think of your eventual long-term goal and work backwards from there, breaking your competences into smaller pre-requisite steps.

2. what do you need to do to get to get to the next step?

certainly one who is more confident in the powder on steeper terrain.'
I was interested in Donnie's appraisal of my riding ability because
he'd never seen me ride before. He'd have no preconceived ideas,
then, and I thought a fresh perspective would be useful. I left the
restaurant feeling positive and excited about the next day.

Before then, however, I had to source a snowboard and some gear.
Distance from the airport is a factor, and consequently I was further
down the delivery queue than other BA customers who were
holidaying closer to Zurich and whose luggage had unfortunately not
travelled with them. Luckily the airline had confirmed that I could
purchase a pair of snowboarding pants, a set of thermals and that I'd
also be able to hire a board and boots. There was time before meeting
Lauren at the hotel, and I headed out into the streets to explore
further. The Landwasser river burbled behind the hotel adjacent to
the train line, and I followed the path beside the river, strolling amidst
both Davos residents and its visitors, taking in the mountain views.
Trains came and went, and I was fascinated by the cross-country
skiers who glided alongside the tracks in designated parallel trails of
their own. A shallow sun wove in and out of the clouds, teasing with
its the warmth. Spying a bench in the near-distance, I sat down for a
few minutes to take in my surroundings, and I felt thankful that I was
here in the mountains, even if my snowboard was not.

Lauren was back at the hotel and keen to accompany me; we hurried
outside, aware that we were on a time schedule. Earlier in the day
the group had agreed to meet up in the early evening, and take the
bus together to the local municipal wellness centre. Eau-Là-Là is
more than the English idea of a municipal pool might suggest —
part spa with outdoor sun deck, and part leisure pool complex — its
indoor pool cuts a swimmable channel through a high timber and
glass wall out to the open, Alpine air, and to views of the Landwasser
Valley. Our aim was to relax and soak in its soothing waters. But
first, the mission at hand. The local ski shop staff were extremely
helpful and assured me I would love the board they had picked out
for me — a Roxy Banana Smoothie which gives a loose, playful ride

but with wavy Magne-traction technology between the bindings to help grip the snow. My regular DC Biddy snowboard didn't have this feature meaning I had to work my legs hard to keep my edge in hard-packed snow. Lauren bustled about, picking up thermal leggings, snowboard pants and goggles, and handing them to me in the fitting room. She kindly offered to lend me a pair of gloves, together with her spare thermal top, and with all essential clothing and equipment to hand, we hurried back to meet our group.

At Eau-Là-Là, the price of admission permits access to both the indoor and outdoor pools, but outdoors is the destination for those seeking underwater jets to pummel aching muscles. Swimming through the channel that connected both bodies of water, I could see the steam rising outside. Icy-cold air blast over my uncovered head, freezing my scalp in an instant, while my body remained cocooned in warmth. Lauren could not see well without her contact lenses, and in the twilight I lead the way towards a powerful jet that massaged our backs. As I peered beyond the buildings, I could just make out the black silhouettes of the mountains rising into the early night stars. The surrounding lights illuminated the falling snow as it disappeared into the banks of steam around our faces, and before long it began to settle on my head, the mat of cold seeping through to my brain. I swam inside. There would be other days for Eau-Là-Là.

Waking the next day, we drew back the curtains to cloudy skies. The morning's high winds were also unwelcome, and we wondered if the chairlifts and even the cable cars would be closed for safety. It had been relatively cold the previous day, so I knew the wind-chill would ensure even lower temperatures. But despite the omens of a difficult day ahead, Lauren (who apologised for her nakedness again) and I hurriedly dressed for the slopes. I took advantage of the breakfast buffet, just like everyone else, covertly making a cheese and ham sandwich for lunchtime consumption on the mountain where the price of a sandwich climbed to the equivalent of £12. Our bus was packed, passengers jostling for space and to hold onto the sharp ends of their equipment as the vehicle progressed through

Davos Platz and took us along to Davos Dorf. We were excited to be released from its enclosed space at the base of the funicular that would carry us on the next leg of our journey, a further 500 metres to the top of Parsenn. Inside the car, we were protected from the wind but we could feel its strength rise the higher we climbed along the steep, winding journey. Towards the top, surface snow whipped up from the ground, blowing across the exposed face of the mountain. Stepping out of the funicular into the station that had been cut into the rock, frigid air hit us hard. The temperature had plummeted to -20 degrees Celsius. Pausing before stepping outside, we listened whilst Donnie talked us through the set-up of our boards, and the angles of our bindings. We couldn't put it off any longer, and braced for the inevitable onslaught of the wind as we left the confines of the building. The air in my nostrils froze instantly, but my eyes were protected from the cold by goggles, and, fortunately, once away from the top, conditions were not as harsh as I had expected; the first few warm-up runs went well. While the wind and light snowfall meant visibility was impaired, the snow conditions were soft and forgiving. But high above the treeline, the landscape and open mountain faces afforded little shelter and the break for lunch was welcome.

Our fellow students included Ronan and Jon, two friends from Ireland and London. Ronan spoke with a soft, lilting accent, whilst Jon was undeniably an Essex man with a cockney turn of phrase. Chris (an American) and Ian had travelled independently bringing the group to six. And finally, Joe, made us seven; Joe was travelling with his wife, Catherine, who occasionally joined us for meals, but we did not spend much time with her. Lauren and I were the only women on the course, therefore. Most of the first day was spent reviewing snowboarding fundamentals, revising speed control, the line or path chosen, and making riding adjustments for the snow and terrain. We revisited what we knew about steering, flow and body management, we practised foot pressure, rhythm, and balance on the board.

As the day drew to a close, the group descended to the mid-station where Donnie gave us a choice. We could continue on the funicular

or opt to ride the black run to the valley floor. I had never ridden a black run, and although comfortable on blues and most reds, I wasn't sure if I should tackle this at the end of the day on an unfamiliar, hired board. I was the slowest rider and the last to reach the mid-station. Many of our group had already strapped on their boards ready for 'the off'. 'I think I should head down on the funicular,' I said, voicing my concerns. 'You'll be fine,' Lauren cut back, abruptly, and taking me by surprise. 'Come on!' she insisted, and headed down the slope, disappearing from view, but leaving her irritation in the air around us. Joe reassured me, 'I've been down here before, and there's only one narrow section which makes it a black run, otherwise it's no different to a red. I'll stay with you.' With his encouragement I decided to give it a go. He was right, there was one narrow section and the rest was relatively easy. At a couple of points, I resorted to sideslipping on my heel edge, but I took my time and stayed focused, listening to Joe's commentary. In what seemed like no time, I'd descended all the way and was heading towards the bar in town. I was floating in a state of grace and achievement. A black run, my first, on day one! I felt proud that I had pushed myself, but was aware that without Joe's support I may well have passed up the opportunity, and I was grateful for his part in my moment of success. As I entered the bar, I noticed that Lauren had been there long enough to get her order in.

TECH TIP

CHIN UP

1. Look up when snowboarding, not at your feet

2. Look where you are going. When driving a car, you do not look at the road 3 feet beyond the bonnet, but further ahead; the same principle applies to snowboarding. Chin up!

Donnie introduced us to his friends, Nigel and Daniel, who were visiting from the UK on their annual boys' snowboarding trip. They weren't part of our course, but we would often bump into them that week on the slope, either at lunch or during après. Nigel had spent significant time abroad, and was fluent in both Italian and German, while Daniel was a surfer. Nigel insisted I try a traditional specialty, mostly because he enjoyed pronouncing it. A Schümli Pflümli is a sweet coffee drink, laced with plum schnapps and topped with whipped cream. Its name, a double diminutive to double the irony, most closely translates to Tiny Little Foaming Plum. This part of Switzerland speaks Swiss-German, which is one of four official national languages that also include French, Italian and Romansh. It is notoriously hard to master, and is different to the spoken German heard in Germany. Approximately 65 per cent of the population speaks Swiss-German, but each canton or area has its own dialect, which residents fiercely protect. Davos lies in Graubünden, Switzerland's easternmost canton, and for historical reasons to do with its geography — which traces the line of Austrian's southern border and touches to its south the ruffles of Italy's northern fringe — it is the country's only trilingual region. Swiss-German is widely spoken, but also Italian and Romansh, and in this part of the country, dialects can change between towns and valleys. As a non-German speaker, I could not make out the subtleties, although I was suitably impressed with Nigel's ability to converse with the locals and exchange the odd joke. I am all for trying local drinks and food, but a Schümli Pflümli, however amusing to order aloud, never became my favourite holiday tipple.

I woke the next day, positive and enthusiastic. The memory of my first black run remained fresh in my mind, and the weather gods were smiling upon us. Gone were the wind and falling snow of yesterday, and in their place a cloudless sky of cobalt blue. As if to seal my good fortune, British Airways had finally came up trumps and delivered my luggage including my cherished DC Biddy snowboard. Leaving the hotel I almost skipped to the bus stop as we retrod the familiar route from the day before heading up to Parsenn.

Descending the run we had stomped so many times twenty-four hours previously, and making my first turns, I expected to feel the familiar comfort that comes with familiar gear, but my beloved board felt somewhat unstable beneath my feet. By the time I reached the mid-station I had fallen three times. My hired board had felt strong and true. In contrast, my own board felt flimsy and skittish. The Biddy is a rockered board its edges very slightly tilted upwards to ensure the rider is less likely to catch an edge and fall. When first riding it, I loved the feel in comparison to my old cambered Rome Vinyl board. Many a time I stayed upright on my Biddy when I would have taken a tumble on my Vinyl. The Biddy had always felt playful. Today it was all hard work. I was unsure why it felt different, but I suspect it was something to do with me and possibly a contrast with the Banana Smoothie.

The next leg was off-piste, part of it directly under the chairlift. As I followed Donnie, Jon and Ronan, the incline appeared to steepen suddenly. I traversed into the powder, riding switch on my heel edge, and looking down the slope I realized that I was not carrying

TECH TIP

INTO THE WILD

Off-piste snow feels very different under your board compared to a groomed run. If you want to try powder, as long as terrain is gentle:

1. Either ride parallel to the marked run just off its side, or better still,

2. Invest in an off-piste lesson from a qualified instructor

3. Keep your knees bent, and be prepared to shift weight around your board to help you maintain your balance and absorb bumps.

enough speed to make it across to the others. Grinding to a halt, I watched both Jon and Ronan snowboard effortlessly to the point where the powder intersected again with the piste. I hesitated, and started to sideslip on my heel edge. Donnie called for me to turn, but feeling unsure, stiff and somewhat frightened, I found it hard to lean forward and continued sideslipping on my heel edge. Reaching the piste, I knew I had wimped out, and became rapidly frustrated and disappointed with myself. The echoes of self-criticism had returned.

They stayed with me on the chairlift, accompanying me back up to the top as I ruminated about my board and lack-lustre performance. To my left, as I exited the lift, a huge wooden noticeboard mapped out the pistes. It marked the only break in the continuous wooden fence that had been strategically placed to stop people falling down a steep, off-piste ridge. Two men stood on the far side of the barrier. Looking closer, I realized they were about to drop in over the ridge, and a number of skiers and snowboarders had gathered to watch the men push off. I saw their backs recede into the distance, and noticed that they appeared to glide effortlessly downwards, their shapes becoming smaller and smaller. I heaved an inward sigh of relief, silently thanking god that we weren't following them. The audience dispersed, and I turned away to wait for my fellow students. Donnie wore a huge grin as he pulled up to the group. 'Alright, who wants to go off the back here and rejoin the piste below the ridge?' he asked. Perhaps the look of horror on my face spoke emphatically because he quickly suggested, 'And those who don't want to, can go around on the piste and join us at the bottom.' I exhaled and set off to reach the group before the last of the off-piste adventurers arrived. Lauren was one of the first over the fence, charging down the slope.

As I rode down, I noticed the only way back up the slope was via a T-bar lift. This type of drag lift is particularly common in Switzerland and Austria, but as someone who had ridden mostly in France, I had no experience with them, and I had never come across one, even in Italy. It felt awkward to have to admit to not knowing how to handle something so basic on a course aimed at a higher level of accomplishment, but I confessed to Donnie that I was a T-bar Virgin. 'No problem,' he said. 'You can ride up with me, and I'll show you what to do.' A T-bar is the shape of an inverted capital letter 'T', its stem running down from the cable and connecting two metre-long bars that extend out either side. Snowboarders need to place one of the short bars between their legs before the cable yanks forwards and upwards. They can ride a T-bar either alone, or with another rider beside them. Skiers, on the other hand, have to ride the lift in pairs, placing the short bar underneath their backsides. At the time, I was oblivious to the fact, but I was actually in the cradle of the ski-lift world. Davos is the location of the world's first ski lift, which came into operation in 1934. It was a J-shaped, single bar, developed by Ernst Gustav Constam, a Zurich engineer, and it was soon replaced with a T-shaped bar (an idea from ski instructor, Jack Ettinger) that enabled two people to be carried up the mountain simultaneously. Before the invention of the first J-Bar, skiers spent only six minutes of a sixty-minute lesson skiing — the rest of the time was spent walking back up the hill. Unsurprisingly, the first lift was an immediate success that transformed the sport. In the first season after it was built, 70,000 people visited the Bolgen lift at Jakobshorn. Here, at Parsenn, Donnie and I travelled up the T-bar together, and it gave me a chance to hear more about his life and passion for mountain biking. Over the years, I'd noticed a pattern emerging — during the summer months most snowboarders seemed either to mountain bike or to surf, replacing one thrilling sport with another.

TECH TIP

THE T-BAR

Riding a T-bar, solo, requires balance:

1. Place one of the bars between your legs

2. Tense your thighs and core ready for upwards movement of the cable

3. Hold onto the cable with your leading hand, and

4. Place your back hand on the other bar

5. Keep your board pointing forward.

Exiting the lift, Donnie ushered us to the right. 'We're heading over to some off-piste,' he said. 'Follow me.' And as a group, we dutifully did as we were told, Lauren at the front and me bringing up the rear. But my spirit was undeterred, and I was keen to make up for my earlier timidity off-piste. Again encountering deep powder and steep terrain, I knew I had to keep pushing through my inner discomfort. But I rode stiffly and on my toe edge, facing the mountain, I caught my heel edge, falling backwards down the slope. As I hit the deck, I heard my neck crack and my teeth snap together — never a good sound. Lying upside down in the snow, I ran a quick damage assessment, making small movements to see what hurt and how much I could move. I had been lucky, it turned out I was fine, although my neck was somewhat sore. Donnie could see I was struggling, and when I arrived at the waiting group which had gathered on the piste, he suggested we all move to the other side of the slope and try the gentler off-piste terrain. As I stood at the top surveying the route, it looked much more manageable. Setting off into the light, soft snow, the floating sensation of riding powder felt sublime, and the grin returned to my face. This was better.

TECH TIP

SO, THAT HURT

Some pain is inevitable:

1. Carry painkillers that work for you in your snowboarding jacket

2. Most pain can be resolved, whilst on the slope, for the majority of injuries.

Still bringing up the rear, I cruised through the powder, delighted to be in familiar territory. Nearing the end, I looked ahead again towards a narrow bridge in the distance below the point where we would rejoin the groomed slope. I studied the others as they crossed, and it became evident that I would have to generate sufficient speed to drive me across the bridge, and uphill, so that I could pop out onto the piste beyond it. There were no handrails, and any miscalculation would mean falling into an unknown drop. Staring at the bridge on approach, I made a quick assessment and stopped short. I wasn't sure enough of my capabilities, and I was not prepared to take the risk. I removed my board and walked. The hike on the other side was short but steep, and in deep snow it was heavy going. Donnie waited patiently, and we rode the chairlift up together to meet the others at a slope-side restaurant. The morning had been difficult, and Donnie, sensing my dejection, tried to distract me. 'What do you do to keep fit?' he asked. 'Climbing out of that snow is hard work. You did it much quicker than I expected.' He could hear the flat tone of my reply and wanted to reassure me, perhaps. 'Don't worry,' he said. 'The group this week is particularly strong and you're doing well.' I knew he was trying to cheer me up, but I didn't feel good about myself.

Exiting the lift, we strapped in again briefly to take the short slope leading down to the restaurant. Before Donnie set off, he gave me one final piece of advice for the morning, 'Keep your speed up around the corner because the run flattens out. You'll need some momentum to carry you up the incline on the other side. The restaurant is on the right at the top.' With the instruction ringing in my ears, I set off determined to make it to lunch without miscalculating the speed needed to cover the distance. I didn't want the shame of unstrapping and walking the last few metres. But as I neared the bottom of the descent, I hit a small lump of ice, caught an edge, and slammed on my back. My head bounced off the ground. I lay winded for a few seconds before slowly climbing to my feet again. Tears of pain and frustration stung my eyes. I had started the morning so well and it had descended into one of self-loathing and humiliation. Hauling my sorry backside into the restaurant, trailing my board behind me, I felt my neck starting to stiffen, and fought back a new wave of tears that threatened to burst at any moment. I sought out Lauren to commiserate, but she dismissed the vulnerability with a cheery and disarming lack of concern. 'It'll be alright,' she said. 'Don't worry.' And she turned to carry on her story with the others. Eating my lunch in silence, I tried to block out the disastrous morning.

Our sandwiches and goulash consumed, Donnie unfurled his map and showed us where he was taking Ian for some backcountry snowboarding. The rest of us were free to spend the afternoon doing what we wanted, before meeting in a bar downtown to watch the Olympic Halfpipe Men's final. With Lauren leading the charge, Ronan and Jon decided to head towards the off-piste. This was the last place I wanted to go. I declined their invitation, insisting I was happy to spend the afternoon on my own, lapping the blue piste from the Totalp chairlift. As Lauren disappeared from view, shouting to the boys to follow, Ronan, whom I hardly knew, was most concerned. 'I'm not happy leaving you,' he said. 'You've had two falls and you shouldn't really be on your own. Are you sure you don't want to come with us?' I reassured him as best I could, 'Honestly, I'm fine, and would rather be on my own.' And it was partly true. 'I'll have some time to practise at my own pace, I explained, solidifying my own intent. 'Go on, you'll miss the others.' Reluctantly he strapped in, and I watched him retreat into the powder. I was touched by the kindness of this relative stranger. Somewhere inside, a mild pang of loneliness had flared, but for the most part I felt only relief. No need to put on a brave face any longer! Taking a big breath, and exhaling, I strapped in, looked up and ahead, and set off down the slope towards the chairlift.

The next two hours were spent snowboarding the same run, trying to regain my confidence on familiar ground and repeating the familiar on-piste moves. Gradually I began to feel better, my positivity and confidence began to return. I was, I realized, retracing my own mark.

At the funicular, I met Lauren and the boys, and descending back into Davos we hurried to meet Donnie and the rest of the crew to watch the Olympic action in the halfpipe final. It was widely expected that Shaun White would follow up on his previous two gold-medal victories from Turin and Vancouver, but this was not his year. Watching the event live, accompanied by much whooping, hollering and collective groaning, the competition progressed. In the end, the competitor who had completely dominated the sport for many years came fourth, and he would go home without a medal. His crown had been snatched by the Russian-born, Swiss snowboarder, Iouri Podladtchikov. I was not aware that Iouri, or 'iPod' as he is affectionately known, had grown up in Davos. Looking back, I realize it was a privilege that we had witnessed his triumph with his home crowd.

There was no rush for me to get up the following day. Donnie had decided to split the group and he would take the boys and Lauren out in the morning, spending the afternoon with me. I had woken with a sore neck and was unable to lift my head from the pillow without using my hand to support the weight of my head. Instead of feeling disappointed, I recognised it was an opportunity to take things easy. Low cloud hung below the mountain peaks, and I cuddled back under the duvet with my book. The morning group were going to learn off-piste safety and avalanche drills. The previous day, Donnie had pointed out areas of potentially unstable snow. He'd explained how various factors can effect the stability of a slope's snowpack: wind can create snowdrifts piling the snow and increasing its pressure on the slope, thereby making it more likely to slide; the direction of slope can also influence stability (south-facing slopes receive more sun, and as temperatures rise, the bonds between the snow layers weaken and reduce the friction in the snowpack); the time of day is important, and snow that has been warmed by afternoon sun is more susceptible to the effects of those same weakened bonds between layers; and finally, the time of year should be considered — spring brings warmer weather, and with it the risks attendant to higher temperatures, but during the winter, large snowfalls increase the weight of the snowpack, bringing greater downward force upon the slope. There were certain signs to look out for, then, which could indicate a greater likelihood of an avalanche, such as shooting cracks, heavily laden cornices, and balls of snow rolling down the slope. Recent avalanches were also an indication of risk. And that particular season, a number of media reports about fatalities meant we were all aware of our environment.

Lauren had obtained her transceiver, shovel and probe and would be trained to use them later on that day. Dressing, she talked me through her unfiltered thoughts, 'I don't know if I should go on another course because I just want to blast around the slopes doing my own thing,' she said. 'I think I've got to the stage where I don't need anymore instruction.' Without the fodder of a response, she turned her gaze my way. 'I'd be annoyed if I were you. You should be having more instruction. I'd say something to Donnie.' More than happy with the set-up I felt no need to say anything to anyone, but kept my mouth shut and let Lauren talk herself dry, blocking the sound of someone telling me how I should or should not be feeling and behaving. As the door closed behind her, solitude and peace filled the room, and I returned to reading my book.

Lunchtime approached, and I sat back in my seat on the bus south along the Landwasser Valley, shuttling past Jakobshorn (site of the world's first ski lift) and on towards Rinerhorn. The sun had made an appearance and began to peak from behind the clouds, its winter rays bathing the surrounding countryside with their warmth. A short ride up the gondola deposited me beside the restaurant where I was to meet Donnie and the group. I surreptitiously ate my homemade sandwich before perusing the array of desserts on display in the buffet cabinet. The apple strudel caught my attention; it looked delicious, worth every last Swiss Franc. In no time I'd devoured the last flake, and wiping my mouth I watched as the others traipsed into the restaurant to gather their own lunch from the various buffet stations across the room. My neck was still very stiff and Donnie took a single look my way before announcing we'd be taking it easy in the afternoon.

Post-lunch, Lauren was dithering uncharacteristically. She wanted to go and find some more powder to ride, and although Joe and Ian were on the same mission, she fretted that she hadn't been invited to join them. I wasn't surprised, but didn't voice my thoughts. The anxiety revolved, she was unsure what to do, and then she seemed to make a decision, 'Can I join you and Kate this afternoon?' she asked

Donnie. 'I haven't really spent much time with her and it would be nice if I could.' Back on form, this was an audacious call, and I was left momentarily speechless, recognizing instantly that she didn't care at all about riding with me, but that she was relentless in the pursuit of her own riding goals. I had seen no evidence of genuine thought for anyone else's feelings, and my own snowboarding vulnerabilities, which had been run through the quick rinse cycle of her processing the day before, didn't seem to wash clean; they lingered. Wanting to join my afternoon session was acceptable, but her lie abruptly closed a door to friendship behind it, while opening another, more smoothly, to understanding the different faces of fear: Lauren, it seemed to me, simply didn't want to be left on her own.

Jon and Ronan also joined us — a welcome relief. The afternoon began with revisiting technique, learning to drive the board around the turn, getting low and being proactive with pressure on the front foot, first, then the back foot. We practised several times up and down the same run before Nigel and Daniel popped out from some off-piste nearby. Donnie decided to take us much higher as a group, still to this day, it's a journey on the longest T-bar I have ever ridden. Nigel started to complain about sharing the lift up with Donnie, who slapped his friend's backside and yelled, 'Yee-haw!' just before the cable engaged, the Western cry dispersing into the emptiness of the white, open range. Still chuckling, I followed on the next T-bar, and called on the vision I had just witnessed to keep my sense of humour intact during the ride ahead. The lift seemed to stretch as far as the eye could see and over every brow I expected the exit to be in sight. Soon my forward hip, which supported the full weight of the board, began to ache and the burgeoning cramp threatened an early departure as I considered bailing out. But I hung on. Suddenly, Donnie turned back again, 'Keep on your toe edge! In a minute we're crossing a piste which slopes to your left.' I had to focus my concentration to stay upright and tried to ensure I wasn't swept away and off the parallel tracks carved in the snow by other users. 'We're nearly there,' Donnie said, a final push to endure. 'The exit is just over this brow.' I had made it, but the 500-metre ascent (by my reckoning) on a slow

T-bar lift had put many off taking this route. Nearing the day's end this remote area was palpably still, and the dividend was apparent — we had the mountain to ourselves.

Nigel and Daniel took off down the piste, the swoosh of their boards carving sound into the vacuum. Donnie took Lauren, Ronan and Jon on a 15-minute hike further up the ridge towards a beautiful line of off-piste powder. I wasn't capable of making this particular descent, and so I'd volunteered to take photos and videos. Waiting at the edge of the slope, I watched their upward progress. In the lee of the mountainside, basking in the sun's rays as it began to set, I watched the retreating dots of my fellow snowboarders as they made their way against the cobalt skyline above me. Occasionally, an Alpine chough soared effortlessly amongst the peaks, its silent flight amplifying the solitude. While I sat motionless, taking in the glorious view and revelling in the quiet and majesty of my surroundings, something magical began to happen. Looking around, I became aware of thousands of sparkling diamonds in the air, as if Tinkerbell had flown overhead scattering fairy dust in her wake. All around me the air glittered. It was mesmerising to behold, and I was lost in time, fully enchanted. And then the spell was broken, within two or three minutes the magic disappeared as quickly as it had flashed into existence. The meteorological spectacle is known as diamond dust, and occurs when ice crystals form in clear, very cold skies where the temperature has fallen below freezing. In both the Arctic and Antarctic, where the phenomenon is common, the display can last for several days. But for me, those few moments were a privilege and I felt blessed to have experienced them even for such a short time.

> *CONFIDENCE TRICK*
> ## SEEKING THE BEAUTY OF IT ALL
>
> *There is beauty all around you if you take the trouble to look for it.*
> *When feeling negative:*
>
> *1. Really search for the elements of joy you encounter, even if just for a moment*
>
> *2. Focus on them! The process will help you feel more positive, encouraging you to continue with your push forwards.*

I focused my attention back on the small group poised at the top of the ridge, about to drop in. Lauren was the first to descend, unhesitatingly carving her way through the snow and making fast, rhythmic progress to the piste below. She was followed in quick succession by Jon, then Ronan, whose faces at the end of the run told their own tale of delight and excitement; they were entirely stoked to have completed the line. Through gasping breath, they explained how beautiful, but tiring, the hike had been. At its end, Donnie had cut a vertical snow pit and had pointed to the way the layers of snowpack had been formed over the season, indicating areas of stability or weakness in the strata. Once he'd judged the snow to be safe, the group committed to the off-piste ride. As we descended together to the valley floor, this new knowledge buzzed through my mind, and I processed my own tiers of learning, and thought again about success, and what it might mean for me.

The following day began similarly to the morning prior. Lauren's complaint on this occasion was that she had been called a potty-mouth by one of Donnie's instructors the night before. Stav had thought her language was unacceptable as we sat in the restaurant surrounded by families, and he'd told her so. Where the day ahead might have offered promise, instead she was clear that having to take a rucksack up the mountain was an effort too far. Off-piste riding requires appropriate safety preparation; it includes carrying a shovel and probe, and it means wearing a transceiver. Lauren was more than happy to wear her transceiver which she strapped to her body, and it ensured she could be located under the snow if caught in an avalanche. However, the probe and shovel required a rucksack. The probe is used to prod the snow once the rescuers have located the area where a victim is buried, while the shovel, not surprisingly, is used to dig the casualty out before she runs out of air. Lauren's selective choice of equipment meant that she could be saved, but that she could not rescue others. In my sleepy state, only half-listening to the grievances, this had passed me by. But it did not go unnoticed by Donnie.

As I travelled on the bus at lunchtime, heading towards the funicular to take me upwards to Parsenn, my gaze drifted to the windows of the shops lining Davos's streets: shops selling outdoor clothing, gift emporiums, book shops, each one faded into the next. My mobile phone rang and drew my eyes from the blur. It was Donnie. He was going to be 30 minutes late, and he'd tell me why when he saw me. Striding purposefully towards me, he smiled, but his eyes remained hard. I could tell he was furious, trying to balance his need to offload with his desire to remain professional and discreet. I knew he would find it hard to concentrate on my lesson with whatever was bugging him still on his mind, so with some careful probing, I soon came to realize why he was so angry. He had immediately noticed Lauren's lack of rucksack that morning, and he explained to me that the behaviour was selfish and unacceptable. From Donnie's words, I understood that she had been left under no illusion about his thoughts on the matter. Later in the morning, she'd also disobeyed an instruction to stay left when tackling a particular off-piste section. Both she and another rider had ended up in the trees, out of sight, and from that point, also out of contact. They'd had to remove their boards and climb across a river to return to civilisation. Donnie had been on the verge of calling out the rescue service, and the delay had forced a late start to my lesson. No wonder he was cross. But once the frustrations had been vented and were off his chest, Donnie was able to relax, and he turned his attention to teaching.

Riding the familiar Parsenn terrain, feeling relaxed and focused, I concentrated on what I was being asked to do. Donnie revised the principles of foot steering with me, along with the necessary posture and balance that make up good body management, and then he moved on to the skills of tilt, lean, and how to carve a snowboard. With few people on this part of the mountain, I was able to use the whole width of the slope to practise carve turns, eventually tracing the narrowest of lines in the snow, feeling the edge of my board bite hard into the surface, grip around the turn, and propel me across the face of the slope with fluid, effortless control. As I came to a stop, I beamed; my first ever carve turn on a snowboard. 'That was amazing,' I chirped to Donnie, 'I want to do it again.' Travelling up the chairlift, Donnie was complimentary. 'You're close to being a good snowboarder, Kate. You have a great base knowledge and skill, and you're a good listener and easy to teach.' Hearing this from someone who works with Olympians, I was internally delighted with the praise.

As we exited the top of the chairlift, Donnie indicated that we would be heading over to the other side of the mountain. 'One of the pistes has a great natural halfpipe. It's not big, but it's fun. I think you'll enjoy it.' Just as we were about to set off, a rather sheepish and subdued Lauren appeared. She had changed out of her river-soaked gear and returning to the mountain, now asked to join us. Donnie made it clear the focus of the lesson was on my progression but if she wanted to tag along she could. To give her credit, Donnie's prodigal student was less voluble, and contrite, she hung back. Scooting across to the top of the piste, we rode down to the natural halfpipe. The halfpipe is a semi-circular trench with vertical sides between 12 and 18 feet. Superpipes (those seen in major competitions such as the Olympics) have vertical walls of 22 feet, three-and-a-half times the height of a tall man. I had only ever seen a purpose-built halfpipe on television. To my eyes, these were icy death traps waiting to maim the next rider or skier brave enough to enter their gaping jaws. I had never yearned to give it a go. Obviously, the feature before us was much smaller than a purpose-built pipe, and certainly it was miniscule in comparison to those used in televised competition. Effectively, our pipe was a small, u-shaped ditch with walls of approximately 4 feet. But by riding up the side, turning and gliding down to repeat the same on the opposite wall, the rhythm gave me an appreciation of play; the comfort of

CONFIDENCE TRICK

ACCEPTING IT'S A PROCESS

Learning is not a linear experience.

1. Accept that sometimes you will feel like you are standing still, or even going backwards. This is normal

2. Embrace the complete journey, rather than dwelling on its obstacles

3. Refocus on tomorrow's road ahead.

flow transferred from the contours of this snow-packed cradle up through my board, feet, knees, hips, heart and mind. Swooping down before sliding up, and then sliding down, before swooping up and around again, I was enjoying the experience far more than expected. I wanted to give it another go, and headed back up the lift to repeat my previous ride. I was learning to read the mountain's fuller terrain, using it to my advantage, and that familiarity with the surface beneath me provided another dimension of joy; I could see the whole mountain might become a potential playground.

It was to be my last day in Switzerland, and I was heading off on an early train the next day. I was ready for home and, as usual, I'd missed my daughter and husband. First thing in the morning, I cheerily said goodbye to Lauren and felt excited to be heading to the train station. It would be a bonus, I thought, to have the company of Nigel and Daniel who would be taking the same Zurich train and then similarly continuing onwards to the UK. 'How do you know Lauren?' they asked, as soon as they entered the carriage. The question had tumbled out, and clearly it had been on their minds. 'I cannot believe you two are friends.' Further questions ensued and the pace picked up, continuing thick and fast with all the delivery of an artful Barrister who then pauses before the final strike. 'Will you go away with her again?' I laughed into my chest, and then looked up. 'What do you think?' It was my chance for a question. But I had made my mind up on this one several days ago.

Sitting on the train as it glided smoothly from snowy mountains, through Klosters, then onwards to the valley's grassy flatlands, and eventually into the fringes of Zurich's urban landscape, I reflected on the week. It had been a mixed bag in many respects. I tried not to dwell on the challenging times and I thought instead about the positive. I took the time to review my original goals. I had been pushed out of my comfort zone almost every day, with exposure to steep, off-piste terrain, to black runs and to T-bars, and I'd completed my first carve turn. In only a few days, I'd also run the full gamut of emotions ranging from excitement, joy and elation, to disappointment, sadness and frustration. I had moved into unconscious competence riding blue runs, but it wasn't as solid as I would have liked. Often, at this stage, people can execute another task whilst performing an unconsciously competent activity. I had seen instructors pull out and use a mobile phone whilst riding a poma tow. I do not have natural snowboarding talent, and so I knew I needed continued practise otherwise I would regress. I'd gained exposure to steeper terrain, but I was far from being unconsciously competent, something I felt would come with still further practise. But a hidden plus was my strengthening attitude — I had remained positive, even regaining confidence after difficult moments on the slope, encountering bad luck on the piste, and I'd been able to regroup after some challenging personal dynamics.

Did I regret going away with Lauren? No. In her presence, I'd learned a valuable lesson in my own strength. I hadn't allowed myself to be sucked into her anger, and I hadn't let myself be emotionally drained during mornings of unmoderated complaints. Lauren remains one of the best recreational snowboarders I know, and I was envious of her skill, I would have loved to possess it. The strong snowboarders in the group had recognized and commented on her abilities, but she had alienated herself from everyone around her. However, underneath her simmering anger, I detected insecurity and a desire for the acceptance that did not come her way. A brash and cold façade masked the vulnerabilities that in fact expose our strengths. Admitting others confidently into our less-than-perfect state of being, and openly into the realm of our fears can be an act of courage, I thought. I'd refused to be diverted by jealousy, and told myself there was no comparison to make, in fact. I was not less-than.

CONFIDENCE TRICK

ASKING, 'MIRROR, MIRROR, ON THE WALL..'

Pay attention to your own progress, without comparing yourself to others — it is not helpful!

1. Examine the current confines of your skills in balance with your burgeoning competence

2. Remember, your journey is yours alone.

What I needed was to focus on my own skill set, and on the work that I needed to do. Lauren had managed to get under my skin to a certain degree, but at the end of the trip I reconfirmed to myself that there was value in living my life according to my own values and ethics. And I would continue to make my own mark with my board.

1. Choose three people who will give you feedback about the skills you want to improve while working through this book. Write their names, here:

    a...

    b...

    c...

2. How far away are you from tearing it up in your chosen area of competency? Write your impression down in the column headings below (use any metric you like, or none, this is a personal marker) — it may help to work backwards from your stipulated goals from the previous chapter when considering this question. Name two things you still need to do in order to feel more confident in this competency — which refinements are needed? Identify them in the rows under the appropriate column.

Distance from Tearing it Up in competency 1	Distance from Tearing it Up in competency 2	Distance from Tearing it Up in competency 3
1.	1.	1.
2.	2.	2.

♦ ♦ 3. Name one area of skill development that you will need to practise continually for each competency? Think about talents that don't come easily to you — these will be areas that will need more practise than those spheres in which you are gifted. Write them down in the following table:

Distance from Tearing it Up in competency 1	Distance from Tearing it Up in competency 2	Distance from Tearing it Up in competency 3
Skill-dev		
Need help?		
Solution 1:		
Solution 2:		

♦ 4. In which areas of development do you need to speak up and ask for help? Add your answer to the table in the appropriate row. Admitting a lack of knowledge is hard, but imperative for progress!

♦ 5. What two solutions can you find and focus on to help you progress towards your goal? Write your answers in the table.

In order to make your mark and move consistently towards progress, you need to revisit your goals as you carve your turns through life, or you may get stuck on the flat or in powder. Look Up! Are they in the same place? Write your answers down and find out.

Scoring

Exercise1. Give yourself one point for each person listed to whom you choose to give you feedback.

Exercise 2. Give yourself a point for each refinement needed to help you feel more confident.

Exercise 3. For the area you've identified that needs continual practise, add one point.

Exercise 4. Give yourself a point for each area of development where you need to speak up and ask for help.

Exercise 5. Give yourself a point for each solution you can find, and focus on, in order to help you progress towards your goal.

Total chapter points................

05

MORZINE

FINDING YOUR MENTOR

how to discover the right instructor for you

I felt such an overwhelming sense of relief that I started to cry. Carving my board in smooth, rhythmic turns through the snow, and down the length of a red run, no less, I felt a strong sense of personal victory, my frustration gave way to joy. In January 2009, I had left Chamonix feeling disheartened, fluid motion on my board elusive despite all attempts, and I had contemplated giving up snowboarding. But I had one more winter holiday booked for March and it was to be a pivotal trip. Trawling online one evening in February, I discovered an interview with the Director of MINT Snowboarding, Tammy Esten. Based in Morzine, she had trained with Neil McNab alongside Keith, and that was all I needed to know. I booked a lesson.

Morzine was a familiar location for me because Gordon and I had bought a flat there in 2003. Situated 30 kilometres south of Lake Geneva's central point it nestles in the valley below its well-known sister resort of Avoriaz, the Swiss border a few kilometres further east, and the peak of Mont Blanc 40 kilometres further south on the Italian border. Straddling the approximate north-south flow of the Dranse river, its architecture retains Savoyard characteristics from the past, and its wooden facades and slate roofs are drawn from the area's forests and quarries. Unlike a number of resorts, Morzine is a working town with a local population of 3,000 people, and it provides warm hospitality from friendly residents in addition to the year-round mountain activities on offer. In wintertime, the tree-lined pistes descend the north-eastern ridge from Avoriaz towards Switzerland, and from the south-east, they pleat the lower skirts of Les Hauts-Forts all the way to the valley floor allowing winter-sports aficionados to snowboard or ski to the tiny hamlet of Les Prodains, close to town. During the summer, as well as paragliding (also known as parapenting in France) the area offers mountain biking and lake swimming. The Tour de France often has a stage which passes through the centre of Morzine and two of the race's most spectacular alpine climbs, Le Col de Ramaz and Le Col de Joux Plan, end or start in the area.

Part of the appeal of buying a property in Morzine had been its close proximity to Geneva airport, the 90-minute drive making long snowboarding weekends possible from the UK. Together with Avoriaz, it sits at the heart of the vast Portes du Soleil ski region, one of the largest skiing networks in the world with 650 kilometres of marked pistes running from Switzerland through the French Alps, and to Mont Blanc. Our flat had that rarest of French Alpine characteristics, a large balcony facing south-west. When winter turned to spring, the sun's rays heralding warmer weather, we could sit outside, watching the snowboarders and skiers blast down the slopes into town. During the hot summer days, we watched the tranquil descent of the ubiquitous parapenters against the backdrop of sapphire skies and bright meadows, while around us window boxes burst with red geranium.

On this particular holiday, my friend and fellow snow-enthusiast, Kirsten, came with me. Small in stature, with long, blonde hair and blue eyes, she skies like a demon, fast and fearless. She talks with a strong Geordie accent, and laughs easily, thriving on good, hard banter; she also enjoys a drink, be it a pint or shot. I had met her through swimming classes for babies and, at the time, we both had young children of similar age. This was to be the first of many trips we would take together. The holiday gave us some respite from kids, husbands, domesticity and work. And after returning from Chamonix,

I knew that I needed some fun to help inject enthusiasm back into my snowboarding. Kirsten turned out to be a great antidote, patiently encouraging me to laugh and lighten up. Going on a snowboarding trip with other mums has distinct advantages. They understand any concerns about injury when you have a young one to look after, where the feelings of guilt may emanate from, and the frequent need to ring home. Whilst away with Kirsten on one of my first girls' trips, I got to know her better than I would have done at home, surrounded by children. We had the opportunity to chat as mothers, but also as individual women, fellow snowsports enthusiasts. We would talk about our travels, regale each other with funny stories from our past, discuss hair colour, moan about our husbands and compare the development of our children. This was all between reading trashy gossip magazines, having a swift vin chaud and lazing over lunch or dinner. But I also needed some professional input to increase my competence, and I hoped Tammy would supply it.

Ascending in the small gondola on the western, Pléney side of Morzine, butterflies flapped furiously in my stomach. Kirsten was taking a lesson with a ski instructor, more to keep her company than anything else, so I had time to think about my own lesson ahead. The last time I'd been riding, in Chamonix, I'd felt drained by the effort and I'd realized I was still incompetent. In Morzine, I felt nervous stepping out of the gondola and during the walk towards the arranged meeting place I scanned the crowd before my eyes lit upon on a mint green uniform. Tammy was taller than I expected, with cropped dark hair and sparkling eyes above a wide smile. Her nose stud was small, and baggy clothes hid her slim frame. Before we headed up the mountain, she asked about my ambitions and what I wanted to achieve in the lesson. Sheepishly, I told her about my lack of confidence, the difficult last day in Chamonix, and my continued nervousness riding along flat terrain. Then, as Keith had done, she passed her experienced eye over the set-up of my board, making very few adjustments, which was not surprising — both Keith and Neil had tweaked it less than two months' previously. Dropping into piste D for a couple of warm-up runs, Tammy was able to assess my style and proficiency. 'Follow me,' she announced, 'we'll head across to Nyon and can practise making smooth transitions from heel to toe edge, there.'

I followed Tammy along and down a number of runs where I had never been, and towards the lift that would take us higher up the western aspect of Pointe de Nyon. The area accessible from Morzine is vast, its pistes a network of arterial pathways allowing skiers and snowboarders to circulate from the heart of the resort to all its extremities on surrounding mountains, and I had not managed to travel them all, despite the fact that I owned a flat there. It also takes time to cover the whole terrain. At one point, I had to keep my snowboard flat, but with encouragement and guidance from Tammy I conquered my first bête noir, arriving at the lift without stopping; I had carried enough speed and I hadn't fallen. Seated on a lift and heading higher, Tammy and I began to talk. We shared common ground with Keith, and I learned more about their friendship. Both had trained with Neil and had obtained the required qualifications, skills and paperwork to teach snowboarding in France. The laws are strict, explicitly designed to protect the quality of teaching there, and only a few European qualifications are accepted. The British BASI system is one of the limited number of international awarding bodies recognized, but instructors not only have to reach their BASI Level 4 International Snowsports Teaching Diploma (ISTD), they must also obtain Fédération Internationale de Ski (FIS) points in either freestyle or racing. The number of points required varies from year to year, and is awarded on an individual basis. Unlike snowboarders, potential ski instructors face the dreaded speed test where they have to complete a slalom course within 20 to 25 per cent of the course opener's speed, and usually, the course opener is a national ski racer. Prospective instructors have to ski at 75 to 80 per cent of that time, therefore. 'Obtaining the required qualifications can take years to achieve,' Tammy summarized. As the lift carried us up towards the exit, I thought about the information she'd told me. From a student's perspective, I knew that French instructors earn more money than their counterparts in other European countries, but I was emphatically reassured that the instructor sitting next to me was highly qualified.

Practising the smooth transitions on a wide, blue run, a piste not too steep for my abilities, gave me confidence, and I was able to concentrate on Tammy's metaphor, making a smooth sweeping motion with my leading knee. I imagined a light in my kneecap shining around each turn. I snowboarded down to her, stopping before the small covered bridge, just wide enough for one person, which connected Nyon to the Pléney ski areas. 'You do realize that this was a red run, Kate?' Tammy said, 'and I bet these were the smoothest turns you've made on a run like this.' Transitioning between the two pistes had been straightforward, and focusing on the light shining from my kneecap, I'd failed to notice the piste markers had changed colour. I hadn't hesitated during the transition from heel to toe edge, which had otherwise become a bad habit. Provided with the image of a light illuminating the way ahead, a corresponding light had been switched on in my mind, and the Pragmatist in me could turn the illustration into performance. It was then that I had started to cry with pure relief.

> CONFIDENCE TRICK
>
> ## YOU AND YOUR MENTOR
>
> *Qualifications are important, but the success of the relationship depends on someone who will fit with your personality and learning style.*
>
> *1. Invest time to find the right instructor, mentor, or coach*
>
> *2. If the first person you find doesn't feel right, don't be afraid to hunt for someone else*
>
> *3. Look around. Be proactive.*

Those few days away with Kirsten, meeting Tammy, practising with her, it had all been the perfect tonic. It had rebooted my motivation, setting me on a positive path to improvement. Kirsten proved to be a great holiday companion, making me laugh, helping me to relax. During the annual girls' snowboarding holiday, Kirsten has become a steadfast member of the crew and continues to ski alongside me and with my fellow shredders. Discovering Tammy had been a turning point.

There is a well-known saying, 'when the pupil is ready, the teacher will appear'. And while the origin of the wisdom may be in doubt, for me the message was true — it was only when I had become discouraged and frustrated that Tammy showed up in my life. In the course of a couple of hours with her, I'd overcome three hurdles that had threatened to put an end to my snowboarding: I'd travelled on the flat with greater confidence; I'd tackled and overcome a fear of steeper slopes; and I'd carved smooth turns down them. I had found the person who could teach, support and encourage me, and knew I would not be ditching my snowboard.

Tammy had started her snowboarding career back in the day, when hard bindings were in fashion and day-glow gear was all the rage. She has snowboarded all over the world and, teaching in France, naturally holds the highest BASI ISTD qualification. A brand ambassador for global snowboard and surf company, Roxy, at the time of writing she is also one of only four women in France who are instructors dedicated to snowboarding. I also came to appreciate that Tammy understands that women learn differently.

It was during that first pivotal lesson with her that I broached the idea of developing and running an age-specific snowboard camp for women over thirty. There seemed to be options for younger women, camps running for a week, but for older women who find it hard to get away for anything longer than a few days, because of family or career, there was nothing suitable. My idea was to hold a four-day course rather than one that ran for six days, which would make the time commitment away from work and families less. Tammy had observed that women are more anxious than men to snowboard correctly and they need to feel a sense of fun to maximise their learning potential. They tend to be more vocal in their support and encouragement of each other. When snowboarding in an exclusively male environment, I had observed that men are more internally focused, with much less talk. They'd concentrate on the task in hand. This is upheld by the same 2013 neurological study undertaken by University of Pennsylvania researchers, and mentioned in chapter two, 'Sex Differences in the Structural Connectome of the Human Brain', which finds that the neuronal pathways in women's brains are connected differently than in their male counterparts. As a result, women are generally more social, possessing better listening skills, and within the sphere of learning, they generally absorb information sequentially rather than experientially, by listening first, then doing; they are suited to working with an instructor. At the time, MINT Snowboarding was still a relatively new company, and Tammy was keen to explore the idea. We settled on a four-day camp aimed at intermediate snowboarders aged thirty plus to be held the following year in 2010. Working with Tammy over the summer we pulled together some promotional material and a couple of pieces ran in the former *Daily Mail Ski and Snowboard* magazine and in *Cosmopolitan*. As far as I am aware it was the first (and remains the only) snowboard camp dedicated for women over thirty. The cost of running a camp, whether it runs four days or six is essentially the same, and it would appear that most people would rather maximise value for money and sacrifice time away from home. I suspect this is the reason why the camp has not been repeated.

My experience of an all-women snowboard camp in Chamonix the previous year had not been wholly positive, our small group had fractured in two, and as the months moved on, towards the realization of this new venture, I was interested to see how the upcoming experience would play out. Tammy had partnered MINT Snowboarding with the chalet company, Mountain Mavericks, who were to be our hosts during our time in Morzine. Part-owners Olly and Emma Lambourne run several chalets, and our camp was located in Chalet Atelier. In March, our transfer bus from Geneva airport drove through Morzine before taking a right-hand turn to head up the Prodains valley towards the chalet. Climbing higher along the road the valley started to narrow, high cliffs squeezing the ribbon of land below into a dark and somewhat forbidding place. Chalet Atelier sits almost at the head of Route des Ardoisières, and is flanked by the towering cliff wall below Avoriaz on one side, and by the steep, mountain rock face of Les Hauts-Forts on the other. There are a few bars and hotels in the valley, but the area is otherwise dominated by the cable car at its end, which transports skiers and snowboarders 800 metres up to Avoriaz in an almost vertical ascent.

Despite the cliffs' overbearing presence, on entering the chalet the atmosphere immediately felt cosy, and with this welcoming, relaxed vibe, I was instantly at home. Gradually all the campers arrived. Each time the door opened, I was curious to see who would walk through the entrance. In total there were nine women, and we ranged in age from 30 to 41-years old. Most had travelled from Europe, but Mariesa had flown all the way from New York. She was dark-haired and with her distinctive accent, probably the most exotic. With Liz, Helen and Manon, she made up a more experienced group of riders, working at reaching a level of unconscious competence. I joined the remaining women — Hardeep, a lawyer from London, Jackie from Luxembourg, and Nikki and Rowena, both from the UK like me — and we formed a second group of five who wanted to develop to a stage of conscious competence. The two groups would alternate between three-hour morning lessons with Tammy, and three-hour afternoon sessions guided by one of her knowledgeable seasonnaires, either Glenda or Kirsty.

The following morning as I lay in bed under the chalet eves, drinking the cup of tea brought by our chalet host, I could hear the rain drumming on the skylight above my head, and it sounded torrential. I wondered what this first day would bring. It was not ideal snowboarding weather, but hoping the higher slopes might have received snow, I dressed, looking on the bright side. I also knew that the weather conditions would keep many skiers and snowboarders in bed. It was highly likely that we would have the slopes pretty much to ourselves.

Stepping out from the cable car in Avoriaz, a drizzling rain replaced the hoped-for snowflakes. Freezing altitude can vary widely, particularly in spring, and I had hoped the level that day would be lower so that the rain falling in the valley would turn to snow as we ascended in the cable car. In general, moving upwards to Avoriaz, any rain usually turns to sleet, and passengers eagerly look out of the windows, waiting for the moment when the temperature dips further, and snowflakes begin to crystalize in the air. A moisture-laden snowfall sticks to and slides down the windows, but if the freezing altitude is

TECH TIP
LAYER IT ON

Dressing for seasonal variations
can mean the difference between a great day
shredding it on the slopes, and needless misery.

1. In winter, I wear three or four layers plus
an insulated snowboarding jacket

2. In spring I wear two layers plus a light shell jacket

3. Always wear a helmet for life-saving protection
(vents can be opened to increase air circulation)

4. Always wear gloves (use lighter, park gloves
if your hands get hot).

sufficiently low, then wet, sticky flakes become dry, powdery snow —
nirvana for snowsports enthusiasts. But that day it wasn't to be, and
light rain continued to fall on the ground. I made sure my jacket was
fully fastened and the vents on my snowboard helmet were closed.
Tammy was buoyant, and led my group through warm-up exercises
prior to working on foot steering and technique. She looked at our
turns, asking us where we felt the pressure through the different parts
of our feet. I knew that encouraging physical self-awareness of this
kind would enable us to call on muscle memory, and we'd be able to
work on improvements even when Tammy wasn't with us. Heading
to lunch, the chairlift swung around and I noticed the large puddle
of water on the seat. I had no option but to sit directly on it. But by
playing word games on the ascent, Tammy distracted us sufficiently,
and we remained relaxed — nobody in the group fell over while
alighting from the six-man lift. Throughout the morning, the rain
had been unable to drown our spirits. Dripping huge puddles on the
restaurant floor, we met up and ate with the advanced group who had
been on their guided session with Glenda. I was completely soaked

— the rain had penetrated the outer layers of my clothing through to my underwear, which now clung to my skin. My snowboarding gear was relatively cheap, at the lower end of the waterproofing scale, and had not been able to withstand the continual rain and the pressure as I sat in all those chairlift puddles.

After lunch, while the other group headed back out into the drizzle, my group chose enjoyment and we made our way back to the chalet for a dip in the hot tub followed by a shopping trip into town. Reuniting at dinner, everyone sitting around the long wooden table in the chalet dining area, I watched the women laughing and chattering and felt pleased that Tammy and I had collaborated to make this happen. Although the group consisted of different personalities, everyone seemed relaxed, we were enjoying each other's company, and snowboarding was the focus of the evening's banter.

CONFIDENCE TRICK

SEIZING THE DAY

If we waited for perfect conditions we would never do anything. Some people can use perfectionism as an excuse to procrastinate and defer action until circumstances are completely right. Circumstances are rarely completely right. Seize opportunities! You really need to make the most of any opening that presents itself.

Waking on our second day, I listened intently. The absence of drumming rain on my skylight offered the promise of a brighter day. There was a definite hint of sunshine when I looked outside. This morning our group was to be guided by Kirsty, and we would ride with Tammy in the afternoon. Instead of ascending in the cable car we rode the chairlifts that took us to a high point in Avoriaz where the jagged peaks of Les Dents du Midi mountain range can be seen clearly on a day with good visibility. Nikki and Jackie badgered Kirsty to take us to the Burton Kids Parkway, a small freestyle park behind residential buildings in the heart of Avoriaz. Some of us were a little nervous, and Rowena, who was quieter and more reserved, decided to forego the risk despite our collective protestations for her to join the group. It was tempting to stay with her, drinking coffee, but I felt that would be a cop-out, a soft option, and not the correct decision to make if I was serious about furthering my snowboarding goals. The Kids Parkway was an ideal introduction to freestyle snowboarding in-resort, a step-up from my prior indoor experience inside the Fridge. In addition, it was small and didn't attract the crowds that congregated at the larger, more exposed Chapelle Park, which was situated beyond the nursery slopes on the Avoriaz plateau. The vibe was far less intimidating, and now, rather than never, is a great opportunity to try freestyle out in the mountains. There was a button tow to master, then reaching the top, we fell in line to take turns snowboarding over the park's small rollers. No air is caught when clearing them (unlike the jump off larger kickers) and they serve as a great introduction to freestyle confidence and future flight. Where rollers are shaped into smooth mounds, kickers tend to be cheese-shaped wedges with a run-in from above the thin end, and a lip that ensures the rider takes off into the air before landing on the downward slope. Often a solid, flat tabletop extends the distance between take-off and possible landing. But that day, all we had to do was turn our boards into the fall line, point them down the shallow incline, and ride over two mounds of snow. Without the distance required for speed checks between the two, the second roller was taken fast. To begin with, we played around trying to find the correct spot from which to start — too close and we ran out of speed, not even making it up the first mound, but too far away and we speed checked like crazy before even reaching the first roller. Once we'd found our sweet spot, we made our mark in the snow and started from there.

So far, I had only managed to ride the first roller, and as I lined up ready for my next attempt, adrenaline prickled through my veins. I'd panicked earlier, accelerating into the second mound and had ducked out, riding around it at the last second. This time I was determined to nail it. Teeth gritted, and focusing on the second roller, I dropped in, keeping my knees relaxed and bent. Over the first roller, I resisted the urge to speed check, maintaining my position and line. As I reached the top of the second roller, I caught air. I was so surprised that I moved my weight backwards, my board slid out from underneath me as I hit the deck, and I landed on my rear. Kirsty and Nikki punched the air, elated for me. 'Yeah! You nearly did it!' they yelled. 'Try again, try again!' Before I even got up, I knew what I had done wrong. All-business, I climbed to my feet and headed to the button tow to try again. This time I nailed it with certainty. Hanging in the air for that very short while was a suspended moment of thrill, and I rode away with a huge grin on my face, proud as hell. Next up was Jackie, enthusiastic and brave, she didn't hold back. She pointed her board downhill, cleared the first mound, and focused ahead, no speed check, catching air over the second mound. We all cheered and hollered, 'Well done, Jackie! Go girl!' When I got to the bottom, I high-fived her and there were smiles, a shared sense of achievement all round. On our way to meet Tammy and the others for lunch, I floated on cloud nine in the midst of my ebullient group, still collectively celebrating its success.

'I'll be using the video camera to capture your snowboarding technique,' Tammy announced, before the afternoon lesson. 'I know none of us likes watching ourselves, but this way you can see what works, and what needs improving.' And intuiting our internal shame, she invoked logic to reason it away. 'Don't forget, everyone here knows how you ride, they see it every time we're on the slope. It's only you who hasn't seen you.' From Avoriaz we headed up the eastern face of Les Hauts-Forts, above the Prodains valley head, almost to its top, where the broad open height of Arare's blue piste looks back beyond the town and over to Switzerland, just beyond it. Our access to the main run was rather mogul-led, the shaped mounds of roughly packed snow blocking a smooth descent. Trying to snowboard well, absorbing the bumpy terrain, was challenging; I was still too conscious of 'getting it right' while the camera rolled. And in the late afternoon we practised riding switch on the shallow nursery slope. For the first time, I snowboarded goofy the entire length of the run without falling on my backside or face-planting. I was ready to return to the chalet, happy with my day's progress, but Tammy, who is good at knowing when people are truly mentally or physically tired,

TECH TIP

FLUSH IT OUT

During your time in the mountains, warm up
and warm down with some stretch exercises before
and after snowboarding in order to prepare your muscles for
the day and help them recover when the fun is over.
Lactic acid builds up in muscle tissue after a heavy
workout and causes soreness.
Here's how you can mitigate the effects:

1. Grab a cylindrical roller after your day on the slope

2. Stretch and massage muscle tissue using the weight of your
body as you roll your quads, calves, hamstrings, hips, back
and even your arms and shoulders over the width of the
cylinder. The action flushes out the build-up of lactic
acid and any subsequent stiffness felt one,
two or even three days' later
will be reduced.

adapted her plans for the group, and changed the pace of our lesson again. Finishing with a fun, light-hearted session during which we practised ollying, we pitched our boards from the flat up into the air, and over a miniature, homemade snowman. He remained with his head intact, and we returned back to the chalet in an upbeat mood, tired but elated with our full day of achievements.

Sarah-Jayne had been one of the campers during my first all-women course in Chamonix with McNab Snowboarding, and at the time she'd given us all some warm-up and warm-down tips which can be done in the car park, at the top of the lift, or in the chalet, later. I'd continued to do them in the intervening period, and back at Chalet Atelier we took the idea a step further, warming down with a full stretch class, which was great for loosening our tired muscles. For me this can often seem rather a chore, but with age, maintaining fitness in order to continue snowboarding without injury has become increasingly important. Gone are the days when I could get away with very little strength maintenance between snowboarding trips, and could still jump on my board in the mountains without lifting a single weight in the gym. As I stood before my mat, Sarah Stephens, a physiotherapist from Mountain Rehab, led our session. Late afternoon sunlight stretched into the lounge area that had been transformed into a makeshift studio, its furniture pushed to the edges of the room. Surrounded by my fellow snowboarders, we shifted and shunted our aching bodies into various positions, the odd groan escaping my lips, my muscles protesting.

In the past, I'd concentrated on building stamina and endurance through cardio-vascular work and had neglected developing my strength. This was purely through ignorance rather than any specific reluctance to put in the effort. My personal trainer, Tina Shaw, and knowledgeable friends have since helped me understand that strength, particularly in my core, reduces the risk of injury, of straining my limbs and back. Nowadays, I incorporate weights in my strength training.

TECH TIP

CELEBRATE YOUR TOTAL STRENGTH

Frequently we focus on our cardio routines at the expense of the muscular strength that can help prevent injury. As part of your pre-snowboarding fitness regime:

1. Remember to complement cardio-vascular exercises with strength training

2. Choose exercises that build lean muscle rather than bulk.

And if all else fails, if I do injure myself or strain muscles, I seek out the services of a physio or a masseur to assist in the healing process.

On our penultimate day, blue skies and soft snow beckoned us back to the small freestyle park in Avoriaz. This time Tammy accompanied us. Arriving earlier in the morning than we had on the previous day, the snow was crunchy and harder under foot. Again, we lined up in turn for the rollers, but Tammy also encouraged us to try the rainbow box rail. A semi-circular disc, the rail's flat metal and plastic rim is about 40 centimetres in width, and broader than the waist of our boards, therefore. All we needed to do was ride in a straight line upwards over its initial arc, and then slide downwards over the other side. Waiting for my turn, large butterflies flapped wildly in my stomach. The fact that the box is a solid object means falling on it will hurt, but its broad rim has a greater surface area than a narrow rail and that translates into less pain in the event of a fall. This was my reasoning as I tried to banish negative thought from my mind before I set off. Keeping my knees bent, I focused my forward gaze on the rail and beyond. Concentrating on keeping my weight centred over my board, I felt it slide over the snow then hit the hard metal and plastic of the rail underneath. I rode up and over with no trouble. It was much easier than it looked and I rejoined a group of applauding women, fists thumping the air as Hardeep, next up behind me, took her turn. She was unsure, but desperate to give it a go. Tammy took hold of her rear hand and ran with her as she dropped in, gathering speed. As she reached the rail, Tammy stopped running and Hardeep travelled over the rail holding her instructor's empty glove. 'I knew you could do it!' Tammy grinned. 'You just needed a bit of extra support on the run-in. But you actually rode it all by yourself!' Hardeep, who judged herself particularly harshly, didn't look as impressed with her achievement as we all did, clapping and cheering her success.

Nikki was practising the rollers. She was brave and progressive, happy to board at speed. Flying over the second roller just before lunch, she landed badly, on her face. 'Are you alright Nikki?' I called out, concerned, and running toward her. 'That looked nasty. Let me have a look.' Smiling, she laughed it off and waved me away. 'I'm fine, really. It hurts like hell but I'll survive,' she said. The swelling started almost immediately, and eventually she had a real shiner of a black eye contrasting nicely with her blue eyes and blonde hair.

But she didn't let it deter her, jumping back on her board and speeding down Proclou as we hurried north-east towards Les Lindarets and over one more long run to Linga, near Châtel, on the Swiss border, where we'd arranged to meet the other group for lunch. We'd spent too long in the park and were now paying the price, rushing to make it in time.

I have never been a fast snowboarder who tears down the mountain, at the outer limits of control. It's not my style and is actively something I do not enjoy. Forced to hurry, travelling faster than was comfortable for me, I decided to bow out at Les Lindarets and lunched on my own — spending two hours in a deckchair working on my tan, my hunger sustained by the now obligatory French crêpe that I ordered daily, was a wonderful tonic from the adrenaline rush of the morning. Recharged, I was also free to do whatever I wished in the afternoon, and I chose to return to Avoriaz, making my way to the nursery slope to practise riding switch. I'd previously ridden switch successfully on this small slope, but I wanted to ensure it wasn't a one-off, to embed it in my muscle memory. My goal was for that stored bank of knowledge to become so solid that I became unconsciously competent, but I knew it would take a while to achieve. Starting on a slope with which I was familiar, a context where I felt safe and had already snowboarded in switch, this was a place from which I could build confidence.

The final day came around quickly. We headed across to Mont Chéry, the ski area and freestanding mountain that lies further west along the valley and back towards Geneva. Although I was familiar with Mont Chéry I had never snowboarded there. The pace is quieter, its crowds reduced in number because (with one exception) only intermediate and advanced pistes run down the mountain. But its slopes are open to spectacular views when visibility is good, and ours was a glorious day. The sun shone brightly, its warmth almost melting the

snow before our eyes as our van sped through the landscape. The sky
was a deep azure, uninterrupted by clouds, and the line where it met
the earth was punctuated by snowy peaks. Spring had arrived, and
summer was around the corner. We piled out of the van, unzipping
our coats and then crossed the tarmacked road towards the gondola
that took us up to the mid-point of the mountain and from where
we headed up the nearby chairlift — an old-fashioned wooden two-
man system. Approaching the exit here, my usual anxieties about
disembarkation came to the fore. I knew from prior experience that
this kind of lift would give us very little time to dismount before the
chairs swung around to travel back down the mountain. The snow
was starting to melt, and a large, slushy puddle came into view. With
no time to think, I splashed my board into the snowmelt and pushed
as hard as I could away from the chairs, managing to glide away
successfully. Turning away from the lift I stopped abruptly — free
from the towering heights of Les Hauts-Forts, which had blocked our
horizon for most of the week, the view here opened south across Les
Gets and its tree-lined runs, all the way to the Mont Blanc Massif; 40
kilometres of white peaks puckered into the distance, the breadth of

the sight elevating my spirit higher. That morning we were free to blast around the slopes doing our own thing, but everywhere we went my eyes were continually drawn to the scenery. Finally, sitting on the restaurant terrace with Rowena, I could stop and drink in the views, savouring the otherworldly vista before me.

And then, after lunch, it was time to focus. Tammy took us to a red run on the shadier side of Mont Chéry where the spring snow still held. 'I want you to snowboard down this section of slope with your hands on your knees,' she said, and to puzzled looks. 'Yes, really. Put your left hand on your left knee and your right hand on your right knee, and start turning down this slope.' Laughing when I set off – it felt so very strange – suddenly I felt what my feet were doing. I don't know how it worked, but it did, and I became far more aware of the way my feet influenced my snowboard, how their movement was affecting steering and direction. 'That is so weird,' I thought aloud, and turned to Rowena, who smiled and nodded her agreement. As I reached the bottom of the run, I realized that we were the only people around. Moving upwards on the rickety Planeys chairlift, the sound of spring meltwater tinkling over rocks drifted upwards. From above, I could hear the chirping of Alpine songbirds calling to one another. Otherwise the valley was silent. I started to shiver as the chairlift continued its ascent, but as it neared the ridge, I emerged from the shadow of the mountain and into the bright line of late afternoon sunshine. It was a perfect end to a perfect day.

This all-women's camp in Morzine had been very different to my first experience in Chamonix the previous year. Group dynamics are influenced by the personalities and interpersonal relationships between participants, and this time around there had been shared camaraderie amongst the group. Everyone had found someone they could relate to and whose company they enjoyed. Women who snowboard all share a common bond, our kinship through the sport. There is never a need to explain why we strap on a board, or why we participate in an activity that many regard as extreme. However, there remained a huge difference between me and the other students on both camps – not one of them had a child. Although it did not detract from my enjoyment or my ability to relate to the other women, I felt they would have found it hard to understand a major part of my life and, at times, why I could be distracted by thoughts of home.

Claire lives fewer than 300 metres from my home in Tyne and Wear and is a snowboarder; she has three sons. Her husband surfs (as does Gordon) and our children go to the same school. We have friends in common, but the big difference is that Claire's oldest child is younger than Freya, so the children do not have any shared friendship groups. Despite our close neighbourhood ties, we very rarely socialize in the UK, something we often laugh about when we do come together on snowboarding trips where we share our love of the sport. When we first went away in March 2011, then, it was a bit of a leap of faith that we would click and get on.

Early in the dark of that morning, and as the taxi drew up, I felt nervous and excited — nervous because I was leaving Freya who was four years' old at the time, excited because I was going back to Morzine to snowboard with Claire. If I was nervous leaving one child, Claire must have had butterflies the size of elephants in her stomach leaving all three children; her youngest was just nine months' old. Airports are stressful when travelling with a young family, the mountains of necessary paraphernalia to carry can result in an anxiety-provoking chase to the check-in desk, which persists through security and boarding. But not this time. I met Claire and our journey was so relaxed and peaceful. We had time to browse the duty free shops, drink a cup of coffee at leisure, and read the morning papers. We were reminded of the independent travellers we had been in a previous life.

Boarding the plane to Geneva, our thoughts turned towards the mountains and feelings of excitement bubbled over. Tall, slim and with light brown hair and piercing blue eyes, Claire used to do a lot of powerboat sailing, but since the birth of her children, she now concentrates on running and triathlons. She'd remained extremely active, then, but she had not snowboarded in the five years since the birth of her first child. Claire was understandably apprehensive, and she wanted to get on the snow as soon as possible, to confine her current anxiety to history. Arriving in daylight after our early morning flight, and feeling comfortable in familiar territory, I didn't share Claire's nerves. By 2011, Gordon and I had sold our flat, and because I'd enjoyed staying at Chalet Atelier the previous year as part of the MINT women's snowboarding camp, Claire and I had chosen to return there. We settled in and took up residence in the kitchen area to wait for our fellow chalet guests to arrive. Kirsty walked in first, a tall, dark-haired woman, she was a skier. Accompanying her was James (also known as Heinzy), a blond-haired, professional sailor from Ireland, who had more than a touch of the blarney about him. He snowboarded, liked to party, and loved a good *craic*, always engaging the people around him in conversation.

Claire and I had both slept well the previous night, an uninterrupted night's rest with no children calling out for 'Mummy!' I was happy to linger over breakfast, but Claire was eager to get going and prove to herself she hadn't forgotten how to shred. 'If I stay much longer, I'll bottle out altogether,' she said. With breakfast complete, we had no excuses, and we grabbed our boards and set out for the ten-minute walk up to the cable car at Prodains. Very quickly I realized I had overdressed and was perspiring profusely. Claire, who was fitter than me, had not even started to break a sweat. I made a mental note to myself — get in shape, and dress more appropriately.

The cable car would take us to Avoriaz perching precipitously high, at 1,800 metres, on the cliff edge above the valley. In Morzine the snow had disappeared in the heat of the late-season afternoon sun, but I hoped that the colder, higher altitude had maintained the snow base for longer. I'd already checked the piste map, and had decided to take Claire down Proclou, an easy blue run. Exiting the cable car we caught the nearest chairlift, a short ride across to the Avoriaz Plateau, past the wooden-clad apartment blocks on our right and over the traffic-free streets below. The chairlift is low in height and the exit a gentle run-out — nothing too difficult for Claire to negotiate. 'We need to head through the tunnel,' I told her, pointing to our descent on the map. 'You'll need to keep some speed up because the piste flattens out before we reach it. Afterwards, it descends again. We'll regroup just before that, about 50 metres beyond the tunnel.' The top of Proclou is narrow before it widens out into a gentle piste flanked by trees. Our visibility shifted as low cloud drifted across the mountains. One minute we could see the sun veiled by thin, high clouds and another we were enveloped in a clinging, damp mist, the light tinged with grey. Claire found her snow legs, no problem, and riding the chairlift back up the slope, then on and over the Chapelle snowpark, she relaxed. 'It's so good to be back on my board,' she told me. I turned on my seat towards her. 'It felt great,' she added, her smile radiating satisfaction.

In a buoyant mood after lunch, we headed up to another part of Avoriaz. 'Follow me,' I shouted to Claire, over my shoulder. As I turned the corner, I realized very quickly that I had taken the wrong route. In front of me was a narrow cat track. Both Claire and I hated them. But this was now our only option to proceed. The route was the main piste leading into a tunnel after which the slope levelled out; most people were trying to get up as much speed as possible. Our progress was slow as we entered the flow, we stopped and started to avoid the other skiers and snowboarders hurtling around us. To make matters worse, I had crossed onto the wrong side of the track for our turn-off back into Avoriaz. After a few false starts, I scooted across the highway without incident, but the fear and lack of control had dissolved our high spirits from earlier in the morning, and shaken, we headed back to base. 'Thank god we have a lesson with Tammy tomorrow,' Claire said, thinking aloud. And, chin to chest, I could only agree.

As we stepped out of the Prodains cable car on day two, the sun shone brightly in Avoriaz, its warmth radiating through my clothes. But this time I'd dressed more wisely, leaving off a layer. The cloud from the previous day had disappeared, resulting in bluebird conditions. 'What do you want to achieve today, Girls?' Tammy asked, her voice ringing with enthusiasm. 'Do you have any goals in mind?' We told her about our disastrous venture down the cat track, and she explained the need for consistency when riding with a crowd. 'It means staying with the flow so that those behind can anticipate movements and avoid crashing into the slope users ahead of them.' Claire and I absorbed the traffic analogy. 'If a rider makes a sudden change of direction,' she continued, 'or is inconsistent in the way they move, it can be hard for those behind and above to anticipate what they will do next.'

We rode up the small chairlift behind Avoriaz, and Tammy (who knew me well by this time) reminded me, 'You have as much right as anyone else to be on the slopes, Kate. Don't be so hesitant. Once you're on the slope, there is no need to wait for others. Just concentrate on being consistent in your turns.' As we prepared to ride this short, wide and usually busy section, Tammy grinned and said, 'Right, Girls, I want you to think of the word, "Dominate!", as you ride! Remember, you have as much right to be here as others. Now, go and "Dominate!"' Setting off, I could hear Tammy's voice in my head, and made the decision to ride more assertively, more confidently. Even today, I still use this trick when I start to freeze and become tentative. I can hear Tammy shouting, '"Dominate!"' And I make the choice to do so. Later on she took us through our paces, and we practised turns, foot steering and speed control. The spring snow was soft and forgiving — it's not called 'poor man's powder' for nothing. We ended the day feeling far more confident and happy, thoughts of home and domestic life had all but disappeared.

On day three we headed over to Les Lindarets on the far slope of the Avoriaz escarpment. The route took us via one of my favourite runs; officially it's called Combe à Floret, but it's known locally as Star Wars, and is named after the speeder bike chase in Richard Marquand's 1983 film, *Return of the Jedi*. The long, 2.5-kilometre piste is densely lined with high trees, snaking down to the valley floor in a vertical drop of 330 metres. There has been many a time when I have found myself alone riding its path. The quiet and solitude take over, silence falls and I have only the swishing of my board for company. Eventually this run joins another, Parchets, which continues to the base of the Ardent gondola, but to make it, snowboarders and skiers need to generate speed to clear the flat approach. Tammy had said that I needed to work on increasing my comfort with acceleration, so that became our work for the morning — Claire and I thought we would see how fast we could go. Naturally more hesitant than my friend, I was encouraged by her enthusiasm and borrowed her excitement. The late-season snow was heavy with moisture, and that meant a softer landing should we fall. Stopping just ahead of an incline down which we could gather speed, Claire and I pulled out our phones and opened Ski Tracks, an app that we both used. There has been comment in the popular press that such apps, which allow slope users to track their route and read their speed, have been contributing factors in a number of fatalities. In some cases, skiers and riders chasing the elusive target of 100 kilometres per hour have had high-speed crashes resulting in serious injury and death. The reasoning goes that if a skier or snowboarder can clock their speed in real-time and see they have almost reached their goal, then they may be tempted to push it a bit further. Ski Tracks, however, does not use live data that can be read whilst skiing or snowboarding. And that morning, Claire and I were content to check our speed after the fact; there was never any chance that either of us would reach anywhere near 100 kilometres per hour. Keeping my knees bent and my weight over my board, I set off, pointing it directly downhill on the broad slope. I gathered speed, feeling the wind begin to whip more forcefully against my face. Faster and faster, resisting the urge to speed check, I pushed down for even more momentum instead, exhilarating in what felt like the edge of flight before the board began to slow in the slush at the base, and came to a natural stop. I had made the lift and 37 kilometres per hour.

Feeling righteous achievement, we rode the gondola back up over Parchets, the site of our success, to meet Kirsty, Heinzy and our chalet hosts for lunch at the Lindarets bowl. Sitting outside, the sun was strong and we stripped down to t-shirts, plastering on the sun cream. 'Come on girls, what'll it be?' Heinzy was keen to get the drinks in. 'Beer, Jäger, wine – what'll you have?' Thirsty after the exertion, alcohol didn't top our list of priorities. 'Water,' said Claire, 'Or a coke,' I added. 'Okay, but you needn't think that's all you're having,' he insisted. Claire and I looked at one another, knowing that we couldn't escape Heinzy's cajoling for ever, and we conceded the promise of a beer at the end of the day. 'I'll hold you to that, now, girls.' He said, standing firm. 'Because you're coming with me and Kirsty to the Park this afternoon before we all head to the Kinkerne bar.'

Arriving at the Chapelle Park, many spectators were watching from above and I felt nervous. By this time I had some limited experience of freestyle, but Claire had not. We were both very aware that we had responsibilities when we returned home, and neither of us wanted to be incapacitated in any way. Not only would it make home life difficult, husbands would be none too pleased. They might become less accommodating in the future, reluctant to wave us off on another snowboarding holiday, we thought. However, I needn't have worried. Heinzy is a professional sailor, used to team work, and to getting the best from people. He encouraged us to follow him, riding over the line of green rollers. 'Come on, Girls,' he shouted, over his shoulder. 'It's your turn to drop in.' I took my place, turned my head to check no one was coming and raised my right hand, indicating it was my line. With heart hammering in my chest, feeling like the world was watching, I jumped around 90 degrees and pointed my board straight at the roller. After finishing, I turned to see Claire follow me. She arrived with a massive grin and we both high-fived each other. 'You see, Girls, that wasn't so bad was it?' Heinzy had been right.

'Are you going to come down the Home Run with us?' Heinzy asked, on our way down the mountain at the end of the day. The blue piste down to the Prodains valley is officially listed as Le Crôt on the map, and up to this point I had not attempted it. During the snowboard camp for women over thirty, the advanced group would regularly take Le Crôt back to base while my group would be relegated to the cable car. We had always been invited, but I'd felt too unsure of my capabilities. However, this time was different. Under Heinzy's supervision and coming straight from the successful adventure in the larger Chapelle Park, I was confident to try it. The early stretch is a narrow cat track but this soon opens out onto a wide slope. We took it slowly at the top, but with no one on our tail, the pressure was off and the going was easy. Carrying on across the lower flanks of Les Hauts-Forts (the mountain anchors the Morzine-Avoriaz area like a tennis player taking centre court) and on past a slope-side bar, we were giddy for every moment of the run's 3 kilometres. Before we knew it, we'd reached the valley and were unstrapping, heading to Kinkerne, where the beers that Heinzy had seared into the evening's future were waiting.

Our final day came round, and this time our practise was focused on freestyle. We made our way back to the Chapelle Park, approaching the second lesson we'd booked with Tammy with a mixture of excitement and fear. Standing at the top of the line of green-graded jumps, she asked us to ride over the three rollers ahead and, as I had done previously, I turned around raising my hand to indicate I was about to drop in. Riding up to the jump, I speed checked madly, alternately swinging from toe to heel edge, and feeling I was still going too fast. I knew I needed to line up correctly, pointing my board straight for the approach, and adjusting at the last minute, I rode up the roller and down the other side. Then came the second roller, but as I cleared it, the acceleration of my board unnerved me, and I ducked out of the final challenge, riding around it to meet Tammy at the bottom. As we lapped the park, trying to become more proficient, she encouraged us to 'Go big or go home,' and Claire eventually made it successfully over all three rollers. We finished by heading to the smaller Kids Parkway where we attempted the rainbow rail and small box rail. It was so warm we removed our jackets and embraced the spring snow conditions, revelling in the last afternoon we had as individuals before we had to head home to reassume our roles as mothers, wives and workers. For now, though, we could just allow ourselves to be snowboarders.

During our time in Morzine, the spring weather had been getting warmer, bare patches of grass and earth had begun to appear on the slopes. We'd experienced the last of the good snow. Claire and I had got along well together: we snowboarded to a similar standard; we wanted the same type of holiday – a mixture of learning, fun and relaxation; and we understood each other's domestic circumstances. We hadn't exchanged any angry words, and we'd colluded to have early nights despite Heinzy's insistence we drank and partied late. For us, to catch up on rest and get a full night's uninterrupted sleep was part of the holiday. Heinzy could go home and catch up on sleep, whereas we would have to take up the reins of mum-duty as soon as we stepped over the threshold back home.

◆ ◆ ◆

I continue to travel with both Kirsten and Claire but also with other snowboarders, among them, most recently, Ann-Marie. She is short, stocky and fearless, perhaps it's unsurprising that she has recently taken up Roller Derby, a contact sport where participants rollerskate around a track, deliberately shoving and knocking opposing team members out of the way. Ann-Marie is physically and mentally strong. Arriving in Morzine in January 2016, at least 75 centimetres of snow had fallen. After a dismal start to the season, the snow gods had delivered, and we collectively heaved a sigh of relief. Again, I turned to Tammy for instruction but on this occasion, our focus was to be riding powder. We met her at the top of the familiar Pléney gondola above town, and although we were under low clouds and grey sky, visibility was nonetheless considerably better than anticipated — we could see part-way across the valley towards Super Morzine. Tammy knew me well, but needed to assess Ann-Marie and after a few warm-up runs she'd made her decision. 'Follow me!' she said and we headed after her into the steeper off-piste terrain under the Mouilles chairlift, beside the trees. The snow was gnarly, clumped into mounds, and we needed to adapt our stance, bending our knees in order to absorb the bumps. It was heavy going. Nervous in the deep powder and on steep gradient, a combination which requires muscular power and strong technique to manage, I reverted to old habits and hesitated before each turn, eventually too scared to turn at all. I stood frozen on the spot.

Behind me, Ann-Marie fell and tumbled head over heels, surfacing like a snowman. Hearing her laugh broke the tension and Tammy called up the slope, 'Come on, Kate, you can do this! We're almost at the bottom.' I gritted my teeth and went for it. Ever the master at reading people, Tammy suggested we play further afield when I reached her at the bottom. 'Let's go further over to Belvedere where it's much gentler.' And she dived off the side of the piste. Both Ann-Marie and I floated down the powder field behind her, my board gliding effortlessly through the lighter, pristine snow, and it felt sublime. Until the moment I panicked. Looking down, the snow flew past my thighs and afraid that I was going too fast, I tried to brake using my edges in a quick, hard motion. Whoosh! Face-plant straight into the snow. The technique that I'd use on-piste did not translate to the powder here. Everything was much gentler. Unhurt, I laughed and surfaced the soft blanket, continuing to the bottom, where I met the piste. 'You know how to snowboard, Kate. Don't look at your feet,' Tammy told me. 'If you were driving, would you look at the white lines down the middle of the road watching them rush past? No. It is the same with snowboarding. Look up!' I looked up. 'And that's going to be your mantra Kate, "Look Up!"' For Ann-Marie, who tended to collapse at her waist and twist her shoulders over her board, a stance which tilted her off balance, Tammy's mandated refrain became, 'Stand Up!' For the rest of the time that week, both Ann-Marie and I would blast down the slopes, periodically shouting the appropriate mantra whenever we saw each other reverting to old habits.

> CONFIDENCE TRICK
> ## YOU AND YOUR MANTRAS
>
> *They do work,*
> *so let's use them.*
>
> 1. *Listen well to your chosen instructor/coach/guide*
>
> 2. *Adopt their suggested phrases or mantras, and*
>
> 3. *Develop your own that you can say to yourself in times of doubt.*

We took further lessons with Tammy that week and during our final adventure, she showed us how to ride treelines. The conditions were perfect, and travelling up the chairlift over to Super Morzine, the slope running away from Avoriaz back towards Morzine, we played in and out of the trees lining the blue pistes of Tétras and Zore, the Prodains valley to our left, hidden below the sheer drop of cliff wall. I was unsure what to expect, I'd never ridden anything like it previously. But by this time, I was very used to Tammy's declaration, 'Follow me.' And we headed off-piste down a narrow cat track between areas of tall, densely packed evergreens, laden with snow. I was surprised when she stopped, grinning ear-to-ear, and pointed. 'We're going in there,' she said.

I could just make out a track cut by riders who had gone before, but I had to peer into the dark gloom to make out the twists and turns of the narrow path. 'As long as I follow Tammy,' I thought, 'I know I'll be fine.' We slid into the trees, Tammy in the lead, then Ann-Marie and then me. Once under the dark canopy, the environment changed instantly. Our world fell silent. The tall evergreens, their boughs weighed down by snow, dampened sound from the piste. All I could hear were our voices calling to one another as the forest swallowed us whole, Brothers Grimm-style. After a few minutes I could see the exit up ahead. Speeding along, I pointed my board directly towards it. Catching a small lip of snow, I blasted into the air and out of the treeline. Surprised, I transferred my weight to the back of the board, and fell on landing, completely submerged in the deep snow. 'That was amazing!' I said, gasping for air as I sat back upright. 'I loved it,' I added, still blowing and scraping the snow from my mouth, 'Let's do it again.' Tammy smiled. 'I thought you'd like it,' she said.

We spent the next hour dropping in and out of the trees, making our way ever downwards, popping out onto deserted tracks before disappearing again into the dark, green cocoon. During one run, I saw a tight, toe-side turn coming up and at the last minute I realized I wasn't going to make it — the trunk of a pine loomed large in my vision. I winced and braced myself for impact, but none came. I was on the ground, and surrounded by tree stumps, lucky to have avoided all obstacles. Maybe this wasn't quite the carefree fun I first thought it had been. Suddenly, I'd become aware that a missed turn could have more implications than a bruised backside. My joie de vivre waned, and with it my confidence retreated into the shade. I started to concentrate on what I was doing, but fatigue was crawling in and I was ready to head for the top of the Super Morzine lift, and the end of our lesson. We all high-fived each other and hugged, and Ann-Marie and I thanked Tammy — we were stoked to have tried something new, and to have had so much fun in the doing. It had been a thrilling morning. As Ann-Marie and I entered the lift, plonking ourselves heavily on the seat, we looked at each other saying, in unison, 'Time for a beer.' Ann-Marie had guided me and pushed me, as I had done for her. And together with the friends, family and colleagues, who have provided positive encouragement and who have helped cheer me onwards, both she, Claire and Kirsten have shaped my performance and made my journey towards accomplishment far easier.

> CONFIDENCE.TRICK
> ## YOU AND
> ## YOUR FRIENDS
>
> With whom do you socialize, hang out or play sports?
>
> 1. Pick your companions wisely. Who will encourage you, be your biggest support and be vocally positive?
>
> 2. Spend time with these people when you are trying to reach a goal,

◆ ◆ ◆

There are two other women who have provided support, guidance and inspiration. Both snowboard, but one is a fellow shredder like myself, whilst the other became a household name in 2014. I have already introduced you to Lauren with whom I snowboarded in Davos. As you may recall I found it difficult to warm to the swearing, which I found unappealing, and to the negative attitude which was even more of a challenge. But although I don't care for her personality, Lauren did inspire me in other ways.

In 2012, Lauren had been one of the women who had participated in the women's snowboarding camp taught by MINT. She had travelled with a girlfriend, TJ, and they had stayed in Chalet Atelier as Claire and I had that year, although Claire and I were on holiday independently, and had not been part of the MINT course. Tammy usually taught the women's camp, but she'd damaged her cruciate ligament earlier in the season and was unable to ride — she'd enlisted a good friend and professional snowboarder to help. At this point, Jenny Jones had won gold medals at the US Winter X Games in 2009 and 2010, a silver medal in 2011, and gold at the European Winter X Games in 2010, but she had yet to win her historic Olympic bronze medal for Slopestyle in Sochi. She had yet to become a household name.

I had a spare day after Claire had left for home and asked Tammy if I could join the group. She very generously agreed, inviting me along. I had admired Jenny for a while, and had followed her career – I was thrilled to finally meet her. It's commonly said, 'You should never meet your hero because you'll be disappointed,' but I'm pleased to report that I was not. Jenny is down-to-earth, easy-going, good fun and far more beautiful in person.

I met the girls for lunch at Changabang's after their morning lesson, and Jenny was anxious she had pushed them too hard — one had broken her arm, and another had a swollen knee. At one of the outside tables and while chatting over lunch in the spring sunshine, we covered a number of topics, each vital in importance, from snowboarding to boyfriends and waxing. But it was post-lunch that the activity really started. Olly (the owner of Mountain Mavericks) had joined the group. I'd always avoided riding with Olly in the past, but purely for reasons to do with his proficiency — he had a reputation for speed and didn't need to take the number of stops that I needed in order to catch my breath. Used to the altitude and also in better shape, he could keep going when I could not. I am not a fast snowboarder and in the company present that day, I was unsure if I could keep up. As we set out towards Linga and Châtel, I decided it was sink or swim. If I wanted to spend the afternoon with them, then I had better try my damnedest.

It was evident straight away that Lauren was a great snowboarder, and I concentrated on going as fast as I could, without taking a tumble, in order to avoid holding up this very strong group of four. En route from the Prodains cable car, Lauren talked to me about her experiences undertaking her BASI Level 1 exam. While she had no intention of becoming an instructor, she explained that the knowledge and experience had made her a better snowboarder by giving her a solid foundation on which she could build. And she encouraged me to go for it. I have to thank her for that, for opening up the avenue of possibility in my mind.

Watching Jenny snowboard was a masterclass in how to shred. Hitting side jumps on the way down (the natural kickers at the side of the piste, born from the mountain's topography) she encouraged Lauren to do the same. Riding into the off-piste and playing with the jumps, Jenny blasted strong, high and stylishly, landing back solidly onto the piste. It crossed my mind that most slope users would have no idea who was riding right in their midst. The only indicators of her fame were the sponsorship stickers plastering her helmet. Heading up the Chaux Fleurie lift, I listened as Jenny talked about her travels, and I hung on to what she said; my hero was sitting next to me. I also became aware, suddenly, that the exit, my historical nemesis, the site of so many collisions lay directly ahead. And the terrible thought flashed through my mind, 'What if I pull her over? What if my bad luck strikes again, and I injure Jenny Jones, Britain's Champion, while getting off the lift?' I had done as much to numerous others in the past. But Jenny was up and away from Chaux Fleurie before my board had even touched the snow. Continuing towards Linga, we took a detour into The Hidden Valley and had fun playing in the off-piste. Arriving at the top of a natural valley, not dissimilar to the shape and flow of a recessed skateboard park, the playground was laid out before us, and we had the place to ourselves. The quiet was only broken by our shouts of joy as we glided up and down the contours of its perimeter, using the landscape as a natural halfpipe.

The afternoon had been tiring, but exhilarating, and in the evening Jenny graciously joined us for tea at the chalet. Our conversation ranged through a variety of topics: men; hair colour; food; travel and, of course, snowboarding. 'I'm tired from this afternoon,' Jenny told us, 'so you must all be knackered.' I certainly was, and although I wasn't sure whether to ask, I took my courage and seized the opportunity. 'Can I have a photo with you, Jen?' And she smiled. 'Of course!' she said. Somewhere on my computer I still have the image. I was thankful to Jenny — she moved in the upper echelons of snowboarding high-society and it was a privilege to ride with someone of her calibre. But at the end of the day, she demonstrated that she was just a regular woman, enjoying the shred out in the mountains, and chit-chatting to us as though we were part of her normal crew. Jenny was an inspiration.

Over the years, however, Tammy has watched me become a snowboarder. She has given me reassurance, support and most importantly belief, even when I did not believe in myself. She has guided me (and I know she has done the same for others, too) through difficult times when trying to progress and accomplish the state of conscious competence that was my goal. When I slip back into bad habits and become timid, hesitant on the slopes, I can hear Tammy's voice shouting, 'Dominate!' and, 'Look Up!' Good instructors in any sport must be passionate about their chosen field, have great ability, and most importantly they must be able to adapt their teaching to each pupil. I have met instructors in a number of sports who can perform individually, but who have difficulty in communicating to others. Tammy instils confidence, knowledge, fun and belief, and for me these are the hallmarks of a great teacher. It's no surprise to me that MINT Snowboarding recently won the coveted 'Best s School' title at the 2016 World Snow Awards.

Obtaining conscious competence (and beyond) requires input from good professionals who can communicate correct methods and expedite learning. Trying to go it alone, in my experience, makes the journey longer, and the probability of picking up bad habits higher. Finding the right person becomes crucial, it can take time, but it is time wisely invested.

EXERCISES

♦ ♦ 1. Which two beliefs about your abilities do you think still hold you back? These could relate to your self-image, your job, or your relationships. Identify them, and describe them briefly in the column headings, below. And then be honest with yourself: is your belief really true?

Belief 1	Belief 2
True or false	

2. Think of four people who encourage and support you? Continue to seek their company. Write to them, or call them, to arrange to see them. Now.

Supporter 1	Supporter 2
Outreach in place?	

Supporter 3	Supporter 4
Outreach in place?	

3. Name two people who are negative and who hold you back? Who is speed checking your progress? Consider limiting contact.

4. Name two people who could act as mentors to help you gain greater ability, and thus greater confidence? Who is going to help you to keep the stoke high? Your choice could be a coach, teacher, instructor, friend, family member or appropriate work colleague. Write their names here:

   a. Name 1..

   b. Name 2..

♦ 5. Positive behaviour patterns need to become a routine part of your life — engrained in your thought processes. What positive behaviours are you going to start incorporating? These could include adopting an upbeat perspective, or becoming more solution-orientated, dedicated or focused. Write your ideas below.
   Try to think of at least two, but there is no limit:

   a...

   b...

   c...

Finding your mentor can take time. The person who helps you shred it with confidence will be able to assess your performance and understand how you learn; they'll speak your language, and encourage you through the gnarly stuff, or assist you across the flat tracks. They'll push you to perform and you can know they'll be just as stoked as you are when you nail life's kickers. Want that?
Write their names down.

Scoring

Exercise 1. Deduct one point for each belief that you think still holds you back.

Exercise 2. Give yourself a point for each supporter you identify and another point for when you have made the arrangement to see them.

Exercise 3. For each person you've identified as negative, who holds you back, and whom you still chose to see regularly in life, score one minus point.

Exercise 4. Give yourself a point for each person who could act as a mentor.

Exercise 5. Give yourself a point for each positive behaviour pattern identified.

Total chapter points.................

06

FEELING THE FEAR

learning to embrace the devil on your shoulder

The webcam showed green grass, wooden-clad buildings and grey mountains. Not a snowflake in sight. It was December 2011, and one week before I would head out again to Morzine and Avoriaz as part of a collaborative Just Snowboard camp run by MINT Snowboarding and Mountain Mavericks. Looking at my computer screen, I was disappointed. Willing the sky to darken and dump masses of snow, I wondered what activities Tammy would line up for us if it didn't arrive. I needn't have worried.

The cable car climbed higher towards Avoriaz and away from the Prodains valley below, and through the window the pine trees disappeared from sight behind a blanket of cloud and falling snow. The large car held a maximum capacity of eighty people and had been installed in 1963 forming a direct link between Morzine and Avoriaz, 1,800 metres above. In 1966 it was considered one of the fastest ski lifts in the world, but after forty-five years, it was showing its age. In the past, I had often waited thirty or forty minutes queuing for it, but not that day. It was almost empty except for some of my fellow campers. (In 2013, the old, rather tired, two-lift system was shut down and replaced by a modern, state-of-the-art structure consisting of thirty-five cabins, which has created more than double the previous capacity. But on this trip, I had to make do with 1960s technology.)

We inched slowly into the docking station and as the doors opened, an icy blast of cold air raced into the cabin. Clutching my board as we descended the wooden steps, our group huddled together under the canopy waiting for the second cohort of campers to join us. It gave me a chance to view my surroundings, which had changed considerably since viewing the webcam seven days previously. Everything was covered in white: roofs; porches; walkways; slopes; trees. Large flakes of soft snow, swept up by the strong winds scouring the Avoriaz plateau, blew horizontally across my field of vision.

Avoriaz was the brainchild of Jean Vuarnet, a resident of Morzine, who won the 1960 Olympic downhill gold medal in Squaw Valley, California. An early adopter of new technologies, he was the first to win the race on metal skis, receiving them only days prior to the event. He extended the same spirit for innovation towards mountain development, partnering with Gérard Brémond, founder and president of the company Pierre & Vacances, and a group of young architects who had been making a name for themselves with the design of avant-garde buildings. This singular resort is instantly recognizable, and its architecture divides opinion — there are those that love Avoriaz, and those that hate the place. Angular, high-rise, quirkily asymmetrical lines are covered with *tavaillons*, wooden tiles made from cedar and weathered by the elements to form a variety of colours from silver-tinged grey on the town's southern-facing walls, to rust-brown on its eastern and western walls. Challenging conventional mountain chalet aesthetics in the way a Lady Gaga meat dress, or a Vivienne Westwood print demands attention from the eye if not the heart, Avoriaz is the signature bearer of its own indisputable style. Its outward aspect is unique, embodying a distinct futurism, which gave it a cultural edge that was embraced by the movie world, and for twenty-one years, between 1973 and 1993, the resort hosted the annual Festival d'Avoriaz. Here, the makers and shakers within the worlds of horror, sci-fi and fantasy movies skirted the establishment laurels of Cannes to honour their own. Steven Spielberg's *Duel*, Brian de Palma's *Carrie*, George Miller's *Mad Max*, David Lynch's *Elephant Man* and *Blue Velvet*, and James Cameron's *The Terminator* — all of them received the Festival Grand Prix in Avoriaz and went on to achieve cult status, later drawing viewers from the larger world beyond the counterculture. It is perhaps not surprising, then, that the resort was one of the first in Europe to welcome snowboarders.

Behind its distinctive high-rise façade, lies modest, self-catering accommodation; chairlifts ascend and descend above pistes that thread their way through the town itself. The resort is car-free, fully pedestrianized and transport consists of horse-drawn sleighs, snowmobiles, sledges and, of course, skis and snowboards that all mingle in a system of organised chaos. Together with Morzine, this buzzing town offers a gateway to Switzerland through to Les Crosets, Champéry and Champoussin, and as one of the highest areas in the vast Portes du Soleil ski region, its geography sits atop one of the two largest connected ski areas in the world. Avoriaz regularly attracts many visitors. Not on this occasion, however. The first day of camp is usually noisy, high energy abounds, there is a buzz, and everyone is talking. But as I waited that morning, human voices and swishing skis were conspicuous only by their absence.

I squinted, screwing up my eyes to peer through the falling snow, and was just able to make out the red-on-yellow lettering of Changabang's sign from my vantage point at the exit of the cable car. Normally, this is a busy area, restaurants and cafes at the intersection of several pistes bustle with clientele, the main route to the cable car is crowded with skiers and snowboarders arriving and leaving Avoriaz. That morning, almost no one passed us. Waiting for the others, we watched the snow descend and remained mostly quiet. The camp's participants were staying at two different chalets, and in the morning we were we were to be split into further groups after the instructors' initial assessment. The two advanced groups had already dispersed and Hardeep (the lawyer who had attended the snowboard camp for women over thirty the previous year) was the only person I knew.

It wasn't long before the others arrived, but the high winds were now roaring through the resort and in order to be heard, Tammy needed to shout her directions. Before leaving the relative shelter of the cable car entrance for Stade, the nearest chairlift that would take us up Les Hauts-Forts, I pulled my goggles down and my buff scarf up. The full force of the wind hit me as I stepped outside. Holding tightly onto my snowboard, I strapped in and as I looked up, the falling snow appeared to be hanging in the air, not moving. I looked down at my feet and up again. 'Am I moving or am I standing still?' I wondered. Disorientated and slightly off balance, I recalled the sensation of sitting on a stationary train in the station and feeling slightly dizzy when the adjacent train starts to move. For a split second, it's not clear which train is leaving. But I had been to Avoriaz many times, was familiar with the short route to the lift, and in my mind's eye envisioned where I needed to be. On the chairlift I hunkered down in my seat, pulling my hood over my helmet, blocking the elements as fully as possible. There was no point talking to my companions. If I had been able to speak through my buff, the wind would have grabbed my words and flung them across the slope face, without the opportunity to catch their replies. Everyone was wrapped up to the max, shrouded behind goggles and scarfs. I couldn't decipher which snowboarders were men and which were women as I watched them dismount from the chairlift up ahead.

Tammy and her fellow instructors, Dave and Mikael, snowboarded to a point below us. One at a time we set off so they could evaluate our riding levels. I could just about see them through the swirling snow as I made my way down the slope. Together with Hardeep, I was assigned to the more experienced group, which was under the instruction of Mikael, a snowboarder from neighbouring Switzerland, and whose English was fluent. I thought how hard his job must be on days like this, when near white-out conditions make it almost impossible to distinguish visually between his pupils, let alone connect a face with a specific voice.

Snowboarding back towards the base of Stade, I rode beside five other people, concentrating on my path and route down. As we arrived, Mikael pointed to the neighbouring lift that would take us to the top of Arare, an open, blue piste below the summit of Les Hauts-Forts. 'We'll take the chair to the top and have a long ride down,' he yelled. 'Let's go'. Despite the blizzard, I could just make out his grin and heard the infectious enthusiasm in his instruction. Arare's ascent was twice as long as our previous lift, transporting us through the same exposure to wind and snow, and this time still higher to the vast, white, mountain face below the summit. Placing my board onto the exit ramp I gawped at the sheer volume of snow. Sinking deep into 15 centimetres of light, soft, fluffy drifts, a huge grin spread across my face — we had off-piste conditions on the piste. The whole group was away and down the run, as excited as I was to see such a sight. On a clear day, the seven multi-summits of Les Dents du Midi rise to 3,257 metres and can be seen piercing the sky above Switzerland, across the border. That morning, I couldn't see the top of Les Hauts-Forts just to our left. Above the treeline and surrounded by low, dense cloud, we rode unmoored from geography, without any fixed reference points, except the ocassional piste marker. The terrain undulated under my board, and an uneven build-up of recent snow had been shaped by the wind, which still blew fiercely and erratically, swirling snow in all directions. Everything felt unstable, in flux; my universe was in perpetual motion. At the outset, I was entirely mesmerized, but soon began to focus in order to keep at least one member of my group in sight. They rode much faster through the drifts, and I pushed forward as hard as I dared. Soon I was staring hard through my goggles, trying to locate a fixed object in order to steady my balance. So much motion was disorientating, but I dismissed the dizziness, relegating the disruption to a nuisance. I wanted to concentrate and I needed not to fall over — in this deep snow, it would take me an age to get up and by that time, I'd have lost sight of my group. Gradually, I started to notice pinpricks of dancing light; my eyes darted backwards and forwards, sweeping my field of vision, searching for my fellow snowboarders and any points of fixed reference with which to anchor myself. We repeated the run again, but at the top, my ears strained to hear Mikael as we huddled around him. He gave us a new route, 'This time we need to keep right and head through the tunnel towards Chavanette. We'll take the lift on the right up to the top of Fornet.'

During the past hour, I had not been aware of anyone else using the slopes. We had arrived in resort at the same time as the snow, so most winter sports enthusiasts (who had followed the same series of updated webcam images as I had) had stayed away. Avoriaz and her slopes were eerily quiet. On the mountain, as weather conditions deteriorated, the other groups had headed lower, towards the trees at Les Lindarets, where they had better visibility and shelter. In contrast, we were heading higher, further up into the deeper snow at 2,250 metres. The rest of the group took off, Hardeep among them, racing down to meet the Fornet lift. I tried to keep up, but fell. And then I fell again. And one more time again. On each occasion, I scrambled to get up as fast as I could, but was losing ground to my companions. I shook my head, blinking, trying to dislodge the twirling lights in front of my eyes, but the nausea and vertigo only increased. Realizing I couldn't keep this up, I made the decision that this would be my final

TECH TIP

KNOW WHERE YOU ARE

Visibility and slope conditions can
change rapidly in the mountains.
It is a good idea to:

1. Pay attention to your routes and options down
the mountain so that you remain on slopes within
your ability level;

2. Keep each piste marker in sight,
moving from one to the next

3. Keep an eye on the progression of numbers
on the piste markers indicating distance to the base –
this way it's much harder to get lost.
If you do find yourself in trouble,
you can give an accurate description
of your location on the run.

run before lunch. Finally, I caught up with Mikael who had remained at the base of the lift. He'd sent the others on ahead to wait at the top. Breathing heavily, my head throbbing, we jumped hastily on the chair. I turned to half-face my instructor, 'I'm going to have to make a confession,' I began. 'I don't feel well. I feel dizzy and sick. It's getting worse. I think this should be my last run before lunch.' Mikael looked concerned and asked how bad I felt. 'I think I'm ok,' I shouted back. 'But I need to get inside and out of the swirling snow.' Mikael glanced downwards and then sheepishly looked up, loudly declaring, 'If we're making confessions, I have one of my own. I don't know if this is a good idea taking you all to the top. The other groups headed for the trees, and maybe we should have gone with them.' I was unwell, poorly, but stubbornly tried to be positive. 'Well, it's a bit late, now,' I replied. 'We're on the lift and we'll just have to get on with it. I'm sure it'll be fine.' A slight feeling of foreboding took hold, several aspects of the day seemed unusual — my illness, the blizzard conditions and deserted slopes — but just as quickly I rejected it, dismissing it from my thoughts.

The group gathered around Mikael, listening to his instructions. Standing at the back, not caring what he was asking of us, I concentrated on my balance. All I wanted was to get off the mountain as quickly as I could. Everyone had waited for me, and they were obviously anxious to descend and get warm. As I fiddled with my bindings, strapping in, I saw their backs disappearing off into the gathering snowstorm. I exhaled. Now on my own, and thankful there was no pressure to keep up, I could take it steady, finding my way down at my own pace. Standing still, the cloud and snowflakes swirling around me, I took a deep breath and checked my surroundings. The piste was new to me, it was imperative I stayed alert and kept my bearings. I broke things down in order to maintain control, and began by noting the piste markers — they were blue — good. The numbers within each of the discs on top of the poles were high, however — not so good. This was quite a long run, then. The descent would have been routine but for my deteriorating health and the worsening weather. I made a few turns, sure to keep the piste markers in sight. And then I fell. The snow was light and the impact didn't hurt, but its depth made extrication more tiring and the process time-consuming. Finally, I was able to stand. My board was buried under the snow but it was still strapped to my feet and I tried to push forward, continuing on my path. Making my next turn, I fell again. I lay in the snow, breathing hard, feeling sick and disorientated, my reserves of strength slowly ebbing away. And it dawned on me — my balance had become so impaired that I could no longer snowboard. Sitting up, I became aware of the quiet around me. Here, in the lee of the mountain, the wind had abated. Still, I saw and heard no one. From the markers nearest to me, I was relieved to discover that I'd travelled further along the piste than expected. But I wasn't even close to the end, and I had to keep going. Heaving myself upwards I repeated the process, only to fall again. I lay backwards, frustrated and ill, the piste marker to my right reassuringly in sight. The snow cradled me in its soft blanket and I closed my eyes. 'I'll rest here, just for a bit,' I told myself. 'If I can keep still, I can clear my mind, start thinking straight.' I was warm, not too hot, nor too cold, almost like Goldilocks. The snowflakes continued to fall, resting on my face, while the surrounding quiet, a motionless solitude beckoned me to stay a bit longer. I felt....cosy.

TECH TIP
TAKE YOUR PHONE

This is one occasion in modern life where there's no admonition to leave it behind.

1. Always carry your mobile phone

2. Punch the local emergency number into your 'Contacts.' You never know when you may need it.

Further nausea and head spins interrupted my drift into slumber. I just wanted to lie in a darkened room, go to sleep, and block out this awful feeling. Not wanting to open my eyes, knowing I couldn't meet the demands to get out of this nightmare, I told myself again, 'Just stay here a little longer.' I'll never know how long I actually lay there – my concept of time had been lost. It could have been two minutes, but

I don't think it was really any longer than ten. I never thought to call Tammy, despite carrying my mobile phone. I didn't even consider getting it out of my pocket.

Gradually, I became aware of voices getting louder. People were coming towards me. I opened my eyes. A French skier and snowboarder came very close, they saw me prostrate and stopped dead in their tracks. 'Ça va?' they shouted, in unison. 'Alright?' 'Mais, oui!' I replied indignantly, and rather rudely. I didn't want to make a fuss and with a true, British, stiff upper lip, I tried to make out the fact that I was lying inert in the snow, during a blizzard, was completely normal. Of course I was alright. They were not fooled. Rooted to the spot, not moving, they waited to see what I did next. I should have been pleased to see them, but instead I was irritated by their interruption of my reverie, and emitting a large sigh, I thought, grudgingly, 'I suppose I am going to have to get up now, and start moving.' As I set off, so did my new entourage. Slightly ahead of me, they often turned back to assure themselves I was there.

Suddenly, I saw movement on the slope below, the bright green uniform catching my attention. Mikael was trudging up the side of the piste, carrying his snowboard, and obviously looking for his lost pupil. The two Frenchmen melted into the gloom, and I never saw them again. 'Mikael! Over here,' I shouted. He looked up and as he drew closer, I could see his broad grin. He looked remarkably cheerful considering the circumstances. 'I'm so ill. I feel terrible,' I said, complaining, unusually for me. As he approached, a wave of relief washed over me and I sat down heavily in the snow, my head resting between my knees. 'I'm too ill,' I said. 'I can't snowboard. My balance has gone.' We debated what to do. 'I know,' Mikael said, 'why don't I give you a piggyback? We can snowboard down like that.' Under different circumstances, that would have been awesome fun. In the moment, however, I couldn't fathom the logistics of his suggestion. 'But how can you get both me and my board down? I'm not leaving it here. It's just not going to work.' Mikael patiently urged me to reconsider, 'Why don't we just try it?' But I was adamant. 'No,' I said firmly. Unstrapping my board, I sealed my intent. 'In fact I'm going to walk.' I picked up my snowboard and started to place one foot in the front of the other, careful to remain at the side of the piste, following the markers. With each step, my foot sunk down and the snow covered the tops of my boots. This was hard work. Mikael shouted after me, 'You can't walk, Kate! It's another 3 kilometres!' Sighing, I stopped. I knew he was right. I couldn't walk. 'If only my head wasn't so woolly, then I could work out what to do,' I thought, exasperated. Despite my bad temper and the challenging conditions, Mikael remained upbeat. In many ways, his cheery demeanour heartened me. Perhaps the situation wasn't as bad as I feared.

Suddenly, I became aware of a *pisteur*, a member of the ski patrol that provides emergency rescue and medical assistance on the slopes. *Pisteurs* bookend the day, making the runs safe at its start by checking their condition, undertaking any avalanche control work, and at its end, they check everyone is safely off the mountain, before the pistes are closed for the night. In his long black coat, this apparition swooped towards us on skis, calling out in French. A quick conversation ensued with Mikael, and with my rudimentary language skills I understood they were talking about my health. No sooner had he appeared than the *pisteur* swept off again, leaving us alone once more. 'He's going to get the snowmobile,' Mikael informed me. 'Thank God,' I thought. 'It's almost over.'

The pisteur reappeared from below, the thrumming sound of his snowmobile getting louder on approach. My contemporary knight in shining armour wore a ski suit and his stead was engine-powered, but that did not diminish the chivalry in my opinion. I scrambled on, leaving Mikael to climb into the sled behind the snowmobile, where he carried both his snowboard and my own. I had never ridden a snowmobile, and I'll confess that a small part of me was excited, but the majority of my energy and focus was concentrated on not throwing up over the pisteur's back. I clung on, sheltering behind him as he drove down the slope. The roar of the engine heralded our arrival near Changabang, where Tammy and Olly were waiting.

Olly chaperoned me back to the chalet where I collapsed into bed, immensely relieved to be out of the swirling snow, roaring winds and unstable environment.

As children we can be frightened of many things: monsters hiding in the shadows of our bedroom; the first day going to 'big' school; even unfamiliar people. Growing up, some of our childhood terrors disappear, but fear never leaves us. It lives on in some shape or form, rearing its head, from time to time, in all of us. It is a tyrannical emotion and a huge obstacle to learning. Mentors and coaches are imperative to support our development, but within a climate of fear, the impact of their teaching is limited. Recognizing and acknowledging what is fearful is the first step to overcoming the psychological block it causes, thereby helping to reduce its power.

But this episode had been different. What I'd experienced on the slopes that morning below the summit of Les Hauts-Forts had not been fear. And perhaps, in fact, fear would have been the useful primal tool it was intended to be, protecting me from danger. On my return to the UK, a clinical colleague informed me that my illness, which had been diagnosed as vertigo, was very likely to have impaired my judgement. My ability to appraise risk had been compromised. Alarmingly, I hadn't felt like that at the time. A number of factors had collided — my vertigo, difficult weather conditions, empty slopes, the ascent of the mountain rather than descent — to compound the situation. But it could have been avoided had I spoken up earlier, not letting pride get in the way. When others are involved in mountain adventures, there is a responsibility not only to yourself but also to those around you. At altitude, in uncertain weather, the consequences of screwing up can be much more severe than those at sea level. This had not been my finest hour.

Waking up later in the day, I still felt the world had shifted on its axis and nothing was in its right place. My balance continued to be 'off.' I was afraid I would have to spend the entire trip in the chalet, and even if I were able to snowboard I was unsure if I would be able to

TECH TIP
AN IMPORTANT CONVERSATION

When booking a snowboarding lesson,
take a moment to think before
you meet your instructor:

1. Be honest about your snowboarding abilities.
Better to be the top of a lesser-ability group
than the bottom of a higher-ability one.
Struggling to keep up may damage
your confidence

2. State your goals and expectations clearly

3. Ask if your expectations
are realistic.

keep up with my allocated group. After a night's sleep, my dizziness had disappeared and I felt almost back to my old self. Descending the stairs, ravenous for breakfast the next day, I looked out of the window. The cloud had dispersed, visibility was good and I was eager to get back on the mountain. At the top of the Prodains cable car, we stood in our allocated groups clutching snowboards, ready to hit the slopes to make up for the limitations set by the previous day's storms. The instructors were talking before Mikael approached me, asking, 'Kate, do you want to come over here a minute?' Separating me from my companions, he continued, 'After yesterday, I think it would be better if you joined the group below.' He paused before asking, 'What do you think?' Glancing downwards, before looking back up to meet Mikael's eyes, I politely said, 'Yes, ok. That's fine.' In reality, I had been expecting it, and deep down I knew it was probably the best course of action for me. As I walked away to hitch myself to the lower group, I felt everyone's eyes looking my way. They all knew what had just happened. Feeling embarrassed by the demotion, I was afraid of what the others might think about me. But what did I think about myself? I was equally fearful that I was always destined to be last, permanently the least able, forever playing catch up. I avoided eye contact with everyone except the snowboarders in my new group.

Moving into unchartered territory means facing your fears. But there are different types of fear: those which play a useful role protecting us from pain, injury and even death; and those, such as self-limiting beliefs, that do not serve us well because they hold us back. It is important to know which type of fear is playing out so that we can take the appropriate action, and in my own case, on this trip, I'd flipped the switch and had been mistaken in both.

As I approached my new group, I was greeted with smiles. Crouching over his board, Dave, my new instructor looked up, a broad grin splitting his face, 'Hi, Kate,' he said, and the welcome was instant. He started telling us about the plan for the morning, when my ears suddenly pricked up. He used the word, 'lush'. It's a Geordie term meaning great, fantastic or wonderful. Listening more closely, I could hear his northern accent. When he'd finished talking, I spoke up, 'Where are you from, Dave?' Turns out he was brought up a couple of miles from where I now lived. As a non-Geordie, I really appreciate their candour, warmth and sense of fun, and the instant rapport made me feel comfortable and welcome. An added bonus was the membership of the group, which included Jo, Ali and Tim who turned out to be supportive and entertaining in equal measure.

Heading up, the difference from yesterday at the top of Arare was startling. Across from us, the peaks of Les Dents du Midi were clearly visible, snow-laden and reaching high into the small patches of blue now peaking through the thinning cloud. We followed Dave, who had to curl his height as he ducked under a rope that sectioned off the racing piste adjacent to Arare. To warm up, we set off at our own speed, and I followed my new instructor feeling so much more relaxed and happy. The slope was clearly laid out before me, and my path was plain to see. Dave stopped half-way down and I joined him moments later. I turned to see my fellow snowboarders still descending. Tim approached, breathless, and shouting, 'I was trying to catch you and Dave. But you're just too fast.' I was startled, 'Really?' This was a first. As the day progressed, I found that I was the most able rider in the group. For once, I was not struggling to keep up. My earlier fear — wondering how others saw me — disappeared. I felt better about myself, more confident. Being demoted was the best thing that could have happened to me.

The well-established concept in Susan Jeffers's book, *Feel The Fear and Do It Anyway*, is not ubiquitously applicable, particularly in situations where there is evidence of real risk. Snowboarding and other extreme sports carry varying degrees of danger, and at the extreme end, their magnitude can be immense. Jumping very large kickers and riding huge pipes all create the potential for severe injury, while backcountry snowboarding carries with it the risk of avalanche. But levels of risk can be managed and even mitigated by the choices we make. One area of difficulty faced in extreme sports is the external factor, those elements outside of a participant's control, such as weather and terrain.

Throughout the week conditions deteriorated and storms continued to plague the camp. In the afternoon of my final day, we were due to meet a photographer, Damian, for a photo session that would capture some action shots. Obtaining good snowboarding photos requires the skill of a professional and as part of the course package, Tammy had arranged for an experienced photographer to come along; his work would enable each of us to acquire a couple of great shots as mementos. At lunchtime, Jo, Ali and I had met with other campers, including Scott, at a restaurant near Les Lindarets. Our brief time to rest after the meal was interrupted by a text from Tammy that asked us to meet her and the photographer at Changabang, back up the slope in Avoriaz. We grabbed our coats, helmets and gloves, and all headed out the door together. I didn't know Scott well because he was in one of the advanced groups and was staying in a different chalet. But he was a good snowboarder, quiet and unassuming. As we hiked across the thick snow towards the chairlift, each of us clutching our boards tightly, the wind scrubbed my face; it was perceptibly stronger than it had been before the break. Rising higher out of the valley, up Les Lindarets, we all sat quietly on the lift, no one uttering a word. The pistes below were empty. With my hood up and hands buried in my lap, I patiently waited for the lift to swoop us onto the exit ramp at the top of the slope. Raising the safety bar at the last minute, the wind gusted harshly across the exposed mountain top. Pushing off and away, we soon came to a halt on the ridge. Two lifts converge here, with a third not far away, and the area is usually swarming with snowboarders and skiers. But on this occasion, we were its only souls.

We huddled together before the short final run across into Avoraiz. Above the howling wind, Scott shouted to the group, 'Okay, everyone? Do you know where you're going? Let's head off.' Strapping in was proving difficult, the wind scouring the top layer of snow, throwing it into a small maelstrom that blasted my face as I bent to put on my board. The squall seemed to blow in different directions and at different speeds as I bent downwards. Once strapped in, I stood up and found I couldn't move. The wind against my torso was blowing me backwards. It was the same for us all. We shuffled forward a bit until the flat ridge gave way to a gentle slope, and here, finally achieving some momentum, we set off together. The visibility was poor, low cloud was descending and swirling fast. In the white-out, even though I couldn't directly see the route, I'd travelled this way many times, and I was confident that I knew where I was going. The slope is relatively shallow and short, widening and flattening out where the ski schools usually hold their many lessons above the Chapelle snowpark on our right. To make the distance across the flat, I knew I needed speed, but I couldn't cover the distance and in the descent I lost the others to the mist. Unstrapping my back foot, a sudden frisson of cold caused me to shudder. Now I was completely alone, the snow and howling gale battered me from all directions, and I was afraid. I focused hard to break my progress down into manageable steps, first I got my bearings, and then I could scoot to where the slope steepened again. At the top end of Avoriaz, I could now just make out the wooden-clad buildings to my left and the concrete underpass in front of me. As

TECH TIP

SPEED CHECK
YOUR FEAR

Everyone feels afraid at some point and
it's what you do with it that matters. Unchecked fear can
engender stiffness and jerky reactions, which will
in turn compromise your snowboarding ability. But there are
numerous ways to work through fear successfully:

1. Breathe in and out evenly

2. Clench and unclench your hands

3. Raise and lower your shoulders several times

4. Count evenly in your head, or even sing a song

5. Listening to music is not a good idea —
it decreases your awareness of your surroundings.
However, if music helps you relax, wear one
ear bud rather than two so that you can hear
the people around you and your
immediate environment.

I stood up, a flash of colour in the grey cloud caught my attention, a pair of luminous orange snowboard pants, contrasting against the concrete wall, identified Scott instantly. He'd waited. I felt reassured and touched by his thoughtfulness and my fear abated.

From where I stood, strapped into my board, I knew that the high-rise buildings on my left carried on down, lining the slope, and after the underpass there would be a small chairlift to my right. The last part of the slope is gentle and usually extremely busy; like a ring road at rush hour, it carries snowboarders and skiers who race each other to the Prodains cable car at the end of the day. But now, there was no one except Scott, who rode on ahead, and me. Changabang, opposite the cable car, was almost within reach. Civilization was but a touch away. The buildings afforded some protection from the elements, but

I could sense their lack of occupancy, and the emptiness provided no comfort. I carried on past this futuristic ghost town, through the blizzard, my eyes straining to locate the restaurant. Suddenly, the cable car entrance came into view and I veered left. Changabang's yellow and red sign indicated my arrival. Unstrapping, I placed my snowboard amongst the sparse handful of others, upturned and temporarily abandoned by their owners who had retreated indoors. Once inside, I shook the snow from my clothes and was momentarily shocked by the bright light, the sounds of laughter and of people chatting. Not 5 metres' away I had passed through a different world, deserted, scoured with snow and inhospitable. Briefly, I stopped in my tracks.

Tammy, Damian and the other members of my group, including Ali, Jo and Tim were sitting together. No sooner had I arrived than Tammy thought it prudent we leave to get across to the Stash, where we would be sheltered from the worst of the weather by the park's natural features, and Damian would be able to take photos without exposing his equipment to the inclement conditions. Riding down towards the chairlift, we were greeted by an unusual sight. Snowboarders and skiers, boards and skis in hand or over their shoulders, were tramping towards us up the slope. 'Stop!' they shouted. 'The lift has just closed. We have to go back.' In the high winds, it was now too dangerous to keep the chairlifts open and the resort was being closed down. There was no way of getting to the Stash now. We must have been some of the last people to return from Les Lindarets back up to Avoriaz. Removing my board, I slogged back up the piste I had just ridden to join the group gathering in a close huddle around Tammy near the entrance to the cable car. 'You have a choice,' she shouted, straining to be heard through the gale-force winds. 'You can either get back to the chalet by going down in the cable car, or you can come with Damien and me down the Home Run, Le Crôt.' 'But Tammy,' I yelled, pointing to the orange netting across its entrance, 'It's closed.' Muffled faces deep inside hoods turned to read the word, Fermé, that spanned a sign in large black letters. Tammy's grin split her face as she replied, 'We can give it a go, but I cannot honestly say what it'll be like lower down. We may have to hike out, but whatever happens it will be an adventure. Who's up for it?' She scanned our faces expectantly, obviously willing us to be as excited as she appeared. Internally, I debated what to do. I had ridden Le Crôt with Dave and my group earlier in the week. The snow had been too shallow for the lower half of the piste to open, so we had cut the run short, only riding part way before catching the chairlift back up the mountain. Returning to Avoriaz from Les Lindarets only minutes previously, I had been scared, well beyond my comfort zone. But for this run, I told myself I would be with Tammy, whom I trusted implicitly. And I knew instinctively that she would keep me safe. I was familiar with the piste and knew that if I had to walk for most of its length I could do it. The worst that would happen would be an accident, but I would not be on my own and help could easily be summoned. It was possible that the weather could deteriorate, but we were descending to the valley floor, and I reasoned that I had managed alone much higher up the mountain. What sealed the deal for me, however, was the fact that Le Crôt is one of my favourite runs traversing a range of gradients it offers a bit of everything, from the challenge of narrow cat tracks to the freedom of open slopes and the enclosed beauty of tree-lined sections. Considering my anxiety in a measured way, I decided this was one opportunity I was not going to pass up. The only other person to join me was Tim, the rest of the group had had enough.

Once Ali and Jo had gone, Tammy turned around. 'Hold onto your boards. Do not let go,' she instructed. 'Pardon?' I said, leaning in close to hear above the howling wind. 'Do not let go of your board, Kate. Hold tight. This gale is strong enough to strip it from your hands.' Clutching its length firmly to my body, I posed with Tim and Tammy for a couple of photos before jumping over the netting with my three companions, off on our adventure. The adrenaline poured as I battled against the gusts, dropping in to the narrow cat track. Slightly lower down, in the lee of the mountain, the wind quietened dramatically, and before us, a pristine field of white blanketed the piste. We turned to face each other, sharing wild grins of anticipation. This was virgin snow and nobody had been down here. It was so clear I had made the right decision to come along. We whooped and hollered our way down, Damian furiously snapping our delight and abandon while he and Tim entertained us with a running commentary. Slashing through the powder, feeling the light snow make way for my board, this was the best run of the trip. When we all came to a stop to breathe, we noticed that others had also ignored the *Fermé* sign and now joined us on the slope, but we had reaped the rewards of riding first tracks. Tammy pointed to her left. 'Let's go this way,' she said. Strung across our path was a low rope that blocked the route to an off-piste section of the mountain. 'We're already in off-piste conditions,' I thought, 'hopping over the rope is no leap of faith.' And we continued on until about two-thirds of the way down before the run turned sketchy. 'Stay behind me in my exact tracks,' shouted Tammy as she guided us around hollows and dips, making sure we were safe. Watching her closely, weaving my way in her trail, I noticed a sudden movement to my right. A skier, travelling too fast for the conditions, hit a depression and was catapulted out of his skis, landing prostrate with a thwomp. Looking over towards the posse of his friends who had gathered around and joined him in laughter, I gave silent thanks for Tammy's topographic skills. And despite her earlier concerns, we rode the entire length of the Home Run, no hiking required. Later that evening, Avoriaz announced the closure of all runs the following day, the adverse weather conditions had brought the resort to a standstill, something Tammy had never known happen before. We had timed our run perfectly and had been lucky with our considered risk.

◆ ◆ ◆

Translating an instructor's shared knowledge into my own physical action has been difficult for me at times. Fear holds me back. I know what I need to do physically but my thoughts interrupt the cognitive chain, preventing me from converting instruction into action. The voice in my head alerts me to risk, it tells me that risk is dangerous in nature, that I could get hurt, and that I'll look foolish. In their book, *Inner Skiing*, Tim Gallwey and Robert Kriegel talk about 'Self 1' and 'Self 2', aspects of the psyche that reside in us all. Self 1 is the voice we use to tell ourselves how we feel, it instructs us what to do and it is the chatter we all hear in our heads. Self 2, on the other hand, is the quiet, knowing trust of our own bodies to do something. It is a physical, cellular wisdom accrued from mistakes of the past, a subconscious internal system of risk information and assessment separate from the mind and it translates into physical performance. Attempting one of my first rollers in Morzine, I'd failed to land – my board had slid out from underneath me because I'd shifted my weight backwards in the air. My body felt instantly its error and recognized what adjustments and shifts in operation were needed. But intellectually, I didn't want to overthink what I'd done wrong. I consciously stepped into repair the chain, to close the loop around what I knew was my own broken process. I stopped Self 1 from blocking the fluid performance of Self 2. And in the next go-round, I stomped the landing as a result. For me, that had been a double-win.

CONFIDENCE TRICK

CURTAILING SELF-LIMITING BELIEFS

Frequently self-limiting beliefs masquerade as fear.
Ask yourself:

1. The nature of the fear you are experiencing

2. Is it fear designed to protect you, or

3. Is it a self-limiting belief imposed on you by yourself?

4. If it is fear designed to protect you, listen to it

5. If it's a self-limiting belief, then it needs to be challenged.

Our internal self-chatter can be hard to control, particularly when considering any form of risk that will be necessary if we want to expand our comfort zone. But in order to grow and to move forwards, we do need to step away from familiarity and take that risk, be it physical in nature, such as a sporting achievement, or be it psychological, such as worrying about failure, how others see us. Feeling fear creates a negative mindset in which anxiety, doubt, reluctance and indecision translate to negative body language. We may become stiff, our movements jerky, eye contact becomes harder. In turn, these lead to reduced performance and falling below our standards can reinforce the initial fear itself.

Obviously, the cycle needs to be broken. We need to be able to feel confident and as calm as possible as we step out of our comfort zone, because that will reduce our fears; we will be free to perform at our fullest potential.

So, how do we do that? By learning through play — the two are interlinked. Children learn most naturally through play, but as adults we gain layer upon layer of inhibitions and ultimately we can neglect this important facet of learning. Connecting to our inner child captures the gifts that risk and play brought to us while we were kids. Creating a learning atmosphere that is predicated on fun and enjoyment allows us to reconnect to this aspect of our past and it can broaden our confidence. Dr Stuart Brown who wrote *Play: How it Shapes the Brain, Opens the Imagination, and Invigorates the Soul,* suggests that play is a biological necessity, it stimulates creativity and enriches our interactions and relationships with other people. In turn, that relaxation lightens the load of risk-taking as we step beyond the limits of our comfort zone. When at play, in other words, we are open to receive. We fall, but we get back up.

For me that process started a few years ago and it continues to this day. At the top of the nursery slope in Avoriaz, beside the Chapelle freestyle park in January 2015, Tammy first outlined my challenge — 'I'd like you to ride from top to bottom in switch.' It was that simple. But I was uncertain. 'Okay,' I replied, 'I'll give it a go.' The visibility was good, the surface soft and forgiving. Looking down at the snow just in front of my board, I set off, and during my progress I continued to look up, briefly, before looking down at the snow again. My turns were shaky and erratic, and I was struggling. Tammy stopped me half-way down. 'I want you to follow in my tracks, but keep looking up at me.' I had noticed Tammy's gloves earlier — depicted on the back of each was an animal. The image of a cute kitten covered her left glove and a panda cub adorned her right glove. 'Go with me on this,' she said, 'I'm going to hold up my gloves, mixing it up, and I want you to shout out the name of the animal.' I looked over at her, deliberately. 'Really?' I asked, my adult brain perplexed, its level of uncertainty increasing.

Tammy sounded serious, but she was grinning and her eyes sparkled when she replied, 'Yes, really. Just trust me on this one. I think it'll work.' She set off and while we rode, I trailed behind shouting, 'Panda, kitten, panda, panda, kitten, panda, kitten, kitten, kitten high, panda low, panda to the side.' I could hear how ridiculous I sounded but it was so comical that I couldn't help but laugh. Concentrating on which animal was being held aloft, I suddenly realized I was at the bottom of the piste. I had made my way down the slope turning in fluid motion, not once looking down at the snow. And I'd felt relaxed and happy all the way — it's hard, after all, to tense up and ride stiffly when laughing.

CONFIDENCE TRICK

CUTTING THE TRASH TALK

Self-1 chatter, is similar to self-limiting belief, and should be discarded rather than recycled. Distract yourself by:

1. singing a song;

2. counting to the same number before making a turn, or;

3. playing games.

Recently, Tammy threw in a variation on this theme within the context of a group lesson, her goal, similarly, had been to encourage us all to look up and relax. Taking it in turns we led the group, miming different animals, letters of the alphabet and dance moves. Everyone following had to copy the actions and shout out the name of the animal, letter or dance move. As we progressed down Star Wars, snaking our way in file through the quiet run to the bottom of Les Lindarets, I noticed Tammy's gloves — kitten and panda had been replaced by giraffe and monkey.

Being given permission to play connects us to our essential, creative selves; we are able to think beyond the confines of present limitations. The very act of snowboarding is itself a playful activity where I can hear the echoes of childhood. Playing outside with a group of friends, exploring nature and testing ourselves, these experiences were all part of growing up and they allowed us to bond with each other and marvel at the world. As an adult, snowboarding still allows me to do that, it is a direct channel back into the land of wonderment, where magical transformations are possible.

The connections made between people with a shared passion can be swiftly spun, they are strong, the gossamer of a spider's web binding us together. In the summer of 2009, I turned forty and was looking forward to entering my fifth decade. Times were good. Gordon had been to New York on several occasions, and having watched the character, Carrie Bradshaw, weave her way through Manhattan every week on television during the 1990s, I was keen to see it for myself. A milestone birthday needed a memorable celebration and we headed stateside. We trotted around Central Park in a horse and carriage, felt humbled and saddened at Ground Zero, took an elevator up the Empire State Building, soaked up the atmosphere in SoHo, and sailed to Ellis Island and the Statue of Liberty. One of the highlights for me was spending an hour in the Jimmy Choo store. As I pushed open the door I was greeted by a well-dressed man. 'Hi, ma'am! How can I help you, today?' he asked with a flourish, American service at its best. Painstakingly, he showed me almost every pair of shoes on display, while two female assistants fussed around, regularly dressing me with flattery. 'Wow, I love your pants!' I was told. 'They're so pretty!' I was informed. Deliberating between two pairs of shoes, I was shown handbags while the names of restaurants and galleries I should visit littered the exchange like the colourful tissue spilling around the shoeboxes on the floor. However, I was rather embarrassed by all the attention. The fiction of *Sex and the City* was starting to become a reality and like Carrie, I ended up with two pairs of shoes. They were both so fabulous I couldn't make up my mind. I am not a shopaholic, but owning a pair of Jimmy Choos had been on my bucket list for a long time.

Flying home, we returned to routine family life. One evening in late May I logged into Neil McNab's blog. I'd left Chamonix in January after my second visit, and was keen to catch up with Neil and Keith's progress, to learn what they had been doing. Reading Neil's updates usually provided a bit of escape from domesticity and work, and learning of his latest adventures kept me connected to the people with whom I'd shared time and to the mountainous landscape they inhabited. These gossamer threads stretched, but they held steadfast. Expecting some escapism, I was shocked to read that Keith had been caught in an avalanche whilst riding at the UK Board Test in Kaunertal, Austria. On 5 May 2009, he had been killed.

I stared hard at the screen and reread the post but could not believe the words in front of me on the screen. I had emailed Mel, Keith's wife, only recently, just before jetting off to the States. She had told me Keith was heading to the UK Board Test with friends and fellow professional snowboarders for the last blast of the season — it is one of the final standing events on the snowboarding calendar before the snow itself disappears. I was also aware that he had been looking forward to what lay ahead, to his mountain biking during the summer months. I found hundreds of tributes to him online. The funeral had been and gone, but Neil brought me up to date, and asked whether I'd like to contribute to a memory box for his young son, Arren, who was only two. The aim of the box was to help him connect to his father. I sent the following letter:

Dear Arren

Forgive me for typing this letter to you, but my handwriting is not so good and can be hard to read. I was so sad and shocked to hear about your Dad's accident and although you don't know me, I feel like I know you because he used to talk about you frequently. I have a little girl who is a year older than you and your father and I used to 'talk babies' when we were driving to the slopes in the morning, or sitting on the chairlifts, or having lunch.

I first met him in January 2008 and you would've been almost a year old. I can remember him talking about getting you some plastic skis to try on your first birthday. On that first clinic I was the only woman and your Dad never made me feel different to everyone else, but he always made sure I was ok. One of the photos I've included was taken at the end of the last day where I was so tired I felt I could hardly stand up!

The next time I saw your Dad was in January 2009 during a girls' technical clinic. He was very patient with us and never complained. I have two really good memories of him. On the first day I got stuck in the powder, and it took me twenty minutes to get out and back to the piste. By this time everyone had boarded off, but after I'd got my breath back and sat up I noticed he'd waited for me. He didn't make me feel bad for holding everyone up and he gave me a hug and laughed with me at my ridiculous attempts to get out of the powder. The second memory is of him teaching me to run my board flat at Grands Montets, which is where the other photo that I've included was taken. I'd caught so many edges prior to that, and was quite nervous, but he told me what to do and to relax. He boarded with me holding my hands and told me to 'Go faster', and we both ended up laughing as I shouted, 'No, I can't, it's too fast.' But do you know what - it worked!

A few weeks after the clinic, I was in Morzine and ran my board flat for 500 metres. I was going so fast that I could feel the wind whipping tears from my eyes, and I remember wishing your Dad could see me. He was such a talented snowboarder, but also a very good teacher, patient and kind. The only time I ever saw him get annoyed was with other skiers and snowboarders who were doing dangerous things and putting others on the slope at risk.

When he used to talk about you and your Mum I could tell he really loved you both — his face changed and became softer. I remember your mother once brought you to the hotel and your Dad was so pleased to see you. Both your parents were and are brave people who decided to leave Scotland and follow their dream of living in the mountains. As you grow up you will realize that lots of people are too scared to follow their dreams and they end up living a half-filled life. Your parents are not like most people and you should feel proud of them both for living life on their own terms.

I know it will be hard to remember your Dad, but he touched lots of people's lives and many will always remember him. I hope your memory box will help you know him in many different ways and that other people can help you remember him, too.

I wish you all the luck for the future. Be happy and find peace in life.

Lots of love,

Kate xxx

I was surprised by how hard I found it to process Keith's death. After all, I had not known him that well. Yet at times I would find tears welling up, empathetic grief for Mel and Arren. It was difficult to believe I would never see him again. I also felt guilt and regret. On our final day, driving back from the slopes, I had sat next to him but had been self-absorbed, contemplating my exit from the world of snowboarding. I'd paid little heed to Keith. Even though I didn't know at the time that this would be the last time I would see him, later I couldn't help but feel guilt at the self-indulgence of my mood.

CONFIDENCE TRICK

DEFINING ACCEPTABLE RISK

Understanding what levels of risk are acceptable to you can help you progress towards your goal rather than prohibit it.

1. Think of risk as a series of escalating steps

2. Move from one to another without skipping any out, tempted to leap high

3. Upon which step do you currently draw the line? Is it where your perceived benefits are outweighed by your perceived losses?

Keith had still been in his thirties when he'd been taken so swiftly and unexpectedly. I felt shocked by his sudden departure from this world. It seemed so unfair. I'd shared some intense times with an instructor who had seen me angry, happy, elated, frightened, and excited; a whole range of extreme emotions which many of my friends might never even witness, and perhaps that comes with the profession, the ability to weather the clientele in addition to the climate. Keith had been kind and supportive and had laid the foundations for my snowboarding. I felt angry that I would never ride with him again, that he would never get to see how his teaching had influenced me. More importantly, he would never get to see his son grow up. I felt this keenly, my daughter was a similar age, and I couldn't help but think about my own circumstances, my own mortality. Keith had been well-trained and was familiar with the backcountry, he was an experienced snowboarder and so the surprise of his death brought the danger of avalanches up close and personal. I had to ask myself how much risk was I prepared to take to pursue my passion, especially now that I had a child.

I still think of my instructor, eight years after the avalanche that killed him. Occasionally I talk to him in my head when I am snowboarding and wonder if he can see me. Sometimes driving through a tunnel I think of that last journey. Nearly a decade has passed but Keith is not forgotten and, in all of us whom he taught, the infectious love of his sport lives on. With Keith gone, however, I have not snowboarded on Chamonix's slopes again. His death severed my gossamer thread to the mountain town.

Risk. Snowboarding is considered an extreme sport, attractive to a young generation. With its display of counterculture that explicitly rejects authority and imposed rules, it is thrilling precisely because of its uncontrollable variables, hazardous terrain and the uncertain weather of the mountains. I had experienced the difficulties weather could bring and had overcome the associated fear of shifting conditions. But I had come to learn that other factors, such as where and with whom I ride are within my control, that a conscious understanding of the degrees of risk can help manage the fear that can begin to overtake the degree of risk itself. At its very heart, snowboarding is an exciting activity that is performed in breathtakingly beautiful surroundings and where adrenalin can flow; it creates life-affirming energy. I can legitimately connect to my inner child while playing with friends in the snow and shredding with my crew. Risk-taking and fear, these are both natural parts of life, and life without risk would be boring and dull. Life without risk is a half-life, it is a life not worth living.

CONFIDENCE TRICK

CHALLENGING YOUR COMFORT ZONE

Once you've identified your fear(s), you can use that knowledge as an opportunity to learn and put plans in place to lessen its impact in the future:

1. If you are fearful, have you done something similar before?

2. Are you making a small step outside your comfort zone, or a huge leap?

3. If it is the latter, scale it back trying something on a smaller level first

4. If it is the former and you are anxious, then enlist the help of a mentor, coach, instructor or a positive friend to see you through the experience.

EXERCISES

♦ ♦ 1. Name any two activities you have done, or list any two occasions where you have felt nervous or frightened. Add the gnarly activities or occasions to the column headings in the table, below. What do you believe made you frightened or nervous? List each reason in the rows below the relevant activity or occasion. There may be one or more beliefs or reasons for each activity or occasion.

Activity/Occasion 1:	Activity/Occasion 2:
Reason for fear 1:	Reason for fear 1:
Reason for fear 2:	Reason for fear 2:
Reason for fear 3:	Reason for fear 3:

2. Cite two remedial actions you took in order to overcome your nerves or fear in the table on the following page. Were they conscious or unconscious? State 'yes' or 'no'. Don't overthink.

Activity/Occasion 1:	Concious?	Activity/Occasion 2:	Concious?
Remedial Action 1:		Remedial Action 1:	
Remedial Action 2:		Remedial Action 2:	

◆ 3. In retrospect were your fears real or imagined? For each
fear, write out your reason, 'My fear was real because.....'
Or, 'My fear was imagined because......'

a. My fear was...

....

b. My fear was...

....

c. My fear was...

....

4. Read the beliefs aloud. Have a trusted friend read them.
Discuss whether they also think your fears are real
or imagined.

♦ ♦ 5. If you still hold self-limiting beliefs about fears, real or unreal, what two actions can you take to confront them? When will you confront them? Make a date with yourself to do so.

Belief 1	Belief 2	Belief 3
Action 1:		
Date to confront:		
Action 2:		
Date to confront:		

6. Name two parts of your life where you would like to embrace more risks. These could be in any sphere: financial, social, or recreational.

a. Area to embrace risk 1..

b. Area to embrace risk 2..

♦ 7. List two reasons that you believe are preventing you from taking those risks. Write out why, e.g. 'I believe 'x' is blocking me from 'y' because...'

a. Risk 1: I believe..

b. Risk 1: I believe..

c. Risk 2: I believe..

d. Risk 2: I believe..

♦ ♦ 8. Which two things will you do to manage these beliefs? When will you do them?

Risk Area 1 Belief 1	Risk Area 1 Belief 2	Risk Area 2 Belief 1	Risk Area 2 Belief 2
Action 1:	Action 1:	Action 1:	Action 1:
Date to confront:	Date to confront:	Date to confront:	Date to confront:
Action 2:	Action 2:	Action 2:	Action 2:
Date to confront:	Date to confront:	Date to confront:	Date to confront:

Feeling your fear takes courage, assessing it objectively means taking fellow riders alongside. Embrace the risk to catch some air! Write your answers down, now.

Scoring

Exercise 1. No points given or deducted.

Exercise 2. Give yourself a point for each item listed where you overcame your fears.

Exercise 3. Award a point whether the fear was imagined or real, but only if you have determined which it is.

Exercise 4. Award yourself a point when you have discussed this with a friend.

Exercise 5. Give yourself a point when you confronted those fears.

Exercise 6. For each part of your life highlighted, give a point.

Exercise 7. For each statement completed, award yourself a point.

Exercise 8. For each action identified, give a point, and for each highlighted date, also give a point.

Total chapter points................

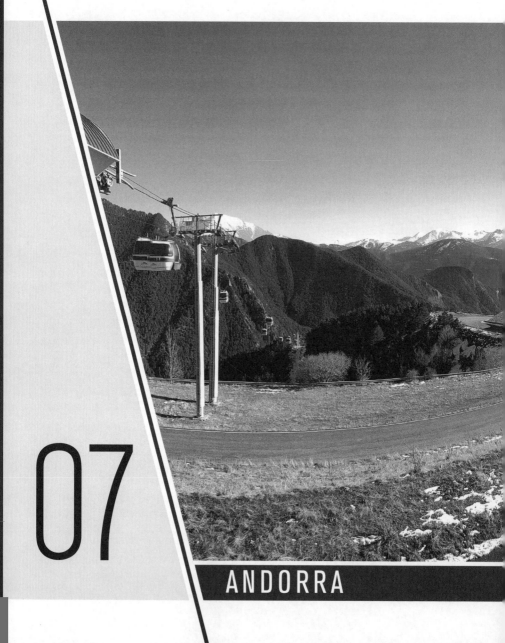

07

ANDORRA

AFTER THE FALL

understanding the strength of failure
and finding what's right in the wrongs

Piercing blue sky, punctured by fragments of white cloud. Occasionally, the view was interrupted by the dark underside of a chairlift suspended below the long arc of its cables. I could hear almost nothing, only the muffled sounds of the snow under the rails of the sledge as we headed down the mountain. Strapped into the blood wagon, this was one of those occasions when I ceded absolute control — I let the ski patrol call the shots. My neck was collared in a brace and my arms lay protectively over my chest. I tried to keep still, but the combination of creeping cold and shock took effect and I began to shiver uncontrollably. Intermittently, the lead skier pulling the sledge carved a turn, his skis spraying freezing snow onto my face and I gasped involuntarily. The snowflakes quickly turned to water on my cheeks, fresh droplets to dilute my tears. As we continued downwards I closed my eyes, giving into the pain and trusting ski patrol to get me to safety.

The day had started badly even before my unscheduled trip in the blood wagon. I had woken to acute pain in my neck and back, all-over muscle stiffness and the broader ignominy of a hangover. My trip had been going well until the previous day, but within twenty-four hours, everything had changed. I'd arrived in the principality of Andorra five days previously, in mid-December 2016, to undertake the BASI

Level 1 Snowboard Instructor qualification. The exam was something I'd been planning to take for four years, but it had taken this long to find time in my schedule.

My flight had touched down in Barcelona late in the evening, and consequently I'd missed the public bus. The surrounding Mediterranean air was warmer than in the UK, but sitting on top of my suitcase for almost two hours, careful to ensure I caught the final transfer to Andorra, I was starting to tire. December is always a busy month — there are preparations for Christmas and New Year to weave in and around various family commitments and work. Leaving for a week during this period had required planning and co-operation from others. I had written and sent all our Christmas cards, bought and wrapped all the presents including those from the Big Man himself, and I'd made sure to decorate the house with Freya and Gordon. The groundwork for this holiday season had started back in October. For the first time Freya had no school nativity performance so I'd been able to book the week away, confident I would not be compromising parental responsibilities. However, as my thoughts tumbled along the quiet, deserted pavement, and I waited for my transport, it occurred to me that I was starting my trip both physically and mentally tired.

Eventually, my bus drew in and I settled into my seat for the four-hour drive that would take me up into the highest inhabited country in Europe. Andorra nestles in the Pyrenean mountain range between Spain and France and administrative responsibility for this tiny principality, its radius only miles-wide, was shared by both its neighbouring countries until 1993, when the existing feudal system was replaced by a parliamentary democracy. There are two co-princes who act as indivisible Heads of State — one is the president of France and the other is the Catholic bishop of the Spanish town La Seu d'Urgell. Neither can veto legislation made by the General Council, and as such they have limited powers, but the dual nature of its political structure makes Andorra unique. Its approximately 85,000 residents live in fewer than 500 square kilometres, but the destination is popular with tourists, and every year estimated ten million visitors flood the region. Part of Andorra's popularity has been its tax-haven status, although the European Union has applied pressure on the principality to introduce taxes in line with international standards and the enjoyment may not last. However, costs remain relatively low when compared to other European countries and the allure of a cheap holiday attracts many people, year-round, to its rugged mountains.

We travelled north along the motorway before turning off onto the smaller, two-way roads. Journeying higher, my eyes strained to see through the inky darkness. Instead of snow, I could see dry, orange-brown earth and scrubby Mediterranean vegetation; before long, the hum of the engine and the bus's loose suspension rocked me to sleep. I woke as we entered the town of Andorra La Vella. A few miles from the principality's southern circumference and its border with Spain, we'd arrived in Europe's highest capital at just over 1,000 metres from sea level, which had been my starting point. It was past midnight and I was struck by the cold, this was mountain air and my breath misted up in the splay of neon light that illuminated the bus station. Retrieving my bag, I transferred to a shared mini-bus taxi for my journey's final leg — while the popular ski resorts of Soldeu and Pas de la Casa tracked east towards Andorra's Grandvalira ski area and its eastern border with France, I was to ride a further twenty minutes north-west to Arinsal, part of the Vallnord ski area. Winding up through the town's main street, I could see the rugged stone walls of the buildings' facades decorated with wooden shutters. The valley was so narrow that many of them backed right into the mountainside. Approaching the Hotel Montane, its sign standing proud, I was the last passenger to be dropped off. Finally, I fell into bed at 2.30 am.

Four-and-a-half hours' later, a shrill ringing punctured the depths of my sleep, slinging me back into consciousness and I grappled with the alarm, trying to turn it off. It was dark and I yearned to roll over and resume my dream. Instead, I dressed quickly and hurried downstairs to breakfast. Only one other person was seated at a table, and I guessed it must be someone on the course. No one else would be up this early. 'Kate?' he asked, calling across the room. I nodded and enquired in the way these exchanges go, if he was also on the Snowboard Coach course. Introducing himself, he explained that he'd arrived the day before. Callum was in his early twenties, had dark, curly hair, big eyes and an even bigger smile. Although I couldn't see, he was also tall. As we'd been eating, the sun had started to rise and back upstairs in my hotel room, I drew my curtains to reveal the scene outside. The road and pavements were completely devoid of snow, but as my eyes rose upwards following the gondola directly opposite, I could see a familiar blanket of white above the treeline. The town remained in shadow, but the surrounding summits, in brilliant white contrast, were bathed in early morning sunlight, jewels atop the crown.

Changing into my snowboarding gear with instinctual ease, now down to a fine art after many years practise, I was nervous about the day ahead, but also excited. At times I find it hard to distinguish between fear and anticipation. I have often felt this way when I've stood before a kicker or box rail — excited to jump or slide, but also frightened I might fall and hurt myself. My daughter and I have created a term to describe the state of uncertainty, when the feelings we are experiencing scrabble for dominance, and we call it 'nervous-cited'. In my Arinsal hotel room, that's how I felt when getting dressed. I had spent many hours preparing for this exam, even attending a weekend pre-course at the Snow Centre in Hemel Hempstead more than 250 miles from home. I had also been warned that students opting to undertake the exam in the mountains, rather than at an indoor snow slope in the UK, are usually more skilled and driven to achieve, and I was nervous about my own skills in comparison to theirs. Despite a reliable ability to distance myself from surrounding competition, I am not perfect in my practise and on this occasion the self-judgement was an unwelcome intrusion.

Taking a final look out of my hotel window, I could see Ash Newnes waiting by the gondola. Ash had been my Snowboard Coach instructor from the Snow Centre in Hemel Hempstead and he was now the BASI trainer for our week in Andorra. I grabbed my helmet and board and headed out the door, taking my butterflies with me. I crossed the small, stone bridge spanning the Arinsal river and joined Ash at the base of the gondola. By now, I had known Ash for a number of years and it was good to hook up and see him on his home turf. We hugged hello and, to the accompanying gurgles of the river, he introduced me to my fellow students, Jay and Felix. Together with Callum, we jumped into the small gondola ascending steeply above the stone buildings and brown fields of Arinsal. Below us, I could see how little flatland exists, the buildings, river and road were all packed tightly together. As we headed up through the morning's shadows the sun's rays met us from above, extending their warmth further into the valley as the day grew bolder by the moment.

Inside the gondola, the customary first-day conversation turned to breaking the ice. Jay was an accountant and together with his girlfriend, Anna, he'd taken time away from his regular work to become a seasonnaire and had been working over the previous winter in Morzine so he could snowboard as much as possible. Both Felix and Callum were water sports instructors during the summer and, although they did not know each other, it turned out they had mutual friends in common. Both had lived abroad snowboarding for at least one season, and both would be returning to Andorra in January to undertake their BASI Level 2 exam, which meant they would be able to teach in the mountains in subsequent winters.

My ears popped as we climbed higher over the densely-wooded, dark green slopes, but as the top station came into view above us, the ground below the gondola transitioned to white. Grabbing our boards we climbed the metal staircase to the Polar Bar where we met Jess, the last member of our group. Jess lived and worked in Arinsal as a ski instructor. In her mid-twenties, with a dark plait draped over her shoulder, she greeted us with a welcoming smile. Looking around my fellow students I realised I was the oldest by about twenty years. All were either already working in the snowsports industry, or they had at least spent a few months snowboarding, working for a full season in a resort.

Before Ash introduced the course, he encouraged us to get a drink and take a seat at the tables away from the other customers. Ordering coffees, hot chocolates and water in Spanish seemed very strange. *Bonjour!* and *Buongiorno!* — the French and Italian slope-side greetings that had become so familiar to me — were now replaced by *¡Hola!* The official language of Andorra is Catalan and the principality is cradled within the bowl of Catalonia's northern border. Deriving from vulgar Latin, the language spread west from the Eastern Pyrenees during the Middle Ages. Centuries later, during Franco's dictatorship of Spain (from 1939 to 1975) its use was banned in an effort to quash the rebellious north-east, but after the end of the regime, it rebounded and reclaimed its officially recognized status there. Today, it is the only official language of the principality but in practise, Andorra's geography and historical ties mean that Spanish, French and Portuguese are all commonly spoken.

Our drinks ordered, and seats located, Ash took us through the structure and requirements of the BASI Level 1 Snowboard exam. 'This is the first qualification on the BASI pathway. If you pass,' he told us, dangling the carrot, 'you'll be qualified to teach snowboarding in a non-mountain environment such as an indoor snow centre or a dry slope. It won't qualify you to work in the mountains. For that you need to pass Level 2. But this is the first step. You'll be teaching people who have never snowboarded and their early experiences will influence whether they continue in the sport or drop out. As such, your role as an ambassador is an important one.' He went on to explain that not only would we need to pass that week's exam, we'd also have to complete thirty-five hours of shadowing, spending time with instructors teaching in an indoor environment or on a dry slope. Additionally we'd need to complete a first aid course, and a children's safeguarding module. With that, he gave each of us each a copy of the BASI, British Snowboard Instructor Handbook, together with an accompanying workbook.

An hour had gone by. 'The time for talking is over,' Ash told us. 'Now let's get out there!' With the sun's pale warmth on our backs, we strapped in and rode the long Les Fonts chairlift up to 2,350 metres where the air was cold, the visibility clear and bright. One of the advantages of riding with an instructor is that they know the pistes and mountains intimately; students can rely on their local knowledge, relax a little, focus on skills rather than location. There is no need to pull out the piste map to check the route. Smiling, Ash provided orientation, 'Up above us is Pic Negre. At 2,500 metres it's one of the highest points in Andorra. From there you can see into Spain. To the left is Alt de la Capa, or Capa, which is closed at the moment because there isn't enough snow.' Turning around, we looked down the mountain. 'There are two pistes we can take from here,' Ash continued, pointing left and then right, indicating our options. 'Officially they're called Les Fonts and Port Vell. But locally,' and he turned towards us again, grinning, 'we call them the Light Side and the Dark Side, for reasons that will become obvious.' We looked at each other, and I wondered quietly if Ash would be our Obi-Wan for the week, or if he was to be our Darth Vader. On the Light Side the snow would have yielded to the sun, becoming much softer, whereas the Dark Side would be icy and crunchy, immersed in shadow. The Light Side would also be warmer, the sun's rays removing the sting from the cold bite in the air. I knew where I'd be happiest on day one. 'I want you to get your legs warmed up, but don't speed down too fast. Stop where I do,' Ash instructed. 'We're taking the Dark Side'.

We set off, the boys at fast pace. I knew the first few runs would be the point at which the group members sized each other up, establishing our unofficial rank and identifying the most and least proficient riders in the group. I had run this gauntlet many times and, having relaxed into the day, was probably less anxious than others about my place in the pecking order; it didn't really matter to me, as long as I was of a sufficient standard to pass the exam. The slope was gentle and the snow softer than I'd expected, I felt no crunch of ice under my board. We rode past the Port Negre chairlift on our left and continued downwards, eventually coming to a halt beside Ash. 'This is a good place to stop,' he said, before turning the statement into a question, 'So why have we stopped here?' In turn we ventured our thoughts: at the side of the piste we were out of the way; the terrain was flat and it was easy to stop; a restaurant with a toilet was nearby. 'Nope. All of these are good points, but not what I'm looking for.' Ash was direct. 'What's the difference between here,' he asked, 'and over there?' And he pointed to a site about 4 metres away. 'Ah,' we'd understood immediately, 'We're in the sunshine, not the shade.' 'Exactly,' continued Ash, 'Think about your students, think about what's going to make them as comfortable as possible. Standing in the shade means they'll get cold more quickly.

On the next descent, we rode the Light Side and although it was open to the sunshine, its snow softer under our boards, its camber was more challenging. Our fall line sloped horizontally rather than vertically and we needed to look for it. Keith's lesson from many years ago remained firmly in my mind and still held true — the direction of the fall line differed to the direction of the piste. It meant I needed to stay high on one side to take account of the gravitational pull. Ash had eased us into the day gently, letting us discover the differences for ourselves. Later we examined the fundamentals of snowboarding, those aspects of riding every snowboarder must master whatever their level: speed control; adjusting technique according to changing conditions and terrain; steering the snowboard, harmonizing balance and posture. All these fed into the notion of flow and ensured co-ordinated rhythm.

We returned to the Polar Bar for lunch, basking outside on its sunny terrace and as we looked over the mountains, Arinsal remained invisible in the deep cleft of one of the valleys beyond. Cushions of snow had fallen on the surrounding peaks, but below these summits, dense woodland clung to sheer precipices, long hunched shoulders in a cloak of dark green, pulled tight. It was still early in the season and more snow would arrive by late December, but for now our playground was a brilliant crown atop the heights of the principality.

Anna, Jay's girlfriend, joined us. A proficient snowboarder in her own right, she had wanted to take the course but felt her 180 half-rotation jumps were not sufficiently strong to warrant the expense of an exam that she could well fail. I warmed to her positive smile and attitude, which were a welcome addition to the conversation, and I was happy that she continued to join us most days for lunch. The Polar Bar became our default location and a routine established itself through the week. Anna and Jay were in the process of buying a house and fielded calls from their estate agent and solicitors, often nipping away from the table. Felix would usually sneak away for a time to eat his packed lunch, Jess checked in with her ski school pals, whilst the rest of us remained to make the most of the Polar Bar's offerings, stocking up on calories before the afternoons resumed.

That first afternoon we headed to the nursery slopes, just behind the Polar Bar where the ski school operates its activity, harnessed by a magic carpet that runs alongside the gentler runs. A form of travellator — similar to those in airports — a magic carpet allows complete beginners to ascend the slope without using a drag lift. At some resorts, a clear, plastic canopy covers the travelator, protecting skiers and snowboarders from the worst of the elements. As students learning to instruct beginners, we only needed to show our competence on slopes with a gradient equivalent to those found on a dry slope or an indoor snow slope, and much of our time was spent on or around the nursery runs. Despite the gentle terrain, even in good weather conditions and with soft snow, the areas can still be hazardous, their dangers unforeseen. Huddled in a group around Ash, we heard a sudden piercing scream behind us. A skier flew past, completely out of control, unable to stop. His elongated howl stretched elastically through the air with him, snapping abruptly into silence after he hit the boards at the end of the run with a loud bang. Every skier and snowboarder, as well as the people relaxing in the deckchairs, gawped. On the other side of the barrier, the piste fell away to a sheer drop. Before anyone could move, the kamikaze skier was up, apparently unhurt. Less than five minutes later, Ash shouted, 'Watch out,' as another skier hurtled down the piste out of control. Both her skis flew off on impact as she fell, one twisting through space and hitting me in the back. Fortunately, not hard. Jess quickly gathered up the skier's equipment, returning her skis to her, and checking she was okay before pointing her in the direction of her teachers. As we ascended on the small El Cortal chairlift serving the minor El Cortalet run closest to the nursery slope, we saw at least four other skiers walking down the side of the piste, their skis over their shoulders. I had never witnessed this before. 'What's going on?' I asked, turning to Ash. 'In the morning, groups of Andorran school children come for lessons on the nursery slope,' he explained, 'and in the afternoon, they are let loose without a ski instructor — at which point their regular teachers are supposed to supervise their activities. But as you can see, the teachers are sitting over there in the deckchairs…Ash turned and pointed to the terrace, before continuing, 'while the children are overly ambitious and over here.' He indicated the random chaos occurring on the run below us. 'They leave the nursery slope and head for this small slope full of excitement, thinking they have mastered skiing. And unfortunately, they haven't.' I chuckled, enjoying the vast chasm between local practise and my own health and safety standards, rigorously applied after years in the NHS. With this snippet of local information, I became circumspect around schoolchildren who were anywhere near my vicinity on the slope.

TECH TIP

SLOPE SMARTS

At times, the pistes can seem like busy white motorways; it's advisable to:

1. Be aware of other slope users and the proficiency levels of the majority in various areas of the mountain

2. Steer clear of any kamikaze skiers or snowboarders.

We rounded up the day with a debriefing in the Polar Bar. Ash had already explained that the course was continuous assessment, and that by Friday lunchtime we would be expected to ride at the required level, but by the end of day one I felt confident and relaxed. He'd given me some exercises to help improve my stance, ensuring my front shoulder stayed aligned with my board, and we had all worked on flexion and extension, learning to absorb pressure coming up from the ground through the knees. We had also been assigned homework (a chapter in our handbooks for reading) but I was starting to feel the effects of little sleep. Heading through the door, Jess invited us for a drink, but I needed to bow out. 'Count me in another time,' I said, waving off the rest of the group as they happily followed her to the bar.

Waking up the following day, I felt refreshed and ready to tackle the next chapter of learning. I timed my journey up the gondola badly, arriving in the middle of an army of Andorran school children ascending to their morning lessons. Rather than wait in line as I would have done in the UK, I took a more European approach and squeezed in alongside five pre-teen girls who giggled and smiled at me shyly. Listening to their schoolgirl chatter, Catalan sounded quite different to Spanish, although I could decipher the occasional, familiar word. The day followed the same format as previously, but we were introduced to the 'central theme', the framework used in teaching beginners, which helps them to progress through a series of manoeuvres from straight running, sideslipping, falling leaf and garlands, and on to basic and standard turns. There was more homework and we had to think which of the central theme manoeuvres related to the fundamentals of snowboarding. Covering safety and teaching styles, we moved forward, progressing to mid-week with ease.

By day three we had found our rhythm, and after our early morning lecture, we rode the chairlift to the top of the Dark Side. Again, it was a glorious day with blue skies and good visibility. As the chair lifted us up and away from the Polar Bar, Jay rubbed his thighs lamenting that his legs ached. 'It's often Day three when everything starts to hurt,' Anna sympathized and even Callum weighed in, complaining of sore muscles. I sat quietly, grateful that my own legs felt fine. Normally, I'd similarly be experiencing stiff muscles and aching limbs, but not this occasion. Before my trip, I'd prepared for spending six hours a day on the slope for five days, and had worked with my trainer, Tina, on a combination of strength exercises and aerobic activity. I had never felt as strong as I did now. And although I was in my mid-forties, I was the fittest I had ever been, relieved that my prior effort back in the UK was paying dividends. We rose higher, feeling the light, cold breeze on our faces, the sounds of voices from the slopes below rising to meet our own.

After the morning's session, the moment to face my bête noir, the 180 half-turn came around — they were part of the curriculum and had to be mastered. As a freestyle trick, we would not be expected to teach them, but demonstrating proficiency indicates a rider's agility on a snowboard, as well as her ability to land and ride in switch. My most recent attempt at a 180 had been with Tammy on the gentle Proclou run in Avoriaz. I'd managed to turn about ninety degrees, occasionally reaching a full 180, but it was very sketchy. My learning had not been consolidated. In the intervening time I'd intended to practise indoors, back at Cas. But I hadn't acted on my intentions and now it was too late.

Ash instructed us to jump a half-turn without our snowboards, demonstrating to us that we could all jump 180 degrees. Now we just had to pull it off whilst in motion, and with a snowboard strapped to our feet. Grabbing our boards, we headed up the El Cortal chairlift, I felt the nerves kick in. Until now, I had felt confident in my abilities, I could show all the required manoeuvres, but I knew this was my Achilles heel. Gathering around Ash at the top of the chairlift, we listened as he explained our process. 'I want to build up gradually using progressive exercises,' he said. 'To begin with, I want you just to aim for a 90-degree turn. And remember, whilst on your toe edge, you will be using your leading arm to punch upwards, taking your shoulder around the turn. It's easier to do a backside 180 than a frontside,' he finished up.

Whenever rotations are required, I have always struggled to orientate myself and work out which way I need to travel. It's a spatial awareness deficiency, and I have to concentrate hard, initially trying to visualize the trick before I attempt it. I set off, looking up across the slope, and then tensed my core muscles as I bent my knees, threw the punch with my leading hand and jumped. Turning ninety degrees, I landed it. Great! So, I tried it again. This time it didn't work so well and I fell. But I got up and tried many more times. As for most people, it was easier to start the trick riding switch and then land in my regular direction. We then stepped it up, attempting a full 180 rotation. All the men succeeded, most of them extremely well and stylishly. Felix already had his CASI Level One Snowboard qualification, the Canadian equivalent to the British system. Watching the men, the move appeared easy and effortless. Like me, Jess had also been concerned about this element of the course, but she was progressing well and had landed most attempts that afternoon. As I tried again, for the umpteenth time, I landed hard on my backside, bouncing off the ground. I rolled onto my knees in a crouching position. I was winded and struggling to find my breath; I could feel my stomach had been wrenched. Slowly standing upright, I felt somewhat frustrated and sore. This was proving harder than I expected. I just needed to practise more. Ash told us we would try again the next day.

As the sun rose on day four, I could feel the pressure mounting. I had one-and-a-half days to show Ash that I could land three out of four 180s, and I knew my time in the afternoon would be crucial. But until then my focus needed to remain on teaching because directly after lunch, I had to instruct a lesson. We worked together in pairs on the nursery slope, and in this sheltered spot away from the wind, the sun was warm on our back, and we all removed our jackets. 'When teaching students, you will need a degree of physical contact,' Ash said. 'You'll need to help those who have fallen get back on their feet, or lend support to those trying new manoeuvres. But you need to keep that contact to a minimum,' he explained, 'and I'll show you how to lift someone safely without hurting yourself.' This felt logical, but his final observation came as a surprise. 'You'll spend a lot of time on your feet without a snowboard because you'll be running backwards and forwards supporting students. In fact the only time you should be strapped in to your board is when you are giving a demo.' Teaming up with Callum, trying out different techniques for lifting the fallen and lending assistance during manoeuvres, we practised. When a snowboarder on her heel edge falls backwards, the instructor can jam her own foot under her student's board to stop it sliding out as she gets up. Sitting in the snow, the student then places her fist behind her hip and pushes upwards from the ground just as the instructor, having taken her other hand, gently pulls upwards. The combined forces of push and pull make for a team effort. The morning flew by.

Ash had given us each a particular section of the central theme to teach, and he'd deliberately chosen an area that we ourselves needed to develop further. Back on the nursery slope after lunch, we were particularly mindful of the crazy skiers now that we were in the zone of imminent threat for that time of day. We all took turns as instructor for the group, and I'd dutifully prepared my lesson plan the evening before. My task was to teach the basic heel- to toe-edge turn because Ash had said I needed to engage my back foot more strongly so that my board could grip the snow effectively. With the exception of Jay, we had all taught in a variety of settings. My own area of expertise lies in training doctors in academic disciplines, including applied methodologies for healthcare improvement. But that experience is very different from teaching a practical skill to members of the general population. The satisfaction of watching someone value what they are being taught and the pleasure of witnessing their achievement is immediate. Feedback from Ash was positive, who told me, 'You have a good manner and come across well, Kate. You just need to make sure you can deliver the other aspects of the central theme, including straight running and sideslipping, with the same confidence. Shadowing will help,' he added. But I had passed the requirement and so had everyone else. One aspect of the course had been completed successfully, then, and I felt relieved.

Swiftly refocusing, I turned my attention back to the 180s for the remainder of the day. Ash offered to video everyone and I knew his feedback would be valuable, and I readily agreed. On familiar territory just off the small El Cortal chairlift, I began to practise. After several attempts, none of which I landed, I gave it another shot. Landing hard on my backside, bouncing off the ground, winded and gasping for breath, I was clearly making the same mistakes as I had the previous day. On the second attempt, the pain had felt worse and I stopped to compose myself. Before a third attempt, Ash asked us to ride to Polar Bar so we could review our performance. As he connected the video to the television, I gingerly lowered myself onto the chair. Sitting through everyone's playback, we could see where improvements could be made. To demonstrate exactly what I was doing, Ash showed my last attempt in slow motion. I felt sick. I wish I had never seen it. As my bottom bounces off the slope, my back is forced upwards, arching before my head snaps back awkwardly. My fellow students all gasped and turned towards me, horror streaked across their faces. 'It's my arse that hurts, not my neck,' I muttered through my hands, unable to look. The video screen went blank. 'I stopped filming when I realized you were winded,' Ash explained. 'But can you see what was happening? You commit, ready with your punching fist, but you don't bend your knees sufficiently. You don't get low enough at the outset, which means you can't spring to the height that will give you time to turn your board a full 180 degrees. You end up catching your heel edge.' He didn't mention my old bad habit, a lack of speed, so I must have improved somewhat in the intervening years. And I could understand precisely what he meant, the video had demonstrated it perfectly. But I still wish I hadn't seen it.

TECH TIP

LESS IS MORE

You're in the mountains, likely at altitude greater than your customary elevation, and your body may not be used to the additional exertion

1. Listen to your body and respect i

2. You should know when it has had enough;

3. Leave the slopes and take a rest.

By now it was late afternoon, about 4.00 pm, and I had one last chance to practise this jump. It was now or never. Anna offered to come with me and in the last rays of the sunshine we headed back out. But my body was stiffening up and, uneasily, I shifted my weight on the chairlift, my bottom sore and uncomfortable. 'I just can't do it, Anna. If I cannot manage it, I'll not pass.' She tried to reassure me saying, 'It'll be okay. I'm sure it'll be fine.' As we descended the slope, several times I tried to make the jump, but I was now too frightened to attempt it. In my heart, I knew my body couldn't take another slam. Almost in tears as we progressed lower, I eventually ran out of slope. It was too late.

Dragging my snowboard across to the gondola, I climbed aboard with Anna and sat alongside Callum who had come off the mountain as we were leaving. Dejected, knowing I was unlikely to pass the exam, I wittered on to my companions. Callum, ever the enthusiast, tried to be positive, but as the gondola descended my spirits sank with it. By the time we got to the base station, my mood had blackened. I was cross with myself, ready to drown my sorrows in the bottom of a Jägermeister. Callum offered to take my snowboard, stowing it away in the locker room at the hotel, whilst Anna and I headed the twenty metres uphill to Cisco's. Before too long, our group united, I had consumed more alcohol than I had intended and found myself holding the microphone singing the Spice Girls' hit, 'Wannabe' alongside Callum, Jay and Felix. I hadn't sung karaoke in twenty-five years, before most of my companions were even born.

I soon realized I hadn't eaten anything, I was still in my full snowboard gear, impact shorts included, and was really rather drunk. This wasn't what I wanted at all. The lyrics still running through my mind, I staggered the short distance back to the hotel where I had agreed to meet Callum for dinner – we would just make the cut-off time of 9.00 pm. I took two mouthfuls before abandoning it and headed upstairs. Quickly undressing and after drinking a couple of pints of water, I lay in bed concentrating, trying to stop the room from spinning. By 9.30 pm I was asleep. Desperately thirsty and still drunk, I arose in the middle of the night to glug more water. Falling back into bed, my dreams took over and churned a strange mix of images within my subconscious. The video of me falling in a tangle on my arse played on a constant loop. Exhausted, I woke at 7.00 am, my alarm heralding the start of our final day. Turning over, I instantly became aware of the stiffness in my body and as I tried to get up, the pain in my neck put an end to any sudden movement. Unable to lift my head from the pillow without the support of a hand, when eventually I made it upright I reached for some painkillers to ease my aching muscles and minimize the atrocious hangover. I had every intention of completing the course and there was never any question that I would not go out on the slopes. I berated myself for getting so drunk the previous evening. It was out of character.

Ascending in the gondola I could feel pins and needles in the outer two fingers of my left hand, a sensation that I knew was not a good sign. My neck continued to stiffen up and, alone in the cabin and thinking about my 180s, I came to a swift but firm decision. It would be foolhardy to even attempt the manoeuvre today. My body was in no state to take another slam and I would talk to Ash as soon as I saw him. I knew the implications and felt my qualification slip away from me. Entering the bar for the usual pre-snowboarding briefing, I saw the look of concern spread across my instructor's face, 'That looks sore,' he said. 'You don't look good.' 'It doesn't feel good either,' I replied. 'I'm sorry Ash, but I won't be attempting my 180s today. I know what this means. I'll just take it easy and ride around with you guys.' He nodded his head in understanding, 'Okay, Kate, no problem.'

Higher up the mountain, it had snowed overnight and we headed towards the fresh runs. Taking Les Fonts, we rode halfway down the Dark Side, and over to the Port Negre chair that ascended to the summit and from where the cliffs dropped suddenly into Spanish territory. A thin cloud veiled the sun, but the heat threatened to burn it away soon and the day held promise. The run opened along a wide, gentle track for 200 metres, dark grey cliffs rising on our left and dropping below us to our right; we set off, carving turns through 5 centimetres of fresh snow. Normally, I'd feel excited and privileged to be the first to make my mark, but not today. I felt subdued and defeated. My body was so stiff and sore that I rode rigidly and defensively. Veering right down a steeper gradient to meet the top of Les Fonts, I reverted to bad habits, hesitating, then rushing my turns. Nonetheless, I made it to the bottom of the run and was glad to be off the steep, with only the gentler slope of the Dark Side to go. Ash gathered everyone by the lift. 'Who wants to go up again before it gets tracked out?' he asked. I knew I didn't want to repeat the run, but waited to hear the responses from the others. 'Should I bow out and head down to the bar?' I wondered. Everyone else wanted to take the run again and I agreed to go with the crowd, not wanting to be left out. It was to be my sliding doors moment. I should have listened to my inner voice and although I could have spoken up, I didn't. On the chairlift, I regretted my decision. But in the back of my mind, I still hoped that I might pass the exam before the lunchtime cut-off.

CONFIDENCE TRICK
SPEAKING UP

Learning anything from anyone is an exchange of information:

1. Know that you have as much right as everyone else for your voice to be heard. It will help you learn more quickly

2. Speak up if you have concerns, worries or do not understand anything; your instructor will also benefit from knowing what may be unclear, and how better to help you.

CONFIDENCE TRICK
EMBRACING YOUR INTUITION

Listen to your 'gut' and trust it.

It's that simple.

Dismounting the chairlift, I fell. This hadn't happened in a very long time, and it was an indication that my mind and body were performing at a lower level than normal. But I pulled myself up and tried to concentrate on what Ash was saying and on the session. Approaching the lower half of the steeper section of the run, only a short ride to our meeting place opposite the top of Les Fonts remained. After the recent snowfall, conditions under our boards had changed, and, as I turned from toe to heel edge, the back of my board slipped out from underneath me; I juddered down the slope. I should have bent my knees more during the turn to absorb the extra pressure exerted by the terrain and new snow. These were basic fundamentals of snowboarding and I paid for my mistake. As my board jolted downwards, I leant back putting my arms behind me in an attempt to break my fall. As a result, my chest cavity extended, opening up sharply. With the sound of a dull crack, my chest popped out and then back in, and I screamed out in pain. I came to a stop in a sitting position, my board underneath me. Hunched over, my breath quickening, my mind raced with the awful possibilities of what I'd just done to myself.

I could breathe without pain, so I knew I hadn't broken any ribs. The rest of the group was ahead of me, further down the slope, and the only person behind me, still to ride, was Callum. Suddenly he appeared, sweeping to an abrupt stop in front of me. Kneeling to my level, he asked if I was all right. He'd witnessed my accident. I looked up for the second time that morning to see concern cross someone's face. 'Just give me a minute. It's my chest,' I said, my voice cracking. Callum turned and shouted down to Ash. By now I was crying, soft tears bleeding from underneath my goggles and I gripped my sternum, pushing back into the pain. 'Do you think you can you stand?' he asked, jamming his board firmly into the snow below mine. 'You won't fall.'

TECH TIP

BE KIND TO YOUR KNEES

As a newbie you will fall more often, so wear hard-shell skateboarding knee pads if you are a beginner.
They also provide warmth when kneeling in the snow.

I knew I had to try and told him that I'd give it a go. But as I put my right hand behind me to push down against the snow, the pain shot across my chest and I fell back, crying out in agony again. Although I was able to breathe, I couldn't inflate my chest much at all. Ash started to climb back up the slope to within clearer earshot of Callum's shouts, and while they dealt with the situation, I gave way to the surging tide of pain flooding outwards from my chest.

Callum turned back to me, 'It's okay, Kate. Ash is getting ski patrol for you.' In the distance below, I could see him running across to the lift operator's cabin at the top of Les Fonts. Callum sat quietly with me as we waited for help. First one, then two and eventually four patrollers arrived, the first asking my name. His English was far better than my Catalan or Spanish, but communication was not easy. He wanted to lay me flat on my back but my neck was so sore that it hurt to move. Supporting my head, I tried to obey, wincing, 'My neck, my neck!' At which point the patrollers promptly wanted me to sit back in order to avoid exacerbating a suspected neck injury. Callum interrupted them, 'It's okay,' he explained, 'she hurt it yesterday. She's got whiplash.' His ability to communicate reassured me, and suddenly I became worried that he would leave, that reassurance going with it; I begged him to remain. His response was calm, 'I'll stay. Don't worry.' By now I was cold and shivering, and my teeth began to chatter. Time seemed elastic, stretching out and snapping back, but eventually ski patrol removed my board, placed me in a neck brace and lifted me into the blood wagon for the journey down the mountain. Lying on my back, I noticed the early morning's thin veil of cloud had indeed burned off to an almost perfect bluebird sky.

On arriving at Arinsal's medical centre, situated at the top of the main gondola from the town, I was transferred to an examination bed and promptly asked about my ability to pay. Andorra, although part of Europe, is not within the European Union and as such my European Health Insurance Card was invalid. I would need to claim on my insurance at a later date, but I had my credit card with me — I always carry it on the mountain — so there was one less worry. Also on the plus side, and unlike many European countries, Andorran Mountain Rescue services are free and I didn't have to bleed further money on ski patrol. They had been caring and expert in transporting me off the mountain and I will be forever grateful. Once means of payment had been established, X-rays were ordered and I was handed two latex gloves filled with warm water to stop my shivering. The makeshift hot-water bottles seeped their comfort through to my bones, and I began to feel less overwhelmed. But lying on the X-ray table, covered by a blanket, the bleak walls and decades-old machine took me back to the early 1980s when, as a pre-teen, I'd broken my leg while roller skating. The injury had required months of intensive physiotherapy and I didn't savour the thought of a repeat. The tears continued to roll and I prayed nothing was broken — my family was due to arrive for Christmas and another snowboarding trip had been booked for late January. I could not afford to be laid up.

Ash had been busy and had contacted my hotel — understanding that any broken bones meant a transfer to the hospital seven miles away in Andorra la Vella, he knew I would require my passport. He dashed down the valley to get my handbag, personal documents and toothbrush, slipping them into the consulting room whilst I was in the X-ray room. Fortunately, the doctor reported that my sternum and cervical vertebrae were intact, nothing broken. However, his nurse explained that I had suffered bruising which would heal in approximately three weeks and she went on to decorate my chest with bright blue kinesiology tape in order to give the area some support. The full extent and complexity of my injuries were yet to reveal themselves, but at the time I felt overwhelming relief. I was free to go. Outside the building, my snowboard was propped up against the railings outside. All on its own, it seemed forlorn and a bit lost, not unlike its owner.

The medical centre is located at the bottom of the ski runs and has road access for any patients who need transport to the capital, but it also lies, conveniently, next to the Polar Bar. Gingerly, I made my way next door to wait for Ash and the group. I looked a mess, dishevelled hair scrappily framing a pale, tear-streaked face, and below it, a paler, fat neck brace. The waitress took pity and delivered hot chocolate on the house. Jess arrived with the others and an offering of sweets to cheer me up. She had noticed that I coveted the bright coloured, sugary, rubber chews every time we'd passed the shop window en-route to the nursery slope. The collective support and thoughtfulness of everyone around me was touching. But now it was crunch time — each of us was called individually by Ash to receive private feedback about our performance during the week. I knew the others had passed the exam from the big smiles that split their faces as they returned to the table. My turn was up. I walked carefully over to my instructor and opened the conversation first. 'I know I haven't passed,' I began. 'It's okay. I just need to know what I have to do now.' I wanted to make it easier for Ash. As a lecturer myself, I always want my students to do well and it's hard breaking bad news to someone. Ash seemed relieved and added, 'Kate, everything else was spot on. It was just your 180s. When you walked in this morning, I was gutted 'coz I knew you wouldn't be able to do it, today. If you hadn't said you weren't going to try, I was going to suggest you lay off the 180s. I even spoke to a couple of other trainers last night because I so wanted you to pass. Not everyone wants to be taught by a young lad, and you'd be a great ambassador.' It was a compliment, but I remained on point. 'It's okay, Ash. I totally understand. The criteria are there for a reason and I wouldn't have passed me, either.' In sports such as athletics and running, participants can measure performance that is age-graded, their times are balanced and adjusted for age and gender disparities. And although age-grading is not appropriate for snowboarding, I do recognize that it is used for a reason — our bodies cannot perform in the same way they did when we were younger. For a woman in her forties, I appreciate the challenge is different to the one faced by a man in his twenties. Ash proceeded to explain that I would have to do a day's re-sit in the UK that would cover all aspects of the exam and I'd have to practise my 180s until I had them nailed. I'd also need to maintain the standards of my general riding. I could proceed with the shadowing requirement and obtain my first aid certificate as originally intended. Disappointed that I had failed, but

CONFIDENCE TRICK

TIMING
IS EVERYTHING

Speed-learning, or leaving your learning to the last minute, exerts an undue pressure that in turn engenders panic – it's a stressful state, unconducive to absorbing information and desired performance.

Robust skills are developed when:

1. You have plenty of time to learn what you are working on

2. You allow plenty of time to practise that discipline in a safe, stable environment.

armed with a plan to achieve my qualification in the future, I limped back to the UK. Down but not out.

Felix and Callum returned to Arinsal in January and passed their Level 2 exam, whilst Jess reverted to ski instructing for the rest of the season. In order to obtain her BASI Level 3 Ski Instructor's qualification she'd had to complete a Level 1 Instructor course in any of the BASI disciplines to give her a second snowsport specialty. For her, the course had been a pre-requisite to progress her ski qualifications, but it had also been a vehicle that would eventually allow her to teach a sport she loves. Jay and Anna completed on the purchase of their house, and in the New Year headed to Canada for their next snowboarding adventure. Back at home, I began to experience more pain and went for further tests, eventually beginning a course of rigorous physiotherapy.

Injuries from skiing and snowboarding generally result from some type of impact, whether from hitting an immovable object such as a tree, from colliding with another skier or snowboarder, or from falling hard on the ground. Skiers who fall risk twisting their knees if their bindings do not release them from their long skis and torn cruciate ligaments are a frequent injury. But for snowboarders — who tend to put their arms out to protect themselves in a fall — common injuries are to the wrist. Protective equipment and clothing can be worn to minimize that risk: wrist guards and knee pads give support, cushioning those joints when pitching forward; impact shorts protect the base of the spine and coccyx, particularly for beginners; and some people, particularly freestylers, also wear back protectors. For those venturing into the backcountry or going off-piste, a shovel, probe and transceiver are standard pieces of kit in the event of an avalanche, and in recent years, airbags (contained within a rucksack) have also been developed, the evidence showing a higher survival rate for people who have been equipped with one that they've deployed — irrespective of weight, objects with a larger surface area rise to the top of avalanching snow and for that reason, when a snowmobiler is caught in the cascade, it's often the heavier machine that's thrown to the top while the rider is buried below. The use of protective clothing and equipment is a personal choice that can provoke fierce debate. During the 2013–4 season, the accident and subsequent head injury of Formula One racing driver, Michael Schumacher, precipitated further discussion of risk and prevention. Deciding between a helmet and a woolly beanie has been a thorny topic within our house for years. When I started snowboarding, hardly anyone wore helmets. With the exception of children and extremely nervous adults, most people opted for the beanie and I was adamant I was not going to wear a helmet, either. I am unsure why I resisted so much. But I changed my mind during my first snowboarding trip after becoming a mother. I fell backwards hitting my head. It hurt, I saw stars for a while and my neck was incredibly stiff for a day or so. It was the wake-up call I needed and, with a baby at home, I decided I needed to protect myself much more. I have never looked back and at times, in subsequent falls, I have thanked my lucky stars I wear a helmet.

TECH TIP

THE BEST OFFENCE
IS A GOOD DEFENCE

If you are worried about injury, consider suiting up with extra safety clothing and equipment, which you may not normally wear:

1. Back protector

2. Impact shorts, or

3. Wristguards.

In 2013, a film called *The Crash Reel* was released. The documentary features American snowboarder, Kevin Pierce, who had suffered a traumatic brain injury after a fall in a halfpipe while he was training for the 2010 Vancouver Olympics. Although the film's main narrative examines the run-up to the Games and Kevin's rivalry with Olympic gold medallist, Shaun White, it also focuses on the risk inherent in a number of extreme sports, examining how the brain reacts to injury. Ultimately *The Crash Reel* is about the years of Kevin's recovery and the question of his return to competitive snowboarding. He has not returned to the sport on a professional basis, but his friends and family began the 'Love Your Brain' campaign, which brings people together in order to build awareness around brain health. Kevin was wearing a helmet at the time of the accident, but sometimes even wearing a helmet will not prevent brain injury.

Returning to the UK less than a week before Christmas, I knew the NHS would be struggling to cope and saw no point in cluttering the system with my own injury. My X-rays were clear and I believed that not much more could be done. That was a mistake. Shortly after New Year, I began to develop pain that radiated along the bottom of my ribcage. I was working but only just. As a self-employed contractor, I was not eligible for sick-pay and could not afford to lie in bed. Various colleagues drove me to meetings, or carried my laptop and briefcase, while clients cut me as much slack as they could. Bending over to put on shoes was next to impossible, wearing a bra was uncomfortable, even walking and talking became laboured after a short while. In the end, a colleague persuaded me to seek further medical attention. At A&E the physician and surgeon disagreed with my diagnosis; one suggested internal bruising and the other diagnosed a peptic ulcer caused by the volume of painkillers I'd consumed. After further X-rays of my ribcage, cervical spine and thoracic spine confirmed no fractures, I assumed again that nothing could be done. But in discussion with a GP colleague who is an experienced clinician and snow sportsman, he diagnosed costochondritis, an inflammation of the cartilage at the joints where the rib bones meet the sternum. He suspected that the popping noise I'd heard on impact was the dislocation of these joints and went on to say, 'Recovery is slow due to the poor blood flow to this part of the body, and you won't be snowboarding in January. Possibly in March, but you won't be attempting 180s until at least May or even later.' Prolonged injury is a dismal prospect for any athlete or athletic person, and I was gutted.

As my holiday approached, I still harboured thoughts that I might be able to snowboard, but it was wishing and hoping. I was exhausted at the end of the day and often needed thirty minutes lying down when I came in from work. Despite taking maximum doses of both Ibuprofen and Paracetamol, I was in constant pain. I was worn down. Then, one morning, I awoke pain-free. I lay still, not daring to move, but knowing I had to get up and face the day. I heaved myself out of bed and within minutes the pain had returned. Every morning for several weeks I awoke to the same process, but I recognized that it was a positive sign, proof that my recovery had started. And I tried to embrace the turn of events. However, the simple knowledge that when I got up, the pain would also rise, made it hard to pull myself out of bed.

The January trip was my annual pilgrimage to Morzine, this year with fellow mums Claire, Kirsten and Tina. As our departure date approached, I resigned myself to spending the week inside the chalet. My snowboard was too heavy to lift, so it remained at home, packed away for now. Nonetheless, staying with Mountain Mavericks at Chalet Kaplamaki was to be a turning point. The chalet was situated much closer to the centre of town, near the Prodains valley, but it was close to the river and offered open views. As I walked in through the large, wooden door and was greeted by our hosts, Stephen and Kirsty, I felt instantly at ease. The sun streamed through a picture window, which looked down the valley and the welcoming warmth contrasted with the freezing air outside. That morning the temperature had plummeted to -17 degrees Celsius. A large table invited hearty participation at mealtimes while an indulgently soft couch would become my sanctuary for reading and relaxation. The days fell into a routine and after everyone had left for the slopes in the morning, I was left in peace to potter at my own pace. Usually I showered, chatted to Kirsty and Stephen, and wrote before breaking for lunch. The quiet days were so different from the high energy and goal-orientation of previous trips. I found that merely sitting, just watching the snowy landscape, listening to the silence and observing the light change as the day progressed was therapy in itself. Come late afternoon, I would either meet the girls for après drinks or attend physiotherapy sessions. Prior to departure, I had thought it would be a good idea to visit a physiotherapist based in the mountains, someone who would be more familiar with snowsports injuries than those based in the UK, and the manager at Mountain Mavericks' had recommended a physiotherapist from Mountain Rehab, Sarah Stephens. When I first entered her treatment room I recognized her from many years ago when she had taken the pilates class for the snowboard camp for women over thirty. Slim and petite, Sarah's dark hair and gentle voice both contribute to her aura of calm. She took my history before physically examining me, and was the first person whom I let touch my sternum after the accident in Arinsal — I had been worried that people might be too rough, that they might add further pain. In the intervening month I had become round shouldered, subconsciously protecting my chest, afraid that if I stood up straight, my costochondral joints would dislocate again. Sarah lightly touched each joint, and examined my spine. I was hoping for some clinical insight and a treatment plan. 'Kate,' she began, 'I have never seen an injury like this before. I really don't know how you have been able to work. You have strained every intercostal muscle in your chest. But whilst you're in Morzine I'm going to get you doing some gentle exercises, and we'll explore what's possible.' We experimented with gentle therapy bands to strengthen my abdominal muscles. At times, Sarah would think quietly before asking me to do something else. I had piqued her clinical curiosity. Throughout the week, I could feel myself getting stronger physically — I began to stand upright, and to reduce the intake of painkillers. During my last session she stressed that I should also visit a physio in the UK. 'You must continue with treatment and I'll email my assessment which you can take with you to whoever you see.' Throughout the weeks my injuries had remained largely concealed. I had no cast, no sling, and no bandages had been on show. The lack of visible evidence had made it hard for others to appreciate the damage. But the central location of the injuries, at the front of my chest, were at the very core of my being and after each small move, the pain never let me forget what had happened.

Back home, I received a recommendation from a friend who directed me to Cheryl Bailey, a private physiotherapist. 'That's interesting,' she mused when we spoke on the phone, 'most injuries I deal with are shoulders and knees. A sternum injury is rather unusual.' I could tell she was intrigued and when I met her she undertook a full assessment. 'You are in the right time frame to start physio, the acute phase of four to six weeks is over,' she said. 'Mobilization and treatment are appropriate at this stage.' But I wanted more than confirmation, I wanted a plan. 'What can I do to help myself?' I asked. 'And when can I snowboard again?' I explained that I had two further holidays coming up — a family trip in early March and a recreational camp later that month. 'Will I be able to go?' I wanted to know.

Cheryl did not throw her hands up in horror, nor did she think I was being unrealistic. 'Okay, we have a date and a goal to aim for,' she said. 'Let's see what we can do.' I knew then I had found a kindred spirit, someone proactive. I discovered later that Cheryl is a keen cyclist and that she had pursued amateur mountain bike races, even making the podium. In the winter, she was also a skier and a snowboarder. I knew she understood my mentality. Soft tissue damage is notoriously hard to diagnose, and injuries can take months to heal properly. The process is slow, but as the weeks went by, I did make progress. After several treatments, continued pain at the base of my ribcage led Cheryl to suspect that I had also strained my diaphragm and may have torn my abdominal rectus, a paired muscle running vertically on each side of the abdomen; it's what is commonly referred to as the six-pack. But by early March, before heading away with Gordon and Freya, I had been given the all clear to snowboard on gentle slopes with strict instructions to limit myself to soft and forgiving snow. If it was icy, I was to forget it.

The March family holiday to St Anton in Austria had been booked months previously but my goal, now, was to use it as a gentle reintroduction to snowboarding, before determining whether I would be able to head out to the recreational camp at the end of the month. A lot depended on this trip. Tired after travelling and suffering some pain, I decided not to try and snowboard on the first day. But it was playing on my mind, and I wanted to get it out of the way. Gordon was eminently wise on the matter. 'You have hundreds of miles under your snowboard. Your fall was one small blip in all that history. Don't forget it,' he told me. And throughout the coming weeks, I reminded myself of this fact on a regular basis. I needed to keep some perspective and to get my fear under control. I had scouted out some of the slopes but many were prohibitively steep and eventually I opted for a small nursery slope next to our hotel. If I hurt myself, I wanted to get off the piste without resorting to ski patrol and rescue services. I walked up the slope to the button tow, my head down against the wind and my boots sinking into the soft snow. As I grabbed the pole, placing it between my legs, the jerk of the lift unbalanced me and I let go, quickly. I had not been defeated by a tow in years. I tried again but with similar result. I could not give up now. If I did, the defeat would hang over me and I would sink deeper into despair. With a sense of déjà vu, reminiscent of the time I'd first started snowboarding, I carried my board and walked up the side of the piste. Head down and puffing like a train, I walked fifty metres before strapping on my board. 'Just do it, just do it,' I chanted to myself, and set off down the slope, wobbling and feeling like a newbie again. But I made three turns and reached the bottom. I had done it. After three months, I was back on my board.

I was neither elated nor particularly pleased with myself. With hindsight I should have been, but I was expecting too much too soon. It had been sketchy and psychologically, very uncomfortable. I needed to try again, and I felt I'd be reassured in the company of someone I knew. We had travelled with other families and I enlisted my good, long-standing friend, Gabby. A true Glaswegian (although now she lives in the North East) Gabby likes good banter, a better laugh and a wee dram of the best hard stuff. An attractive brunette, she used to model in her younger days before her children came along. She is warm-hearted, loud, funny and gregarious, and has been known to utter the odd swear word. Gabby was game-on for my plan. She had snowboarded for a number of years and could easily outpace me. But she hated button tows and dreaded exiting chairlifts. We left St Anton behind, and boarding the local bus, headed east to the gentler slopes of neighbouring St Christophe, making sure we arrived after any hard crust of surface ice had been softened by the sun.

We'd scouted out a small nursery slope serviced by a button tow, and nearby there was a blue piste to which we could transfer if we were done with the nursery slope. The sun's glare bounced off the snow and, avoiding the button tow, we joined the run midway, preferring to head up its side on foot, until the top of the tow was in our sights and the full length of the green run fell away below us. Ducking under the perimeter rope, I sat down to put my board on. Gabby was quicker than I and no sooner strapped in, she stood up, ready for the off. 'Well, I can snowboard,' she said, 'but can I get up that button tow? You know what I'm like.' Gabby's aversion to button tows meant she nearly always avoided them. 'But it's good to practise,' she added, looking down the slope. 'You just take your time, Kate,' she said. 'We can spend as long as you like, here. Okay?' And I was reminded why I'd been touched she'd agreed to come with me. 'I'm fine, Gabby, you go,' I told her. After a few moments, I set off behind her, finding my line, and on this slope, also my balance. The familiar feel of the board gliding over the soft snow and the bite of its edge as I made my first turn, rhythmically flowing downhill, precipitated a giant grin, ear-to-ear. This felt more like it. As I reached the bottom, I could see Gabby above me on the tow, teetering. Her back arm stretched behind her, she wobbled before bailing out at the top shouting as she lost control, 'oh! Oh! OHHH!' We lapped the nursery slope three or four times before tiring of its challenge, and decided to head up to the blue piste via the chairlift. The run wasn't very long but it was heavily smattered with moguls that were spread thickly across the slope. Half-way down, cursing the run, I fell. Quickly, I ran a mental check on myself but I was fine. I didn't hurt, no more than normal, and in many ways it was reassuring to realize that I could fall without causing damage.

Returning to the UK, my mission accomplished, I knew I would be able to snowboard in late March. But back in Cheryl's capable hands, she reminded me, 'It's as if you have sustained three car crashes. Your body is going to take time to recover, it's been brutalized. You must be patient. The complexity of your injuries has meant it has taken time to discover what's really happening. It's like an onion, as I peel back the layers, I find something else. I'm not happy with your left shoulder and this may need further investigation. Let's see how it is after your recreational camp.' Normally I would train before a snowboarding trip and I had started to work with Tina in preparation, but I knew the exercises I was able to perform would not give me the strength I needed to snowboard comfortably all day for six consecutive days. Her expertise had worked in the past, however, and my injury in Arinsal could have been far worse without that base strength she'd helped me accomplish. Now her plan for me was to complement Cheryl's guidance, and I left for France prepared as well as could be.

Arriving in Morzine with Ann-Marie, we were greeted by a different scene to the heavenly white I'd watched so intently in January. All the snow in town had disappeared. As winter moves forward into spring, the warmth of the sun intensifies and heavy snow showers become scarce. Our group at camp this year was large, and comprised ten other women in a wooden chalet above the centre of town. Tammy was running her first women-only camp in several years, and I had been keen to join. It was perfect timing — I'd have a chance to test out my recovery in a familiar environment with someone I trusted. I balanced my stated desire to develop my skills further with my need to rehabilitate, and I was comfortable not pushing myself. Before I left England, I'd also promised Gordon that I wouldn't ride off-piste, nor would I venture into the snow park for any flirtation with freestyle acrobatics.

Our large group was divided into two smaller cohorts, according to skill, and I was, by now, intimately familiar with the process. One group would ride with Tammy in the morning, the other group riding with her in the afternoon. Ann-Marie and I were to ride in the afternoon and with free time to play, in the late morning we took the gondola up for an hour of practise before lunch. I was nervous. Spiders of doubt crept through my mind. Would the pain return? Would I exacerbate my injuries? Would my stamina hold out? Could I keep up? All those harmful thoughts scuttled around, but I held onto the fact that I had been given the blessing of my physio, I was also amongst friends, and I was certainly on familiar territory. As we ascended in the new Prodains cable car that lifted us silently and swiftly above the trees, the snow came into view. It felt fantastic to be back on my hallowed ground, and my excitement swirled with my uncertainty causing my stomach flip. I felt a bit sick — nervous-cited. Exiting the cable car and catching the escalator up to piste level, I was blinded momentarily by the sun and stepped outside straight into a large puddle of slush. Spring riding had well and truly arrived. At the entrance of Le Crôt, our familiar Home Run, I strapped in, taking one final look behind me to confirm a quiet start, no other skiers or snowboarders to nip at my heels. The piste was soft, but it was littered with moguls. Ann-Marie led the way, but I couldn't keep up with her pace. I hesitated at every turn, tightening with fear before I was able to gather my courage. I looked down rather than up and felt tense rather than relaxed. I found my favourite run mentally and physically challenging.

After lunch at Changabang, Tammy took us up to the top of Arare, the long piste beneath the summit of Les Hauts-Forts. Again I found it hard to stay with the others, and presented with an off-piste foray, I made the decision to bow out. By the end of the three-hour session I had made up my mind to transfer into the other group, which travelled at a slower pace and where I'd be much happier for the week. My new companions included Karis, a tall blond in her mid-twenties; an overhead linesman, she told us that she spent her days up pylons and telegraph poles across Scotland. Linda, on the other hand, worked as a physicist at CERN — the European Organisation for Nuclear Research, in Switzerland. Both of them typified the diversity of the women in the camp as a whole.

During the week, while I became aware of old habits creeping in, instead of becoming frustrated, I was kind to myself and absorbed what Tammy was telling me — where I struggled, she gave me hints and tips, and I tried them out. On steeper sections of the mountain, I struggled to turn and Tammy reminded me to check my front shoulder was in line with my board; performing a mental check before every turn helped. Focusing my energies on tasks required in the moment stilled the chatter in the rest of my mind, and the lighter perspective helped me relax overall. Feeling more confident as the camp progressed, I enjoyed riding with women who were supportive and fun, and was reminded of a more lasting purpose — the contentment that accompanies team, a shared goal of community and assistance.

When we fail at something, the mantra, 'get back in the saddle', is a familiar directive. But it's true, and the longer we postpone the restart, the more time our inner critic has to rattle within its own echo chamber. I'd spent the better part of three months separated from my board, and I was determined to ride before the season was out because I knew there would be psychological repercussions if I didn't ride until the following season. As the week progressed, my confidence growing with the days, I attempted a few side hits, approaching the piste over a natural jump from the off-piste terrain. I knew, then, that I would continue to improve, and my plan to return to the BASI Level 1 qualification was securely in my future. At the time of writing, I'm still unable to practise my 180s and I don't know when I will be able to pick them up again — I am waiting to be referred for more tests, my left arm has limited movement and my left shoulder may need surgery. But while I live

> *CONFIDENCE TRICK*
> ## *TURNING THE SITUATION AROUND*
>
> *Failure is not the end; it is the point at which we can decide if we want to come back stronger:*
>
> *1. Take time to let the experience settle*
>
> *2. Regroup, and if the original plan failed, consider what you can do differently to achieve your goal*
>
> *3. Look at your learning points, enlist others to help you*
>
> *4. Make a new plan to achieve your goal*
>
> *5. Remain flexible in your approach – you will live to fight another day.*

with the long-term uncertainty of that outcome, my failure has given me a renewed sense of determination. I have a plan to move forward, practising my 180s in the UK and nailing them before I book my resit. I'll continue my strength training with Tina, and I continue to harness the support of other mentors and friends who will help me achieve my goal.

Life is full of risk and depending on the choices made and the training received, as that risk relates to snowboarding, it can be managed and even mitigated. Riding a blue run on a sunny day with good visibility will carry less risk than venturing into the backcountry, or the snow park, in a whiteout. In life, as on a snowboard, calculated risk has to be made, but I say again, life with no risk would be boring. I do not regret my trip to Andorra, I have learned some valuable lessons and recognize my restored determination to achieve my goal.

EXERCISES

♦ 1. What does failure mean to you? Perspective is everything, so there is no right or wrong answer. Be clear with yourself; what is failure for you and what is it not. Write your answer down.

For me, failure means..

♦ 2. In the table below, name two occasions when you failed at something. When did the face-plant happen? Or when do you think it happened? Write the moment.

Failure 1:	Failure 2:
Time of face-plant:	

♦ 3. Look at your rows. For each occasion that you failed, which two things did you learn about yourself?
Write them down below.

Failure 1:	Failure 2:
Learning 1:	
Learning 2:	

◆ 4. How could you turn your failures into something positive? How would you reframe the experiences to learn for the future?

Failure 1:	Failure 2:
Reframe:	

◆ ◆ 5. Name two aspects of your life in which you fear failure? Write them down in the column headings, below.

Fear failure 1:	Fear failure 2:
Step 1:	
Step 2:	
Step 3:	

◆ ◆ 6. If you do fail in those aspects of your life where you actively fear failure, what two or three steps can you put in place that will enable you to reach your goal at a later, specific date? Write them down in the table above, under the appropriate headings.

We can't grow if we never fear or fail. Life's not always a groomed slope, it can be littered with moguls or obstacles. But take heart and take a risk - see what you might have to learn about yourself when you decide to grapple with the gnarly stuff.

Scoring

Exercise 1. No points given or deducted.

Exercise 2. Give yourself a point for each failure listed, and a point for each time of your face-plant that you were able to list.

Exercise 3. Give a point for each thing that you learned.

Exercise 4. Award yourself a point for each reframed experience.

Exercise 5. Give yourself a point for each named aspect of life in which you actively fear failure.

Exercise 6. Reward yourself with a point for each step you have put in place to achieve your goal at a later date.

Total chapter points................

08

DOLOMITES

TAKING IT ALL ON BOARD
how to accelerate progress and maintain control

Italy's Val Gardena area has been host to the FIS World Cup Men's Downhill Ski Race since 1969 and to the Super G since 1983. In February 2013, I was standing on one of its famous slopes weighing my options. 'Red or Black,' I wondered. There were about twenty people in our ski-hosted group, none of whom I knew — except Gordon and a family friend, Mark. The full-day session was designed to help visitors with mountain orientation, and we knew it would give us a chance to familiarize ourselves with the resort slopes. We'd met our guide, Carlotta, in the small town of Sëlva that morning, and as we'd gathered at the bottom of the Ciampinoi gondola and more people had arrived to swell the group's numbers, I observed that nearly all of them carried skis while Gordon, Mark and I clutched our snowboards. Scanning the assembled crowd, I caught sight of only one other snowboarder, and by the time we were ready to set off, I'd resigned myself to being the sole female rider. The situation wasn't unusual, but I always retained hope that I'd come across a like-minded woman. Exiting the gondola, we headed over to the Saslong slopes where Carlotta offered us the black run, Saslong A, or the red run, Saslong B, either of which would take us from 2,254 metres down to the village of Santa Cristina Gherdëina. At this stage, after ten years, I was consciously competent as a snowboarder, turning my board on most red pistes with ease, but I still conferred with Gordon and Mark, uncertain if this was the moment to try for a black run. 'Red,' I decided, sticking to my strengths, and for feeling greater confidence in this large group. 'Let's take Saslong B.'

We set off, and I followed the boys' line. On the wide, open slope, the skiers blasted past us before we came to a narrow, steep, icy section bathed in shadow, the brilliant sun yet to extend its warmth and soften the hard ice into submission. Mark and Gordon slipped, slid and occasionally fell their way down ahead of me, and I questioned whether I had taken on more than I could handle. Riding on ice was never pleasurable and the balance between keeping my edge and losing control was a fine one. Concentrating hard, focusing on the end of this section of slope, I was determined to continue on, keeping pace with the group, showing that a woman snowboarder could keep up with male skiers. I had noticed a few disdainful looks earlier in the tour and had channelled the anger in my belly, allowing it to fuel my resolve. I powered downwards and into Santa Cristina Gherdëina, metaphorically giving two fingers to the naysayers.

Anger is an emotion, which if used positively, can elevate performance. It can translate the burning fire within to something that is, in fact, serviceable. I frequently go through phases of timidity on the snow and feel nervous when I'm recovering from injury. To wit, on the first day of my Winter 2017 women's snowboarding camp in Morzine, I'd returned to old, unhelpful habits, tensing, physically, and feeling very unsure of my abilities, emotionally. My battered body was far from healed and, to my mind I was a diminished snowboarder. I rode hesitantly, regressing psychologically, not only in terms of my external capabilities. That is, until the moment when a male snowboarder pushed me. Riding down a long cat track, I became aware of someone close behind me. It was busy, but there had been enough room to manoeuvre. Shielding my injured shoulder, I screamed involuntarily and twisted so that my right arm could take the brunt of the fall. I caught sight of the snowboarder's raised hand of apology — 'Sorry,' he yelled casually, the accent clearly British. And just as quickly he disappeared.

Riding off! — this had been a snowboarding hit-and-run. Trying to weave his way through a narrow gap between myself and another slope user, he'd realized too late that the squeeze was tight and he'd shoved me out of the way to save himself. The red mist of rage descended, all thoughts of hesitancy — Bam! — gone. I was filled with indignation and roared blasphemy. Jumping up as fast as I could, I determined to give chase. Adrenaline coursed through my system and the burning anger I felt ignited a dormant force within me. I kept the oaf in sight for a while, but he had a lead on me and it was difficult to catch up. Eventually his back melted into the crowd and I'd lost him. When I met up with my group later, I was still seething, but in many ways he'd done me a favour — all my psychological angst had disappeared and the innate flow of the inner snowboarder I had become could now surface and show itself.

CONFIDENCE TRICK
HARNESSING YOUR FIRE

It's ok to be angry. You can channel the energy created into service towards the greater determination you need to overcome a particular hurdle.

Direct it into rapid and powerful focus on the task at hand.

Reaching Santa Cristina Gherdëina, keeping pace with the group of faster skiers during the hosted tour, I'd been on my way to becoming that inner snowboarder, that woman. But there was little time for rest and, almost immediately, we headed up the funicular, taking the subsequent gondola to Col Raiser. From our vantage point at the top, we could see the peak and towering cliffs of Sassolungo on the opposite side of the valley. The sunlight gave false hope of warmth; it was -19 degrees Celsius and frost nipped at uncovered flesh. Eventually, the broad open vista of the plateau gave way to tree-lined pistes, and our descent from the exposed upper reaches brought shelter and marginal comfort. Carlotta had promised lunch and with growling stomachs we approached what appeared to be a wooden hut. The slats were worn and weathered, a crumbled relic from the past. 'You've gotta be kidding, I thought. But as I stepped over the threshold, I was beamed into an unexpected, sharply-designed world: slate-grey, Italian tiles lined the floor; gleaming, polished steel abounded; and glass tables were laid with stylish, Villeroy and Boch porcelain. Streaks of the outside world could still be glimpsed between the primitive slats of the hut, the contrast highlighting the warm comfort of the room. The Italians had cleverly constructed an interior that was more akin to a city nightclub than a mountain eatery. And where, in France, I'd become used to the ubiquitous menu offering of pommes frites that were frequently served with a scowl, here, homemade pasta was brought to the table with a smile. The local relationship with time was also flexible, and this was a delightful, relaxing lunch. Without a guide we would have ridden past this ancient, wooden hut, her secrets preserved and hidden from the crowd.

In the afternoon, we continued onwards, down the valley and into Ortisei, our 10-kilometre trip complete. For the return leg we took two long, consecutive gondolas up and over the limestone escarpment looping back to Secëda. The cold chased us all the way back to Sëlva before the sun began to drop over the high plateaus and pinnacles. As the light started to change more rapidly, the white vertical cliffs that had reflected the day's sun intensified in colour through light pink to deep apricot, and as the sunbeams lingered their final caress, the canvas melted into red. Feeling truly blessed to have witnessed this magical, natural light display we headed back to the chalet, our day's adventure complete.

The trip was our annual family snowboarding holiday. Since 2011 we'd taken it with our friends Gabby and Mark, together with their two children, Arianna (Freya's close pal) and Isaac. Gabby's husband, Mark, was much quieter and more reserved than his Glaswegian wife. A Geordie, tall and slim, he bears a passing resemblance to the tennis player, Pete Sampras. We were two families then – including two 7-year olds and one 4-year old – who had enlisted the winter childcare specialist tour operator, Ski Esprit, and had headed to the South Tyrol.

As the plane had touched down in Innsbruck two days previously, the sun's rays were retreating from the narrow valley. During our approach, the mountains had seemed too close and glancing nervously out of the window, I saw the wings of the aircraft almost kiss the steep mountains on either side. Leaving the airport, I could taste the bite of the cold air and heaving a sigh of relief, my breath billowed out, misting before me. Back in the mountains, I felt the familiar excitement course through my veins again as I anticipated the week ahead. Innsbruck, although in Austria, is one of the nearest airports to Sëlva, and our transfer was relatively short at less than two hours. During the ride south, I had some time to reflect upon our chosen destination, a place I had always longed to visit.

Sëlva nestles in the Dolomites, a geologically distinct mountain range with an interesting history and a particular vibe that is very different from anywhere in the rest of Europe. Approximately 170 kilometres south of Innsbruck and 170 kilometres north of Venice, they form part of the Southern Limestone Alps in north-east Italy and are distinctive in their shape and colour. Sheer, vertical cliffs, spires and pinnacles protrude alongside horizontal plateaus and ledges, and give the range their characteristic silhouette. Rising out of the valleys some stand as isolated rock formations, but others can also be seen grouped together. Everywhere, extensive scree and gentle foothills separate the valley floor from some of the highest limestone walls in the world. A natural canvas for the colours that are reflected from surrounding lakes, meadows and sunlight, the pale rock can change appearance in dramatic displays of light through the year, and at the start and end of each day. At dawn and dusk, the Dolomites often glow through a series of whitening or intensifying hues, saturated red to white and from pale pink to deep apricot in a transformation of light known locally as the *enrosadira* (pinkening). For many people, this is considered one of the most beautiful mountain landscapes in the world and, as such, the range was declared a UNESCO World Heritage Site in August 2009. The region attracts visitors year-round, offering skiing, snowboarding, climbing, paragliding, hiking and, for the yet more adventurous, BASE jumping. It was here, in 2009, that world-class freeskier and jumper, Shane McConkey, died, while ski-BASE jumping from Sass Pordoi, one of the best-known mountains in the area.

The social history of the region has always been influenced by its extreme geography. During the First World War, the front line between Italian and Austro-Hungarian forces ran right through the Dolomites as fierce battles raged high in the mountains and defied the challenges of the terrain. Metal ladders were constructed and pinned to the rock, extending the existing system to a broader network that enabled military personnel to navigate through the high passes, and these routes are still in use today. Collectively known as the *via ferrata* (iron road) they are scaled by modern-day foot soldiers, hikers and walkers treading in the same steps taken by fighting men one hundred years ago. Most of the original ironwork has been replaced by modern equipment, including fixed cables for use with karabiners, while modern ladders and updated high bridges span the steep ravines. The routes are protected and can be traversed by relatively inexperienced alpinists, allowing almost anyone access to the high peaks across the range. However, for those who dare, the *vie* (nailed, flat against exposed rock face, or strung high above sheer drops) demand a head for heights and some routes do, in fact, require technical climbing expertise.

The Dolomites are also culturally distinct. On the journey from Innsbruck, I'd heard the bus driver speaking on his phone. '*Güten Abend,*' he began, and then, following that initial greeting in German, a mixture of Italian, and a language I couldn't understand ensued. '*Grazie,*' he said, ending his call in Italian. We were in Italy, but close enough to the Austrian border, so I had assumed the driver was bilingual. But I'd been confused by the scramble of indecipherable sounds and it wasn't until later that I discovered the Dolomite population is, in fact, trilingual and a third language, Ladin, is spoken in certain areas, where some places also bear three names, one in each language (our destination, Sëlva, for instance, also carries the Italian name, Selva di Val Gardena, and the German name, Wolkenstein in Gröden). The northern reach of the South Tyrol, the province in which the Dolomites lie, was originally part of the Austro-Hungarian Empire, and until the First World War, its residents spoke German. After 1918, however, the area became part of Italy and adopted the national language of its new state. Ladin, on the other hand, is an ancient language spoken by the first inhabitants of the Dolomites and it derives from the Latin spoken during the period of the Roman Empire. Closely related to Swiss Romansh, it used to be spoken more widely across the Alps, although its reach today is more limited and the choice of language used in each valley depends upon its particular cultural history. Despite the small number of people speaking it (estimates suggest 20-30,000 people) Ladin is officially recognized and taught in schools. Freya's ski instructor informed us that, as a schoolboy, he used all three languages and certain topics tended to be taught in a specific language — mathematics was always taught in German, for example.

As we turned east into the Val Gardena we passed through its main settlement, Ortisei and upwards to the next village, Santa Cristina Gherdëina. Whitewashed walls, typical of Tyrolean buildings, lined the road, and my eyes grazed their wooden shutters and balconies, and their red roofs scattered with snow. But by the time we drew into Sëlva, which sits at the head of the valley, darkness was falling and the white had cooled to grey, the dark wood melting into the shadow of the evening. A thriving town of 2,700 inhabitants, its modern hotels nestling alongside more traditional dwellings, Sëlva is only 1,500 metres above sea level and snowfall can be unpredictable. Some years, coverage can be poor (although there is good snowmaking) but because Sëlva is part of the larger Dolomiti Superski area and connects to the famous Sellaronda circuit, many winter tourists take the risk — the Sellaronda is one of the most spectacular ski tours in the world.

Approaching our small chalet, the darkness was complete and the immediate geography of our surroundings had become invisible, the limestone spectres of the mountains looming silently behind the town. I'd waited a lifetime to visit the Dolomites, to witness its thrilling mountain scenery for myself, but I would have to remain patient a few more hours. The following day, urgently throwing back the curtains, I drank in the magic. The early morning sun reflected a light apricot blaze from the limestone cliffs that carved into the skyline before me. Paling gently, minute by minute, the game of shadows and light played out until the true colour of the limestone shone through, and the day was officially sealed.

Keen to get out the door, I wanted to experience this unique landscape for real. But first, ski school — all the children were skiing, which may seem unusual for children whose parents rode snowboards, but at the time, children under the age of eight were considered too young to start snowboarding. The consensus was that younger children were not sufficiently strong, and their muscles had not developed enough to steer and control a board. In the past few years, however, that thinking has changed, and Burton has developed snowboarding equipment for younger children — smaller, softer and more flexible boards, one-catch bindings, and softer boots are all now available. The company has also created a system called the Riglet Reel, a leash that attaches to the snowboard and allows an adult to pull a toddler along the flat, and up gentle hills. On small gradients, they can also walk behind their child while holding the leash taut, and control the speed of descent. The combined result of this innovation is that children as young as two-years old can now ride. Burton has additionally invested in dedicated snow parks for children aged between three and five. Riglet Parks are scaled down freestyle parks that feature small boxes, low rollers and mini rails, but they're animated up in terms of colour and other more traditional, kid-friendly playground features. Rolled out across the USA, they're now also available for families in France, Switzerland, Austria and Italy and some dedicated snowboard schools (including MINT Snowboarding) are investing in this area of early instruction and have developed teaching programmes for little ones. The outreach to a much younger cohort was not widely promoted in its infancy, however, and my own daughter missed out, but I'm sure many snowboarding parents will embrace the development and a whole generation of children will be brought up as snowboarders without passing through the ski stage, first.

Back in Sëlva, we deposited the children with their ski instructor. In his mid-fifties and with a wide grin to equal his girth, Tony specialized in teaching children, and people with physical disabilities. A widower with a disabled son, relentlessly cheerful and optimistic, he carried plastic beakers, juice and biscuits for the children. Freya, Arianna and Isaac went off without a backwards glance, and we watched their first shaky turns down the small nursery slope. By the end of the week, all Tony's charges snaked behind him, gliding across the slope and following him as if he was the Pied Piper.

Mark, Gordon and I headed up the Dantercepies gondola, west of Sëlva, and towards the dazzling peaks that offset the cornflower blue heavens that morning. Wisps of cloud dotted their patchwork across the broadening expanse of sky. Exiting the lift, the numerous sheer cliffs of the Sella Group towered overhead rising to 3,151 metres. The classic Sellaronda circuit revolves around them, and riders can elect to travel clockwise, following its orange route, or anti-clockwise, following its green route. At around 40 kilometres in length, the tour can be accessed via lifts from each of four valleys near its circumference — Val Gardena, Alta Badia, Val di Fassa and Valle di Fodom — but accepted practise states the loop must be started by 10.00 am with the last pass completed by 3.30 pm, otherwise late arrivals risk being stranded away from their 'home' valley, unable to complete the circuit

Setting off beneath the Dantercepies gondola, the snow was deep and plentiful. Out of sight, beyond the summits directly above us, I could sense the invisible presence of the Marmolada glacier, which at 3,342 metres is the highest point in the Dolomites. I followed Gordon and Mark's path, keeping to my own pace, flowing from heel to toe edge, popping into the fluffy off-piste every now and again, delighting in the float and feel of my board. Mark had waited for me, sitting to one side of the piste, near its end. I came to a stop and plonked myself down.

'That was fantastic,' I enthused, 'what great conditions!' And then added what was more profoundly on my mind, 'It's a shame Gabby didn't want to join us.'

Gabby had chosen not to accompany us, and she had been missed. Our inaugural family holiday together had been in France's La Rosière where she had been fearless and rode with speed, confidence and joie de vivre. Now, things were different. She had become a hesitant rider, nervous and tense. An accident will do that to anyone. Riding up one of the old, rickety chairlifts, and recognizing it would deposit its occupants swiftly before returning sharply downhill, I'd quickly pushed away down the steep, icy, exit ramp. Gabby hadn't been as fortunate and as she'd tried to stand, one of the wooden slats had caught her impact shorts through her snowboard pants, twisting her around; she'd fallen backwards, smacking her head on the ground. The sickening thud and scream was alarming and for a moment, we froze. Gordon reached Gabby first and managed to pull her up and away from the lift. On examination she seemed somewhat dazed and shocked, which was not surprising when we took a look at her helmet. It was new, she had bought it only the day before, but now the hard shell and cushioning foam was completely cracked, leaving a split 6 centimetres in length. If she had not been wearing it, the crack would have been to her skull. At the time, there appeared to be no physical or psychological fallout from the incident and Gabby had continued to ride happily and confidently for the rest of the week.

A year later, however, delayed shock had set in and in Tignes, on our next holiday, Gabby had become tentative and fearful on the snow. She had replaced her snowboard with a newer model, but had retained her beloved Flow bindings, which allowed her to step in and out from the rear and she could then flip up the highback to secure her feet. Finding it hard to bend down when using a conventional binding, Gabby had opted to retain her decade-old equipment that was now starting to fail; during one run, the rear binding swivelled around and almost detached completely from her board making it virtually unusable. Descending a narrow cat track, I watched her

TECH TIP
PRACTISE THE ART
OF MAINTENANCE

Your safety, and that of people around you,
can depend upon well-maintained gear:

1. Check all your equipment and clothing
on a regular basis for wear and tear

2. If in doubt, consult your local snowboard shop

3. Maintain your board on a regular basis to sharpen
its edges, wax the base and remove any dings

4. Check bindings for signs of stress and weakness

5. Replace worn out equipment
before it fails.

fall repeatedly. 'I can't do it,' she cried. 'Just go on ahead.' Under no circumstances was I going to leave her. 'Let me look at your bindings, Gabs,' I urged her. 'They don't look right and your back foot seems to be moving all over the place.' Examining her equipment, I could see it was practically at the end of its natural life. 'Gabby, before you came away, you needed new bindings, not a new board,' I admonished her. A determination to stick with familiar equipment had compounded an already failing belief in herself. My vivacious friend was a very different snowboarder to the one I had first encountered. Confidence is a fickle companion, sometimes walking quietly at your side, strong and true, but at other times it's a deserter, fleeing in an instant not to return anytime soon. On the slopes, doubting both her abilities and her equipment, Gabby was struggling in every direction.

But she was a fighter. And while she had declined to join us for the hosted ski and snowboard session, she had instead opted to get a snowboarding lesson. And while we were exploring the Dolomite's famous World Cup runs, and diving into hidden restaurants, Gabby was hard at work. This was her chance to practise technique, taking a step back so that she could push off forwards against a more solid foundation. By using the skills of a qualified instructor, she could work through her fears in a safe environment. Although her children were still young, she knew a day would come when she would be left in their wake if she didn't address her declining confidence.

It had worked, and Gabby had made the right decision, thoroughly enjoying her lesson. She felt like she'd made progress. On our final day, I persuaded her to join me and we headed over to a wonderful, quiet piste at the edge of Sëlva that Gordon, Mark and I had discovered earlier in the week. It was graded black, but felt more like a steep blue, only a small section of slope riding like a true black. The run was also short, it offered a café at its base, and it was serviced by an easy chairlift; I thought it would help build her confidence without any pressure.

Esprit staff had informed us previously that, as a UNESCO World Heritage Site, the Dolomites were protected terrain and that venturing off-piste was *proibito, verboten*. Forbidden. The Carabinieri would arrest those caught leaving the marked runs, we were told. Italian officers stood at the bottom of the lifts and watched the slopes through binoculars, lying in wait for offenders to appear before making their move. Gordon, in particular, was unhappy. But Tony, Freya's instructor, had subsequently added a different perspective. 'Nonsense!' he'd said. 'People ride off-piste all the time!' Later, descending the black run with Mark and Gordon, we three came across ten Carabinieri during a ski-training exercise. As soon as we caught sight of their ink-black uniforms, a flock of vultures lurking on the piste, I knew what was running through Gordon's mind. 'Please don't,' I pre-empted him. 'Just wait until they've gone! If you get into trouble, you needn't think I'm getting involved.' 'It'll be fine,' he replied, looking over his shoulder, an impish smile spreading across his face, before he ploughed his board into the soft snow to the side of the piste, and rode in flagrante past all ten Carabinieri. I sighed, rolled my eyes and disinclined to involve myself in any hullaballoo with the Italian cops, continued on past the flock, adamantly sticking to the piste. Fortunately, the Carabinieri appeared oblivious to Gordon's off-piste display. No shouting ensued, no wild gesticulations, and no handcuffs. Gordon was still grinning as he reappeared, blasting back onto the piste. 'I told you it'd be alright,' he said.

En route to the site of Gordon's crime, Gabby and I exited a small button tow, riding through a narrow cat track between tall, snow-laden conifers. Dappled sun speckled through the branches onto the snow, lighting our way through the shade. After 50 metres, we popped out half-way down the black piste, and rode to its base to catch the chairlift that would take us up to the top. We rose through a cut in the trees and could see the tramlines made by off-piste skiers tracking ever downwards. Occasionally, their paths intermingled with scattered animal footprints, silent evidence of the marmots or deer that shared the mountains with us. Now and again, a light breeze swayed the branches of the trees, causing a dusting of snow to fall to the ground below, the flakes sparkling in the sunlight during their descent. We tilted our heads into the sunshine towards the warmth of spring, the surrounding quiet deafening in its magnitude. And then our brief ride through the magic came to an end as we approached the lift hut.

Successfully gliding off the ramp, all past experiences briefly forgotten, Gabby strapped on her board and asked, 'Can you watch me, Kate? See what I'm doing wrong?' I saw her disappear at the pace I had known her to ride pre-accident in La Rosière, and glimpses of her former self shone through. Equipped with new bindings fixed to her old, familiar board, it was clear she felt more comfortable. Finishing her turns, she still reverted to swishing her back foot, but this could be corrected with instruction. What I noticed more than anything was her attitude and her rising confidence. As I joined her at the bottom of the run, I asked her how it had felt. 'Much better,' she grinned. But gazing towards the café, she wanted a break. 'Let's get a drink. Come on,' she said. 'Or, we could do one more run, and then we'll stop,' I countered. Gabby was on a roll and I didn't want her to bow out before she realized this hadn't been a chance exception, but a platform from which she could consolidate positive experience and build further competence, returning fully to her former, confident self. We continued lapping the piste several times, but it wasn't until the following holiday that she really made up the ground she'd lost, fluid and happy on her board.

Italy had been a revelation. We loved her food, landscape, people and language and wanted to return. The following year, in 2014, we opted for the Aosta Valley, a lesser-known area in Italy's north-western corner, and the country's smallest region. As we drove north from Turin airport across the bright extent of flat plains, the mountains stretched tall before us, and dark, heavy clouds gathered on the horizon ahead. Castle ruins rose up abruptly from the landscape announcing the area's feudal history. The region has been occupied since 900 BCE, including five centuries of Roman Rule, and is littered with medieval fortresses. At Pont-Saint-Martin, the autostrada curves west and on for 90 kilometres to Courmayeur, the ski resort bathed in sunlight on the south side of Mont Blanc. But our transfer bus turned sharply right, heading north up the Valle del Lys and taking us along narrow roads that wound through knots of small mountain villages. As we drove higher, we could see the extent of the Gran Paradiso National Park behind us. Italy's first, created in 1922, it was originally designated to protect Alpine Ibex, a species of wild goat that had been hunted almost to extinction in the nineteenth century. Today its boundaries extend even further west towards Val d'Isère and Tignes, and the expanse combines with the French Vanoise National Park to form the largest protected area in Western Europe.

Climbing higher through the valley, the wall of mountains on the right defined Aosta's natural eastern border with its neighbouring province, Piedmont. We gazed out of the bus windows, passing traditional cottages and old, stone farmhouses caged in horizontal wooden slats. In an area with little flat ground, the unusual buildings had originally been designed for storage purposes — the hay cut from the meadows could be piled up the height of the wall and allowed to dry out. This traditional Walser architecture has been preserved since the thirteenth century when the early Germanic settlers arrived from the north, and its oldest example, located in the village of Gressoney-Saint-Jean, dates back to 1547. Our road crossed the river Lys several times, climbing higher still and pushing further into the valley. The dark clouds could hold their load no longer and sleet started to fall, sliding down the windows of the bus. As the temperature dropped, the roadside grass disappeared under a delicate blanket of white. Inside the bus, our ears began to pop, while outside, evidence of human activity gradually decreased, the world retreating inside to dry, warm houses. Pulling into Gressoney-La-Trinité, 4 kilometres before Stafal, the final village and the end of the road before Italy becomes Switzerland, the snow was falling thick and fast. This was our stop. We dragged our bags off the bus and battled a final 50 metres through the snow to our hotel, which lay at the head of a small side road. At the base of the Punta Jolanda chairlift, and immediately in front of the steep rise of the mountain, Hotel Valverde's white exterior was splashed with red shutters, and the warm light coming from within its windows issued a welcoming beacon to signal the end of our journey.

Collective excitement mounted in the hotel, its guests eager for their first day on the slopes, everyone hoping for a powder day under bluebird skies. We were in luck. The heavy snow had stopped sometime during the night, the clouds dispersing to reveal bright sunshine. I fell into routine, grabbing my favourite snowboarding underwear before pulling on my gear (including impact shorts and knee pads) in set order. A small water bottle and snack stashed into their designated pockets, lastly I grabbed my helmet and checked my goggle lens, opting for a red, solex insert that would shield my eyes from the sun's glare. My ritual complete, all equipment assembled and in order, I was reassured, ready for whatever the mountain had to throw at me. Through the process of doing something mindfully, my focus had been refined.

One further task accomplished — the kids off to their classes — Gabby, Mark, Gordon and I headed towards the chairlift, snowboards tucked under our arms. 'All ready?' said Gordon, impatiently. It wasn't really a question. 'Come on. Let's go. No friends on powder day!' I've heard this refrain many times, an excited child who's upset that he's missing all the fun. It was almost 9.30 am and Gordon could hardly contain himself. But he needn't have been concerned. Gressoney sits at the centre of three north-south valleys, and is connected to Champoluc, a resort in the valley over the mountains to the west, and popular with weekenders from Turin and Milan, and to Alagna Valsesia, an off-piste mecca on the Piedmont side of the mountains to the east. These three interlinked valleys constitute the Monterosa ski area and we were about to discover why its reputation as a hidden gem of bountiful off-piste terrain and quiet slopes is absolutely deserved. There were so few people around that Gordon had no need to worry the fresh snow might have been tracked out.

TECH TIP

DEVELOP YOUR OWN
COPING RITUALS

Snowboarding, and the mountains,
can throw up gnarly situations
and you need constructive techniques
for navigating anxious moments.
Practise:

1. Positive self-talk

2. Sitting quietly with no interruptions

3. Carrying something,
maybe a talisman, which makes
you feel special.

I jumped on the two-man lift beside Gabby, its red, foam seats lifting us steeply up through the pines, their branches bowed deeply with snow. As the long ride carried us over rock gardens, cliffs and deserted pistes up to 2,200 metres, we had plenty of time to sit back and enjoy the views. 'This is beautiful,' sighed Gabby, 'but I need to get on the snow and get my boarding legs back. I'm always nervous before we start.' And then the exit came into view. 'There's the lift hut,' she groaned, looking straight ahead and becoming visibly agitated, 'and you know how I hate getting off these things.' Familiar anxieties returned for me, too, and I chanted to myself as much as for her, 'Remember, board flat, stand up, glide on front foot.' The self-talk helps me to focus on manoeuvres needed to fulfill the task ahead, and it's a coping ritual I perform in times of stress. On button tows, if I feel concentration wavering during the slow ride, my chant becomes, 'Knees bent, loose legs, strong core.' Another favourite, this one for the slopes is, 'Relax into the board, soft knees.' And, of course, the mantra I borrow from Tammy, when I need to be more assertive, 'Dominate!'

The practise works, it's been effective in tangible ways and I've extended my lessons from the slopes to my work life, applying similar coping rituals whenever I feel nervous. Before presenting in front of an audience I can repeat to myself, 'Breathe, one, two, three' as I inhale and again, 'Breathe, one, two, three' when I exhale. I'm reminded to slow down, rather than gabble when I talk. And on a higher level, when I first started in business for myself, the new context felt strange and uncomfortable, just as it had when I first strapped on a snowboard. So I translated that experience and understood the feelings of discomfort and imbalance would pass with time as I became more familiar with my new environment.

At the end of the Punta Jolanda lift, both Gabby and I adhered to our mantra. We placed our boards flat, stood up and glided across the soft snow, exiting the lift smoothly. With Gordon and Mark we rode a series of red runs to reach the top of the Stafal-Gabiet gondola, north of Gressoney. Gabby set off at a fast pace, and momentarily taken aback by her speed and renewed confidence, I hesitated; her back had already disappeared around a bend and I smiled, happy to see her anxieties gone. The pistes, true to form, were almost deserted, and the recent snow made the steeper sections more forgiving. Nipping into the off-piste, my board tracked a sunken path and light powder, knee-deep, flew over my thighs. Catching the Gabiet-Passo Dei Salati gondola, we rose up to the pass connecting Gressoney to Alagna, and there, at almost 3,000 metres we were rewarded with spectacular, panoramic views across the Southern Alps. Squinting into the bright sunlight bouncing off the Passo's snow, I could hear the excited chatter of nearby Italians. Snow-capped peaks stretched out into the distance around us; Mont Blanc was a tiny triangle on the horizon to the west. We were well above the treeline, and in the other direction, far beyond Alagna, which was obscured deep in the folds of the valley directly below us, the flat plains of northern Italy flared from the southern hem of the Alps towards the horizon. And in between, to the north, the slender dagger of the Matterhorn, synonymous with Zermatt, pierced the skyline beyond the border in Switzerland. Momentarily stunned by the beauty, our group, to a person, stopped in its tracks. Camera shots would never capture the majesty, and we seared the views into memory, emotional reserves to call upon in the future. At 3,300 metres and another gondola ride away, Punta Indren provides access to the northern, off-piste terrain. But only those carrying the correct avalanche equipment (a shovel, probe and transceiver) were allowed on the lift. Instead, we dipped into the short, wide blue runs of Cimalegna and Bodwitch, which ran east into Piedmont. We had the slopes to ourselves and could pop off their sides, driving our boards through the deep powder and return safely onto the groomed pistes at leisure. Cruising unfettered to their end, just above the Cimalegna cliffs, we stopped near a danger sign, a picture of a person tumbling to their death, which signalled in succinct graphic the Janus face of mountain exploration. This area of the summit is often closed in high winds owing to its exposed aspect and, coupled with a potentially long wait for the cable car rising up from Alagna, many snowboarders and skiers are discouraged from venturing to this corner of the peaks. As a result, we blasted down, each taking our own line, with no worry about those coming from behind.

Later that week we returned to Passo Dei Salati. Alagna, directly below us, was hidden from view and my stomach churned. Our descent would be a 10-kilometre ride with a drop of almost 1,800 metres — well in excess of the UK's highest elevation, the peak of Ben Nevis. Contiguous black and red runs would take us plummeting from the very top, deep into the valley and onto Alagna. As a group we pushed off, keeping Cimalegna and Bodwitch to our left, while we tracked right down the black slopes of Olen. My board ate up the relatively wide, quiet and gentle slope ideal for cruising speed, and the ride was easier than I'd feared. Around every corner, I anticipated a change in gradient, breathing a mental sigh of relief when none came and soon my butterflies disappeared. Eventually, approaching a rise, which I couldn't see beyond, the slope dropped away. Instinctively, I dug into my back edge, sideslipping downwards through the steeper section. And it was here that I had my aha moment — I felt less in control than I did carving turns, when I could feel my board bite into the soft powder beneath it. Under icy conditions this slope would have been different, but for now the moment was ideal to step up my practise, to trust my equipment and teaching, to invest in my progress and divest my past.

Half-way down to Alagna the slope flattened out, restaurants and bars were scattered down either side of the piste, and yellow deckchairs and wooden tables clustered around each eatery. We had reached an intersection where the small gondola from the valley floor unloaded its passengers and a large cable car departed, whisking skiers and snowboarders up higher to Passo Dei Salati behind us. But we rode on past the diners and sun-worshippers, legs strong, continuing downwards, the slope flattening to red through the treeline. Suddenly, Gordon shouted back to me, 'Road!' Pointing ahead, he indicated a car moving slowly across what appeared to be the piste. Reducing my speed, I saw a small ribbon of snow exiting a narrow gap in the fence and bridging the tarmac beyond it. I slowed even further before committing, looking both ways like a pedestrian, then crossing the tarmac, and riding on into our final descent. At last Alagna came into sight stretched across the narrow width of the valley floor, its church spire reaching ambitiously upwards between the giant flanks of the Alps. Gordon, Gabby and Mark were waiting for me and I slid to a halt beside them, exhausted and elated. 'I definitely want to do that again,' I laughed. 'But maybe not today.'

CONFIDENCE TRICK

REWARDING THE SELF

Coping rituals help us get through life, but we need to foster positive, rather than negative habits. Positive rituals can reduce anxiety, in turn leading to better performance. The key is to discover what works for you because they are highly personal. Sometimes we can still get stuck in a rut. Continue to:

1. Find new channels of inspiration

2. Engage with ideas or people that refresh your life

3. Reward yourself in positive, healthy ways that make you happy.

That evening we rewarded ourselves for the day's exertions with a celebratory drink. Gressoney is a small village with fewer than 500 residents and it supports only a handful of shops and bars, and after a short stroll of 30 metres (an easy walk on tired legs) we stepped inside a contemporary bar. The local drink, a Bombardino, is a blur of Advocaat and brandy, topped with cream and often served hot; I couldn't think of anything more sickly. Silently, I toasted my achievements with a Prosecco, acknowledging I had come a long way since my early days riding a board.

A bit tipsy, we walked fewer than ten steps from the bar to an interconnecting shop next door. Owned by the same people, it was a local ski-hire establishment that also sold outdoor clothing. A slim, older woman with blonde hair greeted us and even in jeans she was stylish. Dani introduced herself, and in her easy company we struck up a conversation, sharing our enthusiasm for the beauty and tranquility of the surrounding area that was her home. Her eyes sparkled, and with her index finger, she beckoned us forward. 'Come. Follow me,' she said, her heavily-accented English reeling us in, even closer to the counter. 'Look.' She pointed to some old newspaper clippings and to a set of skis fixed to the shop roof. Peering in, we discovered Dani's brother had been a ski racer in the late 1970s, and had competed as part of the Italian national team. Leonardo David was nineteen when he won a World Cup Slalom in the 1978-9 season, taking the podium from alpine legend, Ingemar Stenmarck; his career was on the ascent. But in a pre-Olympic Downhill very shortly after that win, he fell and sustained injuries that induced a coma; six gruelling years later, he died. It was a horrific end to a promising life that had been destined for greater accolades on the world stage. As Dani's eyes misted over, however, we fell respectfully in the presence of something far more human and intimate than prestige, we were in the company of a woman, a sister, still grieving her sibling who had died at the age of twenty-five.

At the end of the week, Gabby needed to prepare for an interview that would be taking place on her return to the UK. Gordon, Mark and

I took off westwards on our own, then, to Champoluc, the remaining valley in the Monterosa area that we had still to explore. Stepping outside the hotel into the shadow of the surrounding mountain peaks, the crisp air reached my lungs and we hurried across to the chairlift by the hotel, anxious for it to carry us up out of the cold. Slowly, the ancient lift cranked us closer to the sun. Rising above the shadow line, I lowered my goggles and sat back, eyes closed, bathing my entire face in the early warmth of the day. We traversed red and black runs northwards, and down into Stafal, which lay at the head of the valley. Much of the final, black run roller-coastered between short, steep sections and long, flat cat tracks. Seeing a flat section ahead, I concentrated on maintaining my speed, looking up and planning my line. Stopping here would result in a long walk, but as the track meandered through the trees, dappled sunlight laced its pattern on the snow, birdsong punctured the silence and I thought that, really, I would not mind to linger a while. Eventually, I dropped into Stafal, and the sound of voices and car engines broke the spell as I joined Gordon and Mark who were waiting for me.

We took the gondola and subsequent chairlift that rise west up to Colle Bettaforca, the only route in and out of the Champoluc valley. From the fork at the ridge, a piste tracks left and back down towards Stafal and another tracks right, the gateway to Champoluc. We made steady progress across the forgiving snow, zigzagging our way up chairlifts and down pistes. The wide, open runs invited us to cruise in the sunshine and take in the views at a leisurely pace. I felt confident on these mostly red runs, taking short bursts into the off-piste, turning fluidly through the soft snow, remembering to look up. A small rise lay ahead, but I couldn't see beyond it and I debated with myself — this was such fun, I felt secure in the knowledge that the groomed piste was less than 5 metres away and I was tempted to continue. But I ducked back onto the piste at the last minute. Looking back, I gulped and silently gave thanks. My training and instinct for self-preservation had saved me. A 5-metre cliff of jagged rocks lay to the side, behind me. As I rode back into the off-piste, I remained acutely alert to any changes in topography.

Reaching the roadside at Champoluc, we could go no further. The tarmac route defined the man-made, outer limit of our day's adventuring in the snow. Our goal had been achieved and we headed back to Stafal where we rejoined Gabby and the children. Spending the afternoon together, two families, complete, we listened to the children's excited voices and chased each other down the slopes, staving off the inevitability of our return to the UK the next day. We navigated back through the red pistes and stopped at a mountain restaurant, our favourite watering hole for a slope-side sundowner. The children hastily removed their skis at the entrance, hopping from one foot to the other. 'I need the loo! Please come with me,' they urged. 'I hate these toilets!' 'Come on then. Quickly,' I replied and hurried them along the bottom of the terrace, then in through a door to grapple with il Bagno. It was usual, as we had discovered across a number of mountain restaurants in this part of Italy, to find unisex toilets at their most primitive — nothing more than an enamelled hole in the ground with footplates either side of the opening. The experience is a challenge for a grown woman, and in snowboarding clothes the process becomes further complicated. For Freya and Arianna, young girls in salopettes, il Bagno was a bridge too far. Freya and I balanced at arms length, so she could clear the hole and keep her clothes dry. It was the ultimate slope-side hurdle, but once cleared successfully, the children could play peacefully in the snow, three kids crafting their snowmen. Overlooked by the wooden carvings of local animals and birds whittled by the proprietor, and which peered down from their lofty perch above the bar, we ordered our final drinks. Carrying them outside into the still air,

CONFIDENCE TRICK

CELEBRATING YOUR ACHIEVEMENTS

As you progress towards your goals with focus and determination, it's equally important to stop and smell the roses along the way:

1. Make time to celebrate your achievements

2. Plan something special in advance, or

3. Be spontaneous

4. Choose something small or large

5. Choose whatever makes you happy.

we watched the sun dip slowly towards the end of the day, an Italian flag motionless against its mast, nearby.

The Aosta Valley is a quiet, undiscovered part of Italy, very different in its charm to the sophistication of the Dolomites, but its simplicity won me over. 'You're right,' said Gabby, taking a glug from her wine glass, 'I really love it here, and definitely want to come back.' My thoughts telescoped briefly ahead, to alternative horizons. 'I'd love to snowboard in North America with all that powder, to ride in the midnight sun near the Arctic Circle. And to heli-board in Kyrgyzstan, in the Tian Shan mountains,' I added wistfully. Across the table Gabby was silent for a moment. 'That's all very well, darling,' she grinned, 'but you'll have to ride off-piste much better than you do right now, and you'd better start saving!' I joined in with her laughter and couldn't disagree. Toasting each other, the conversation carried on as the sun melted silently and away.

Just as tomorrow inevitably arrives, so will next season and I'll greet it looking up, my snowboard in tow, taking it all on board.

♦ 1. Identify three bad habits you are going to stop in order to help you accelerate your progress towards your chosen goals.

   a..

   b..

   c..

2. Consider three positive coping rituals that you have developed, or that you can develop, to help you maintain control in your journey. Write them down.

   a..

   b..

   c..

2. Name three achievements of which you are proud, and describe how you celebrated each. You stomped it, you felt the stoke, so name those celebrations:

   a. Achievement 1..

   Celebration..

   b. Achievement 2..

   Celebration..

a. Achievement 3...

Celebration..

♦ 4. Which three steps can you take that will continue to push
you out of your comfort zone and keep you moving forwards?

a...

b...

c...

Taking It All On Board is your 360 turn, your ability to fly, to embrace and to execute life's manoeuvres with smooth confidence and unconscious competence. It's your long-term maintenance plan in which day-to-day balance is assured, and you have all the people and skills in place to navigate your life successfully, stomping its black diamonds and life off-piste.

Scoring

Exercise 1. Give yourself one point for every bad habit listed. Reward yourself with another point when you have stopped the bad habit.

Exercise 2. Give yourself a point for each positive coping ritual listed. Reward yourself with another point when you have put the coping ritual into action.

Exercise 3. Give a point for each named achievement, and add another point for each celebration listed.

Exercise 4. Give yourself a point for each of the three steps you will keep taking in order to push yourself out of your comfort zone.

Total chapter points.................

GLOSSARY
a guide to snowboarding parlance and technical terminology

180: a half-circular aerial rotation completed either over the ground or off a jump.

360: a full, circular aerial rotation completed either over the flat or off a jump.

A-frame box: a snow park feature that slopes up, across and down, approximating the shape of an upper case letter, 'A'. The area within the box frame is solid and its profile from either end is rectangular, like a box; the riding surface along the upper contour of the box is flat.

Backcountry: mountainous terrain that is free from artificial infrastructure and which lies beyond the boundaries of a resort.

BASE jumping: parachuting or wingsuit flying from a fixed object, structure or cliff. It is an acronym that stands for the four types of objects from which people can jump: Building, Antenna, Span, and Earth (cliff).

BASI: an acronym for the British Association of Snowsports Instructors. BASI is the UK body sanctioning the recognized grading system for professional snowsports qualifications. BASI also provides training for instructors and coaches.

Bindings: equipment harnessing a rider's feet (one binding per foot) securely to her board, and through which she can translate muscle movements to steering power. There are many different types of bindings and the angle of their position can be tailored to a rider's needs.

Blood wagon: a slang term used to describe an emergency sledge which transfers injured snowboarders or skiers off the mountain.

Bluebird day: a bright, clear, sunny day after a night of snowfall.

Boardslide: a freestyle trick; a slide along or over a feature when the rider's board is 90-degrees perpendicular to the direction of travel. Boardslides can be either frontside (facing up the mountain) or backside (facing down the mountain).

Box: a snow park feature with a wide, flat surface that can manifest a variety of upper contours including A-frames and Rainbows. Under the contour, the area of the frame is solid and its profile either end is rectangular, like a box. Skiers and snowboarders alike can slide down the box.

Butter: a flatland trick performed by pressing the nose or tail of the snowboard so that the opposite half lifts off the snow. It is a foundational manoeuvre that can then be incorporated into other, more complex spins.

Button tow: a lift that takes a solo rider up the side of a piste (often a nursery slope). Commonly called a Poma tow after its main manufacturer, it consists of a pole attached to a moving cable and has a circular disc at the bottom. The pole is placed between the legs and the disc pulls or drags the rider up the slope while their board or skis remain in contact with the ground.

Camber: refers to the slight convex shape, or the arch, of a piste's horizontal cross-section.

Carving: a turning method whereby the tail of the snowboard follows the same path as the nose, its edges cutting into the snow leaving the outline of a precise arc in the rider's wake.

Cat track: a run on a shallow incline; the term originates from their use by Sno-Cat maintenance vehicles to access various parts of a resort. They can be short cuts between pistes, or longer, winding routes around the mountain. But they are often narrow, and frequently they have a steep drop-off to one side.

Drag lift: a generic term for a lift which pulls a snowboarder or skier up the mountain: button tows; T-bars and rope tows are all types of drag lift.

Face-plant: a face-first fall into the snow, the result of a snowboarder catching the front edge of their board.

Fakie: a skill whereby the rider adopts the opposite stance to normal, travelling tail first. The term 'riding fakie' is also known as 'riding switch'.

Feature: a generic term for any of the items in a snow park, it usually refers to rails, boxes or jumps — anything a rider can use to perform tricks.

Fall line: the direction in which gravity pulls a rider when descending a slope. If you placed a ball on the slope, it is the line (not necessarily straight) the ball would take when released.

Flatland tricks: tricks performed on flatter slopes, such as buttering.

Freeriding: a type of snowboarding on natural terrain, away from the pistes.

Freestyle: a type of snowboarding using man-made or natural objects to perform tricks on the slope, off-piste or in the snow park.

Gnarly: a slang word meaning extreme, challenging, or dangerous. It can also mean cool.

Groomed: a term describing the manicured surface of the snow on a slope that allows snowboarders and skiers to use the run for easy recreation within its grade.

Halfpipe: a semi-circular trough or ditch with 3-to-6-metre walls; its length is ridden travelling from one side to the other, up and down the height of the walls, often getting air and performing tricks above their extent.

Heli-boarding: a pursuit in which mountain slopes are accessed via a helicopter.

Hucking: a move in which a rider or skier leaves the ground, launching over an object (usually a kicker or feature in a park) without attention to form or style.

ISIA: International Ski Instructors' Association — the world governing body for snowsports.

ISTD: International Ski Teacher Diploma — the highest snowsport qualification, it allows instructors to set up a ski or snowboard school in order to teach in France.

Kicker: a wedge-shaped jump with a lip from which a snowboarder or skier takes off into the air. Usually kickers are made from snow and found in snow parks. Like runs on the slope, they can be colour-graded for difficulty — green is easy and black is expert.

Liftie: a slang term for the person operating the chairlift.

Nollie: a trick whereby the snowboarder springs off the nose of the board and into the air.

Off-piste: any area of the mountain away from prepared runs and where the snow is not groomed.

Ollie: a trick whereby the snowboarder springs off the tail of the board and into the air. The leap can be performed from flat ground, off kickers or from other obstacles.

Park: a prepared recreational area within a resort that has a number of semi-permanent features such as kickers, rails and other obstacles, and where snowboarders and skiers can focus on performing tricks. It can also be referred to as a snow park or a terrain park.

Piste: a marked run where snow has been groomed to allow snowboarders and skiers to travel safely down and across the mountain. Pistes can be marked by coloured and numbered poles indicating their difficulty and length. In North America they are often called trails.

Poma tow: Poma is a French company that manufactures lift systems. Nowadays, Poma tow is a generic term usually used to describe a button tow, just as a Hoover is used to describe a vacuum cleaner.

Powder: the term for snow that is usually recent and very soft. Snowboarding or skiing on powder gives the rider a feeling of floating or weightlessness. Discovering fresh powder untracked by others is highly coveted — hence the phrase, 'No friends on powder days.'

Probe: an item of safety equipment carried and used, particularly by those going off-piste, to help find anyone buried in an avalanche. It is a collapsible, long pole which probes the snow to locate someone underneath the surface.

Rail: a feature often found in a terrain or snow park, or in an urban environment. Constructed from metal, it can have either a rounded or flat surface along which skiers and snowboarders can slide and perform tricks.

Scooting: the term used when snowboarders move across flat terrain using their unstrapped back foot to push against the snow, propelling them forwards.

Shred: a slang term often used as a synonym for snowboarding, for example, 'Let's go shred' instead of 'Let's go snowboarding.' The term is usually associated with someone who snowboards hard and well.

Sick: a slang term meaning cool, impressive, extreme, hairy, or dangerous.

Slopestyle: a discipline within both snowboarding and skiing where participants ride or ski a course of kickers and rails performing acrobatic manoeuvres. Slopestyle became an Olympic event in 2014.

Snow park: a designated area, usually in a resort, containing features that are used by snowboarders or skiers to perform freestyle. This is also known as a terrain park.

Speed checking: a braking manoeuvre, quickly turning from heel to toe edge (facing the mountain), or from toe to heel edge (facing downhill) that takes the speed or momentum out of travel.

Stoked: a slang term meaning intensely enthusiastic or excited.

Switch: a skill whereby the rider adopts the opposite stance to normal, the board travelling tail first. The term 'riding switch' is synonymous with 'riding fakie'.

Tail press: a trick performed while sliding along a feature when pressure is applied to the tail of the board so that the nose is raised. The manoeuvre is sometimes performed on the flat before progressing onto a rail or box.

Transceiver: a type of beacon that emits an electronic signal and can be worn by those heading into the backcountry. Anyone wearing the device can be located under the snow in the event of an avalanche.

ßTSA: an abbreviation of the UK retail chain, The Snowboard Asylum, which stocks snowboarding apparel and equipment.

UIAGM: the French acronym for L'Union Internationale des Associations de Guides de Montagnes (International Federation of Mountain Guides Associations).

Adams, Linda. *Learning a New Skill is Easier Said than Done.*
Solana Beach: Gordon Training International, 2011.
Available online: http://www.gordontraining.com/free workplace-
articles/learning-a-new-skill-is-easier-said-than-done/.

Basich, Tina with Kathleen Gasperini. *Pretty Good for a Girl:
The Autobiography of a Snowboarding Pioneer.* New York:
HarperCollins, 2003.

Brown, Stuart and Christopher Vaughan. *Play: How it Shapes
the Brain, Opens the Imagination, and Invigorates the Soul.*
Reprint edition. New York: Avery, 2010.

Fredrickson, Barbara L. et al 'Open Hearts Build Lives: Positive
Emotions, Induced Through Loving-Kindness Meditation,
Build Consequential Personal Resources'. *Journal of Personality
and Social Psychology* 95, no. 5 (2008): 1045-1062.

Gallwey, W. Timothy, and Robert Kriegel. *Inner Skiing. Revised
edition.* New York: Random House, 1997.

Honey, Peter, and Alan Mumford. *The Learning Styles Helper's
Guide.* London. Peter Honey Publications, 2000.

Hunt, Kenneth A, and Will Secor. 'A Business Case Analysis of
the Snowboarding Industry'. *Journal of Business Case
Studies* 9, no.2 (2013): 112.

Ingalhalikar, Madhura, Alex Smith, Drew Parker,
    Theodore D. Satterthwaite, Mark A. Elliott,
    Kosha Ruparel, Hakon Hakonarson, Raquel E. Gur,
    Ruben C. Gur, and Ragini Verma. 'Sex Differences
    In The Structural Connectome Of The Human Brain.'
    *Proceedings of the National Academy of Sciences of the
    United States of America* 111, no. 2 (2013): 823-8.

Jeffers, Susan. Feel The Fear and Do It Anyway. Revised edn.
    London: Vermilion, 2007.

Keri, Gabe. 'Male and Female College Students' Learning Styles
    Differ: An Opportunity for Instructional Diversification'.
    College Student Journal. 36, no. 3 (2002).

McNab, Neil. *Go Snowboard*. London: Dorling Kindersley, 2006.